Gender, Identity and Place

For Olive Morgan Leigh, my mother

Gender, Identity and Place
Understanding Feminist Geographies

Linda McDowell

University of Minnesota Press
Minneapolis

First published in 1999 by Polity Press in association with Blackwell Publishers Ltd.

Published simultaneously in the United States in 1999
by the University of Minnesota Press
111 Third Avenue South, Suite 290
Minneapolis, MN 55401-2520
http://www.upress.umn.edu

Printed in Great Britain

Library of Congress Cataloging-in-Publication Data

A catalog record for this book is available from the Library of Congress

ISBN 0-8166-3393-2 (hc)
ISBN 0-8166-3394-0 (pb)

The University of Minnesota is an equal-opportunity educator and employer.

Contents

Plates

Credits

Plate 2.2: The Tattooed Woman, original postcard *c.*1920, colouring Al Barna,
            © Quantity Postcards, Tilt Works, San Francisco, California.
Plate 3.1: Rosie the Riveter, World War II poster, *c.*1942, the National Ar-
            chives/Corbis.
All other plates are photographs by the author.

Figures and Tables

Preface and Acknowledgements

Some years ago, before feminist work in geography was as well-established as it is now, I was asked in a job interview 'what is all this stuff about women and geography?' While a questioner might not be so offensive nowadays, it is still a common experience to be asked by all sorts of people 'what has gender to do with geography?'

This book is an attempt to provide an answer to that question. My aim is to outline some of the main connections between geographical perspectives and feminist approaches and to illustrate them with empirical work that I have read and enjoyed over the last few years. The emphases reflect, as is common in texts like this one, my own interests and some of the work I have been involved in. I work on gender issues in contemporary Britain in the main, and to a lesser extent in other 'advanced' societies. I am also an urban and social geographer, interested in the changing nature of work in global cities and so the examples that I draw on reflect this emphasis. I have tried to be eclectic, but there is still not enough in the pages that follow about, for example, gender relations in 'Third World' nations or about ecofeminist approaches and campaigns. One of the delights but also frustrations of our subject is its vast encompassing range and no one can be an expert across all its subfields. So this book will not provide you with everything you may want to know about geography and gender, but I hope it will prove an interesting and enjoyable place to start and will lead you to explore what is, in my view, some of the most exciting scholarship in our discipline at present. I have introduced the 'classics' and some recent work and I hope that the case studies will prove a stimulus to all those geographers thinking about doing feminist research.

Although my name is on the cover, a book like this one is the result of the development of feminist networks that link geographers in many countries. One of the great pleasures of my academic work has been participation in these networks and the academic enthusiasms and many friendships that I have made thereby. It's hard to mention all the people who have made such a difference, and perhaps invidious to single out a few, but I should like to mention and to thank in particular Gillian Rose whose astute comments on the first draft were just the right mixture of friendly support and scholarly criticism, Doreen Massey with whom I worked for several years and whose energy and enthusiasm have always inspired me to greater efforts, Joni Seager, both for her personal generosity and the example of her work, Sophie Bowlby, Jo Foord, Susan Hanson, Jane Lewis, Suzanne Mackenzie and Janice Monk who have been there from the start, Michelle Lowe for a long friendship, Jo Sharp for more recent pleasures of collaboration and five amazing feminists and graduate students with whom it is my pleasure to work at present: Dorothy Forbes, Flora Gathorne-Hardy, Rebecca Klahr, Paula Meth and Bronwen Parry.

An earlier version of chapter 9 was published in the *Journal of Geography in Higher Education* (1997) as 'Women/gender/feminisms'. I should like to thank the editors and publisher for permission to reprint parts of it.

The author and publishers also wish to thank the following for permission to use copyright material:

Black Rose Books for a table from T. Amott and J. Matthaei, *Race, Gender and Work: A Multicultural Economic History of Women in the US* (1991), p. 325, table 10.3;

Routledge for tables from S. Reinharz, 'Experimental analysis: a contribution to feminist research', in G. Bowles and R. Duelli-Klein (eds), *Theories of Women's Studies* (Routledge and Kegan Paul, 1983), p. 168, table 11.1, and pp. 170–2, table 11.4, and material from J. Fiske, *Reading the Popular* (1992), p. 57;

Royal Geographical Society for a table from J. G. Townsend, 'Towards a regional geography of gender', *Geographical Journal*, 157 (1991), pp. 26–7, table 1;

University of California Press for excerpts from C. Enloe, *Bananas, Beaches, and Bases: Making Feminist Sense of International Politics* (1989), pp. xi–xii, 16, 17, 95, 97, 184, 189–90, 190–1. Copyright © 1989 Cynthia Enloe.

Every effort has been made to trace the copyright holders but if any have been inadvertently overlooked the publishers will be pleased to make the necessary arrangement at the first opportunity.

1
Introduction: Place and Gender

The place of gender

How is gender linked to geography? Do men and women live different lives in different parts of the world? And if gendered attributes are socially constructed, then how does femininity and masculinity vary over time and space? What range of variation is there in the social relations between women and men? Are men usually centre-stage and women confined to the margins in all societies? What have geographers had to say about these issues?

These are the sorts of questions I want to examine in this book. They are issues that seem to have become important in a wide range of disciplines in the social sciences and humanities, where there has been a remarkable flowering in recent years of discussions and debates conducted in pre-eminently geographical terms. In all sorts of disciplines, scholars are writing about migration and travel, borders and boundaries, place and non-place in a literal and metaphorical sense. These debates reflect the huge disruptions and transformations in the links between specific peoples and particular places that have taken place in recent decades. Vast migrations of people and of money – labour and capital in the more abstract language of the social sciences – are a consequence of the increasingly global scale of those sets of social relations and connections that tie places together in the modern world. And these migrations have displaced and disrupted the lives of millions of people. Nationalist movements, wars, famines, as well as the development of transnational capital and global corporations have resulted in the enforced movement of many peoples, while hundreds of thousands of others have voluntarily, and usually temporarily, set off across vast geographic distances, travelling for pleasure and to broaden the mind.

Both types of movement have radically changed the relationships be-

1

tween individual and group identity, everyday life, and territory or place. It is becoming commonplace for increasing numbers of people to leave 'home': some to settle and make their lives far from where they were born, too many others to become 'placeless', 'dis-placed' peoples of the world, condemned to the limbo of not belonging, whether to a nation with a national territorial base, to a class or to a region. For many of the women involved in these journeys, movement has been associated with proletarianization, as local and multinational capital draws them in increasing numbers into the waged labour forces of the new international division of labour. The global reach of capital means that women in Korea, Kampuchea and Katmandu may end up working for the same corporation as women in Western Europe.

For some of these women, their travel may not involve vast geographical movement; it may involve only local travel or indeed no physical travel at all. Instead, the displacement experienced is the result of changing economic, social and cultural circumstances, as women enter factories or the homes of the elite as domestic workers, and as they are connected to other times and places through the penetration and cultural dominance of Western forms of information technology and popular culture. Whether the movement is physical or not, it is almost always associated with the renegotiation of gender divisions. These renegotiations are the subject of the chapters that follow.

Before turning to the ways in which these changes have been theorized and investigated at a whole range of spatial scales and at different sites in the home, the workplace and in public places, I want to look at how these huge material changes have affected our understanding of the links between place and identity.

Space, place and 'the local'

It is often assumed that the net result of the increasing scale of global interconnections and movement is a decline in the significance of 'the local' – in the amount of time people spend in a restricted geographical area, in the number of friends and family in the environs, and in the control that might be exercised at the local level, whether over political decisions and actions or the economic consequences of the actions of capital. The corollary is assumed to be the end of a sense of local attachment, of belonging to a place with all its local idiosyncrasies and cultural forms. While some of the former features are certainly apparent for some people for some of the time in certain parts of the world – most notably, of course, for affluent Western males – for many people in the world, everyday life continues to take place within a restricted locale. Even for the most mobile – an international financier is perhaps the most extreme example – a large part of daily activities, both at work and at home, must inevitably be within a finite area. The global money trader may be moving money around the world at a fantastic speed, but he himself (and it usually is a he) is sitting in front of a screen in Hong Kong, London, New York or some other financial centre, and in the evening, more often than not, these traders presumably go home to somewhere within daily travelling distance of their office, rather than to the international airport to jet off to another part of the world.

While the 'localization' of most of everyday life is indisputable, a perhaps more interesting question to ask is how have the enormous changes of the twentieth century impacted on the notion and existence of a 'sense of place'? Do people any longer feel a part of and a responsibility to their local area? And has the loss of stability, or perhaps more accurately the immobility, that once rooted peoples to a particular place for the whole of their lifetime and for generations of the same families meant the decline of locally based customs and practices, of those local mores that created the particularity of one place and distinguished it from others?

While these are perhaps particularly anxious questions for anthropologists whose whole disciplinary raison d'être has been to investigate the distinctiveness of 'other' local ways of life and the differences from their own (Okely 1996; Olwig and Hastrup 1997), geographers too have felt some anxiety about the consequences of modernity, the growing dominance of global forms of capitalism and the assumed loss of belonging to a local place. Empirical evidence, however, has assuaged this anxiety, as there are many signs of a continued, and even intensified, sense of locality in many parts of the world. These signs vary from the revival of local customs, practices and languages, in more or less acceptable forms, to the appalling effects of ethnic nationalism and widespread poverty and deprivation that trap growing numbers in their place. Further, as growing numbers of geographers and anthropologists recognize, the consequence of all those changes summed up under the term globalization is not that the world is becoming one, reducing local differences, but rather that 'difference, diversity is generated not from the integrity and authenticity of the local community, rooted in tradition, resisting and accommodating a modern world system ever more powerful in its force, but paradoxically from the very conditions of globalising change themselves' (Marcus: 1994: 42).

One positive effect, however, of the anxiety about the meaning of place, and the understanding that globalizing forces reconstruct rather than destroy localities, has been a shift towards a more sophisticated conceptualization of the notion of locality or place itself. The commonsense

3

geographical notion of a place as a set of coordinates on a map that fix a defined and bounded piece of territory has been challenged. Geographers now argue that places are contested, fluid and uncertain. It is socio-spatial practices that define places and these practices result in overlapping and intersecting places with multiple and changing boundaries, constituted and maintained by social relations of power and exclusion (Massey 1991; Smith 1993). Places are made through power relations which construct the rules which define boundaries. These boundaries are both social and spatial – they define who belongs to a place and who may be excluded, as well as the location or site of the experience.

As Smith has recognized, 'the making of place implies the production of [geographical] scale in so far as places are made different from each other.' Scale, therefore, is 'the criteria of difference not so much between places as between different *kinds* of places' (Smith 1993: 99, original emphasis). Thus 'it is geographical scale that defines the boundaries and bounds the identities around which control is exerted and contested' (p. 101). In this sense, as the socio-spatial definition of difference between different *kinds* of places, scale has recently been adopted in a number of geographic texts about difference as a central organizing device. In our reader *Space, Gender, Knowledge*, Jo Sharp and I used scale as the organizer (McDowell and Sharp 1997), as did David Bell and Gill Valentine in their book about food, *Consuming Geographies: We Are Where We Eat* (1997). I adopt the same strategy here.

But defining places, distinguishing the difference between them by scale, does not imply that they are constituted by processes that operate at a single spatial scale. Thus a home, or a neighbourhood, is a locality that is bounded by scale – that is rules/power relations that keep others out – but its constitution is through the intersection of a range of factors that may coincide there but are not restricted to the local level in their operation. As Doreen Massey (1991) has argued, localities are produced by the intersection of global and local processes – social relations that operate at a range of spatial scales. This produces what she terms a 'global sense of place'. Places may no longer be 'authentic' and 'rooted in tradition' as Marcus suggested in the quotation above; they are instead defined by the socio-spatial relations that intersect there and give a place its distinctive character.

So in Kilburn, the example used by Massey in her paper, the peculiar or particular sense of place that is experienced by her and other local inhabitants is defined by, among other things, the combination of in-migration from Ireland and Pakistan, by the 'Chinese' chip shop that sells curry and baked potatoes as well as noodles, by an internationally owned clothing firm employing local women who may have moved to Kilburn from Cyprus, Southern Africa and the Indian subcontinent to finish garments for a high street chain store. The 'authenticity' of places in contemporary global cities like London, therefore, is made up from flows and movements, from intersecting social relations rather than stability and rootedness. And even though a locality in inner London may seem an extreme example of the globality (globalness? glocalization? They are all horrid words but capture what I mean) of local places, at the end of the twentieth century there are few 'untouched' places.

Anthropologists, too, have come to a similar understanding of place. Thus Judith Okely, an anthropologist interested in the changing nature of place or localities in Britain and elsewhere, has recognized the relational nature of place and also noted that places are defined, maintained and altered through the impact of unequal power relations. She has argued that 'different groups inhabiting the same spaces can create and shift boundaries by subtle means' (Okely 1996: 3) and, of course, by less subtle means such as force or legal exclusion. New nations in Central and Eastern Europe are defined by excluding 'others' – Bosnians from Macedonia, for example. And at a smaller spatial scale, the nationalist and 'Loyalist' spaces in Ulster's cities are another extreme example of places defined by exclusion. In other places, different people do live together, but distance between them may occur. Social distance does not always imply geographical distance, and occupants of the same Cartesian spaces may live in very different 'places'. Further what have been termed relational places – locales constructed through social relations between groups and individuals – slip up and down the spatial scale as it were, as particular sets of social practices connect the local to the regional, or to the national and the global in different ways for different inhabitants.

This new sense of place and scale might perhaps be imagined diagrammatically as a double helix rather than an old-fashioned three-tier cake plate which maintains spatial separation. Feminist theorist Elizabeth Grosz, albeit discussing the body rather than place, has used a rather similar image – the Möbius strip, rather than a double helix – that also captures this sense of interconnection and change. It is important, however, not to be too carried away by the fluidity of this new conceptualization and representation of relational place, as customs and institutional structures clearly persist through time and 'set' places in time and space as it were. But rapid change is also possible, as the dramatic events in Central and Eastern Europe made clear when the map of this part of the world was redrawn between 1989 and 1991. Perhaps there are relatively established and stable regimes of places, or socio-spatial associations, which persist through time but which are then overturned and replaced in a period of crisis.

This notion of a regime to refer to a relatively stable set of social relations that are maintained despite minor alterations and variations, but which are subject to periodic upheavals, often in times of crisis which may be related

5

in particular to economic changes, is also a useful way to think about gender relations. In the next section of this introduction, I shall look at this argument in more detail. Before I do so, however, I want to briefly mention the argument of a French anthropologist, Marc Augé (1996), who has suggested that the extreme result of the sorts of changes we have experienced in capitalist societies is the replacement of places by non-places.

Non-places are those locations in the contemporary world where the transactions and interactions that take place are between anonymous individuals, often stripped of all symbols of social identity other than an identification number: a pin number for a cash card for example, or a passport number. Indeed cash points and airports are classic examples of non-places, according to Augé, where each of us interacts as an anonymous individual with a technological object or an official or employee who is not interested in us as a person but merely as a number or a statistic, an anonymized flow-through. In these spaces, our individual social attributes and our membership of a social group become irrelevant: as long as we have the money, of course, to make the cash transaction or purchase the ticket to travel. In non-places therefore, gendered attributes and perhaps even our sexed bodies become unimportant, opening up a paradoxical space of control and liberation. Although we might be able to escape our sets of personal connections and obligations momentarily or for a few hours, these transactions are also carefully monitored and controlled and our movements are subjected to various forms of electronic surveillance.

Augé's arguments are interesting, however, as they have parallels with the freedom and surveillance of cyberspace. As we surf the net, our bodily attributes become irrelevant, or rather, fluid and alterable at will. There is nothing to stop us entering the chat rooms of cyberspace in any form we like. The only limitation is our imagination, which, of course, tends to remain tethered to the limited subject positions available in 'real' space. But unless and until the exchange of views on the net becomes materialized, the gendered attributes that define us as feminine or masculine in other forms of interaction do not matter. Let's move on, then, to explore the material aspects of gender and gender relations, but keep in mind the idea of 'place' as the grounded intersections of a whole variety of flows and interactions that operate over a range of spatial scales: I shall return to this conceptualization of place at the end of the chapter.

Defining gender

If the conceptualization of place has become more nuanced in recent geographical work, then so too has the definition of gender. The focus of feminist scholars, geographers among them, has also changed, from a dominant emphasis on the material inequalities between men and women in different parts of the world to a new convergence of interest on language, symbolism, representations and meaning in the definition of gender, and on questions about subjectivity, identity and the sexed body. About ten years ago, in a review of the work of feminist anthropologists, Henrietta Moore (1988) suggested that the scope of feminist scholarship in her discipline included the analysis of 'what it is to be a woman, how cultural understandings of the category "woman" vary through space and time, and how those understandings relate to the position of women in different societies' (p.12). She suggested development of this understanding required the concept of gender and gender relations: that is the different ways in which women and men, and the accepted attributes of femininity and masculinity, are defined across space and time. Gender, she argued, may be seen from two perspectives: 'either as a symbolic construction or as a social relationship'.

These two aspects – gender as a set of material social relations and as symbolic meaning – cannot really be separated. In defining gender, and in the preceding discussion of the changing definition and understanding of place, it is clear that social practices, including the wide range of social interactions at a variety of sites and places – at work, for example, at home, in the pub or the gym – and ways of thinking about and representing place/gender are interconnected and mutually constituted. We all act in relation to our intentions and beliefs, which are always culturally shaped and historically and spatially positioned. What I feel about, say, young men is related to social assumptions about their behaviour, my own experiences as the mother of a teenage son and how local youths conduct themselves on the streets of Cambridge at night! This influences how I react to them and them to me, and these actions in turn have an effect on my attitudes, beliefs and future intentions, on my knowledge of and understanding of the world and different people's place in it.

So, what people believe to be appropriate behaviour and actions by men and women reflect and affect what they imagine a man or a woman to be and how they expect men and women to behave, albeit men and women who are differentiated by age, class, race or sexuality, and these expectations and beliefs change over time and between places. It is only as an icon or an image, as the Virgin Mary perhaps, that notions of femininity are universal (almost), untouched and unchanging. For everyone else, accepted standards change over time and space.

As well as a so-called 'cultural turn' in feminist scholarship and indeed in geographical research more generally (Barnes and Duncan, 1992; Duncan and Ley 1994) – that is a greater emphasis on symbols, meanings and

7

representations – there has also been a shift in the political aims of the feminist movement over the last three decades or so. My aim in this section is to give a brief summary of these changing emphases. It is brief because there are many other places to look for a comprehensive treatment of the history of feminism in geography (Bondi 1990, 1992; Duncan 1996b; Jones III et al. 1997; McDowell 1992a, 1992b, 1992c; G. Pratt 1993; G. Rose 1993; Massey 1994; Women and Geography Study Group 1984, 1997) and more widely (Alcoff and Potter, 1993; Gunew 1990, 1991; Jackson 1993; Lovell 1990; Barrett and Phillips 1992; Pollock 1996). The new book cooperatively written by members of the Women and Geography Study Group (1997) is an excellent place to start. But as well as the summary I provide in this chapter, in each of the substantive chapters that follow the shifting emphases of feminist geographers will be reflected in the concepts, theories and case studies that are discussed. And then in the final chapter, I also illustrate the changing emphases through a methodological lens, showing not only how research questions have changed but also the research methods that are used in approaching these new questions.

Feminist scholarship

The key aim of feminist scholarship in general is to demonstrate the construction and significance of sexual differentiation as a key organizing principle and axis of social power, as well as a crucial part of the constitution of subjectivity, of an individual's sense of their self-identity as a sexed and gendered person. One of the most interesting definitions of feminist scholarship that I have come across recently is that by Griselda Pollock in the preface to her edited collection *Generations and Geographies in the Visual Arts*:

> Feminism stands here for a political commitment to women and to changes that women desire for themselves and for the world. Feminism stands for a commitment to the full appreciation of what women inscribe, articulate, and image in cultural forms: interventions in the field of meaning and identity from the place called 'woman' or the 'feminine'. Feminism also refers to a theoretical revolution in the ways in which terms such as art, culture, woman, subjectivity, politics and so forth are understood. But feminism does not imply a united field of theory, political position, or perspective. Feminism has been identified with a women's movement and it is important historically that it should be so; but at this moment, its autonomy as the place in which the question of gender is posed acquires a particular political and theoretical significance. (1996: xv)

8

So feminism is, as Pollock makes crystal clear, both a political movement and a theoretical field of analysis. Her definition, not surprisingly, reflects her training as an art historian and as geographers and social scientists concerned with everyday behaviours and political actions – the material as well as representational interventions – we might perhaps want to insert a phrase implying as much: perhaps after Pollock's second sentence. Otherwise her definition seems to me to be remarkably succinct and complete and, most importantly, as we shall explore further in a moment, she emphasizes the diversity of feminist theory. Indeed, many geographers now speak about 'feminisms' and 'feminist geographies', preferring the plural rather than the singular to emphasize the diversity of their perspectives and approaches. Notice that the title of the jointly written introductory book I mentioned earlier is *Feminist Geographies: Explorations in Diversity and Difference*, whereas its 1984 predecessor was more starkly titled *Geography and Gender*.

As Pollock noted, however, feminism within the academy is not only the place where questions about gender are posed – about its definition, variation and effects – but is also where political questions about who is represented within its walls, both as scholars and as subjects of scholarship, must be addressed. I want to postpone the question of women's position as scholars until the end of this chapter and discuss first gender as the subject of scholarship.

As Pollock argues in her book, 'feminism has had to fight long and hard to win an acknowledgement of the organizing centrality of sexual difference, with its effects of gender and sexuality as one of the planes of social and subjective constitution' (1996: 4), and this is no less true in our discipline than in others. As Susan Christopherson (1989) bitterly suggested in an article in *Antipode* – a radical journal of geography – questions about gender, justice and equality remained 'outside the project' for most geographers, even for self-identified radicals interested in class inequality and social transformation. It has been a long struggle to get mainstream geographers to accept gender divisions as a key axis of social differentiation, on a par with, for example, class and race/ethnicity. It is too often assumed that gender is only an attribute of femininity and therefore only of interest to women scholars and students. Those of us who teach a course, perhaps boldly titled gender and geography/ies, even feminist geography/ies, or introduce feminist perspectives into substantive courses such as economic geography, have too often had to compare notes about how to get our teaching taken seriously, and how to keep the men, as well as the women, in our classes on board.

To this misunderstanding about the audience for our work is added a further, and perhaps more crucial misconception. It is usually, but incor-

9

rectly, assumed that feminist scholars have a sole focus on gender to the exclusion of other axes of subject constitution and of discrimination. This assumption is also a misguided one. As Pollock emphasizes:

> Feminism is not for gender what Marxism is for class, and postcolonial theory for race. First, there is a range of feminisms, in varying alliances with all the analyses of what oppresses women. Socialist feminism has always concerned itself with matters of class, and black feminism details the configurations of imperialism, sexuality, femininity and racism. In their breadth, as the plural, feminisms deal with the complex and textured configurations of power around race, class, sexuality, age, physical ability and so forth, but they have of necessity also to be the particular political and theoretical space that names and anatomizes sexual difference as an axis of power operating with a specificity that neither gives it priority, exclusivity or predominance over any other nor allows it to be conceptually isolated from the textures of social power and resistance that constitute the social. (1996: 3–4)

This is a complex claim and it is worth reading Pollock's argument again. It raises important and difficult questions, too, about the connection between theoretical analyses and political mobilization for change which, as you remember, Pollock defined as the dual focus of feminism, for women may be divided in their interests along class and ethnic lines. But I think that there is no doubt that Pollock is correct. It is crucial to understand the intercutting relations of all axes of social power and oppression and the ways in which sexual differences and gender relations are constituted in different ways across space and time because of their interconnection with these other axes of power. But still we must insist that it is the question of the ways in which sexual difference and gender relations are constituted and form a basis of power that distinguishes *feminist* scholarship. And further, we have to hold on to the political commitment to alter the relations between sex, gender and power. Feminists not only analyse but also want to dismantle the structures that reinforce the inferiority of women, and to mount a challenge to the very definition and constraints of femininity as it is conventionally understood. As Nancy Miller (1988) has argued, feminists 'protest against the available fiction of female becoming'. In this project, though, we are increasingly joined by men who also want to protest against available fictions of male being.

The feminist project – its theoretical examination of diverse ways of being a woman or a man and the protest against the currently available options – is, of course, no small enterprise. It demands nothing less than the dismantling of the basis of everyday social relations, most institutions and structures of power and the theoretical foundations on which current gender divisions stand. This is because the assumption of a categorical difference between women and men – women are one thing, and men are the opposite – is deeply embedded in our sense of ourselves as individuals, in daily interactions, in institutional structures and in Western intellectual thought. Despite a growing recognition of the plurality and diversity of social experiences, the belief that a distinctive version of femininity for women and masculinity for men is appropriate remains extremely powerful. As Doreen Massey has argued, 'deeply internalised dualisms . . . structure personal identities and daily lives, which have effects upon the lives of others through structuring the operation of social relations and social dynamics, and which derive their masculine/feminine coding from the deep socio-philosophical underpinnings of western society' (1995: 492). Despite the fact that feminist scholars have convincingly demonstrated the flawed nature of binary assumptions, the belief in binary gender divisions has remained a key element of contemporary social practices. Thus women and their associated characteristics of femininity are defined as irrational, emotional, dependent and private, closer to nature than to culture, in comparison with men and masculine attributes that are portrayed as rational, scientific, independent, public and cultured. Women, it is commonly argued, are at the mercy of their bodies and their emotions, whereas men represent the transcendence of these baser features, mind to women's body.

As many feminist scholars have demonstrated, the belief in categorical difference, which is binary and also hierarchical, constructs women as inferior to men, and the attributes of femininity as less highly valued than those of masculinity. This belief is deeply embedded in the structures and practices of Western thought, in the divisions between social science disciplines, and in social institutions. Thus the public attributes of the market and the state are the basis for study by economists and political scientists respectively, whereas 'private' decisions taken within the home are the province of sociologists or psychologists. Pateman and Grosz's (1987) edited collection provides a very clear introduction to the binary structure of Western social science.

This binary division is also deeply implicated in the social production of space, in assumptions about the 'natural' and built environments and in the sets of regulations which influence who should occupy which spaces and who should be excluded. Thus, in common with the other social sciences, binary categorizations structure geographical scholarship (see for further explanation and examples, Mackenzie and Rose 1983; McDowell 1992a 1992b, Massey 1994; G. Rose 1993; Women and Geography Study Group 1984, 1997). It is clear, then, that feminist geographers have set themselves an ambitious task: tearing down and re-erecting the structures of our discipline, the very ways in which we theorize and make connections between people and places.

11

The specific aim of a feminist geography, therefore, is to investigate, make visible and challenge the relationships between gender divisions and spatial divisions, to uncover their mutual constitution and problematize their apparent naturalness. Thus the purpose here is to examine the extent to which women and men experience spaces and places differently and to show how these differences themselves are part of the social constitution of gender as well as that of place. In a commonsense way, there is a clear geography to gender relations because there are enormous variations between and within nations in the extent of women's subordination and relative autonomy, and correspondingly in male power and domination; there is as well an evident multiplicity in the social construction of gender, in gender divisions and in the symbolic meanings associated with femininity and masculinity. Constructing a geography or geographies of gender, as Pollock has noted, 'calls attention to the significance of place, location and cultural diversity, connecting issues of sexuality to those of nationality, imperialism, migration, diaspora and genocide' (1996: xii).

But gender relations are also of central concern for geographers because of the way in which a spatial division – that between the public and the private, between inside and outside – plays such a central role in the social construction of gender divisions. The idea that women have a particular place is the basis not only of the social organization of a whole range of institutions from the family to the workplace, from the shopping mall to political institutions, but also is an essential feature of Western Enlightenment thought, the structure and division of knowledge and the subjects that might be studied within these divisions.

Thus a list, like the following, of binary distinctions which are gendered, should be familiar to you:

The masculine	The feminine
Public	Private
Outside	Inside
Work	Home
Work	Leisure/pleasure
Production	Consumption
Independence	Dependence
Power	Lack of Power

I constructed this table of binary oppositions, but similar lists are to be found in all sorts of discussions of the organization of social relations and institutions in modern Britain, as well as in explicitly feminist texts. The characteristics and attributes associated with the women and the feminine side are assumed either to be 'natural' and so to need no explanation, or to

12

be trivial and so unsuitable for serious academic analysis. Think, for example, of how long it took feminist economists and sociologists to persuade their peers that housework or domestic labour was as much 'work' as the waged labour that took place in offices and factories and so should be part of their analyses (see Oakley 1974; Rowbotham 1989). Similarly, leisure activities and shopping have only relatively recently become a central area of geographical analysis (Wrigley and Lowe 1996).

The significance of uncovering the ways in which commonplace assumptions about gender structure the very nature of thought, of knowledge itself, is huge. It means that rethinking gender divisions requires nothing less than the reconstruction of Western knowledge itself: perhaps an even larger task than the overturning of structural inequalities between men and women. But one, of course, depends on the other.

Let's turn now to a brief history of this reconstruction of knowledge in our own discipline and more generally.

Thinking about gender

Since the resurgence of feminism in the late 1960s the term gender has been introduced and redefined and is now used in two different, although interconnected ways. In a very clear essay 'Interpreting gender' Linda Nicholson (1995) has outlined the history of its usage and I shall draw on this here.

Separating sex from gender

The first way in which the term gender tends to be used is in contrast to the term sex. While sex depicts biological differences, gender in contrast describes socially constructed characteristics. In 1949, Simone de Beauvoir, the great French existential thinker and feminist, published *The Second Sex* in which she claimed women are not born but made, and so challenged the assumption of biological determinism.

> One is not born but rather becomes a woman. No biological, physiological or economic fate determines the figure that the human being presents in society: it is civilization as a whole that produces this creative indeterminate between male and eunuch which is described as feminine. (de Beauvoir 1972: 295)

While de Beauvoir's positioning of women between men and eunuchs may have been challenged, as have the ethnocentric assumptions in her work,

13

her recognition that femininity is socially constructed was extremely important in the advent of second wave feminism in Britain and the US. The 1960s resurgence of feminist thought and action, which was so called to distinguish it from the 'first phase' or struggle for suffrage, drew on de Beauvoir's book. Her argument about the social construction of femininity was taken seriously and developed through the adoption of the term gender, as distinct from the term sex, to refer to the ways in which women were 'made'. Thus the key aim of a great deal of early theoretical work by contemporary feminists was to challenge what seemed like immutable sexual differences based in biology, to undermine the claims of absolute sexual difference between women and men, and, importantly, to demonstrate that women's supposed inferiority in matters of physical strength and mental agility were not 'natural' phenomena.

By differentiating gender from sex, gender could be theorized as the cultural or social elaboration of the latter and as such amenable to change. Anthropology's notion of culture was of key importance here as variations in male and female roles and behaviours were clearly evident cross-culturally, although even here certain 'natural' process tended to be taken for granted. Thus as Ortner and Whitehead argued in 1981

> natural features of gender, and natural processes of sex and reproduction, furnish only a suggestive and ambiguous backdrop to the cultural organization of gender and sexuality. What gender is, what men and women are, what sorts of relations do or should obtain between them – all of these notions do not simply reflect or elaborate upon biological 'givens', but are largely products of social and cultural processes. (p. 1)

In one of the best-known and influential early articles of second wave feminism, Gayle Rubin (1975) showed how these processes were interrelated through what she termed a sex/gender system. Such a system is, she argued, that 'set of arrangements by which a society transforms biological sexuality into products of human activity and in which these transformed sexual needs are satisfied' (p. 159). Through this transformation and social regulation, 'sex' becomes 'gender'. In a vivid analogy Linda Nicholson suggests that this model or relationship between sex and gender is like a coat-rack. Sex or biological difference is the basic frame on to which different societies in different historical periods have hung various coats – the socially defined arrangement of gender characteristics. The great advantage of this distinction was that it enabled feminists to challenge the 'naturalness' of gender divisions and to theorize them as variable. It also enabled both commonalities and differences among women to be postulated and, for geographers, it proved invaluable as gender relations were theorized as spatially variable phenomena across a range of different scales. Thus it was recognized that gendered characteristics vary not only between countries and over historical time, but also in everyday spaces and interactions. So, for example, in bars, clubs, parliamentary buildings, student hostels, offices, the use of gender symbols and expectations of gender-appropriate behaviour vary.

Subsuming sex in gender

In its second, and later, usage, however the term gender is not seen as distinguishable from sex; rather the latter is subsumable within the former. Nicholson (1995) draws from and quotes Joan Scott's explanation in *Gender and the Politics of History* of this second way of understanding or defining gender.

> It follows then that gender is the social organization of sexual difference. But this does not mean that gender reflects or implements fixed and natural physical differences between women and men; rather gender is the knowledge that establishes meaning for bodily differences ... We cannot see sexual differences except as a function of our knowledge about the body and that knowledge is not pure, it cannot be isolated from its implication in a broad range of discursive contexts. (Scott 1988: 2)

In this way, the biological foundationalism of the first perspective on gender differences is challenged and the attributes of sexual difference which were assumed to have universal applicability have been revealed for what they are: 'matters specific to Western culture or to specific groups within it' (Nicholson 1995: 42). This recognition means that

> we cannot look to the body to ground cross-cultural claims about the male/ female distinction ... differences go 'all the way down' ... tied not just to the limited phenomena many of us associate with gender (i.e. to cultural stereotypes of personality and behaviour), but also to culturally various understandings of the body, and to what it means to be a woman and a man. (p. 43)

Thus the body too is open to analysis and theorization as a variable, not a constant. Recent work on the body will be discussed in the next chapter.

Patriarchy, gender regimes and gender bargains

In the earliest work undertaken by feminist geographers and others, gender was defined and analysed mainly in the first sense and the major emphasis was on uncovering variations in the ways in which material social practices resulted in inequitable gender relations. In this work the idea of patriarchy was an important concept which was useful both in connecting gender to class and in theorizing the reasons for women's oppression in a range of societies. In its most general sense, the term patriarchy refers to the law of the father, the social control that men as fathers hold over their wives and daughters. In its more specific usage within feminist scholarship, patriarchy refers to the system in which men as a group are constructed as superior to women as a group and so assumed to have authority over them. In advanced industrial societies there are several ways in which this superiority and control is constructed and enforced: through the legal system for instance, in the tax and social security systems, as well as through everyday attitudes and behaviours.

If we take the legal system as an example, in Britain throughout the nineteenth century and well into the twentieth, a woman's legal status was as a dependant and her life and property were in the hands of her father or her husband. Until the Married Women's Property Act was passed in 1885, for example, on marriage all a woman's worldly goods passed into the hands of her husband. In the UK women could not vote until after the First World War; women did not become full members of Cambridge University until 1948; they could not have a legal abortion until 1967; they could not gain access to mortgage finance without a male guarantor until into the 1970s.

In her book *Theorizing Patriarchy* (1990) Walby suggests that patriarchal relations in advanced industrial societies are constructed and maintained by six sets of analytically separable structures in which men dominate and exploit women. The six structures she identifies are household production (in which men appropriate the value of women's unpaid domestic labour); patriarchal relations in waged work (in which women are segregated into particular occupations and are less well paid); patriarchal relations in the state (in which men dominate the institutions as well as produce gender-biased legislation); male violence against women; patriarchal relations in sexuality (male control of women's bodies); and patriarchal relations in cultural institutions (male domination both of the production and form of different media and of the representations of women therein).

The concept of patriarchy has been criticized on general grounds for being too overarching. In early theorizations, patriarchy was assumed to be a universal feature of the relations between men and women and so seemed to leave little scope either for variations or for women to evade its reach. Walby's distinction of the six separate structures partly evades this general criticism as she argued that patriarchal relations take specific forms in each of the six spheres she identified, but even so her formulation was also criticized for its overarching nature, and for its ethnocentricity (based on advanced capitalist societies). Walby has also been criticized for ignoring the interconnections between gender relations and other social divisions, such as those based on ethnicity, age and different sexual orientations.

In her later formulations, Walby accepted the burden of these criticisms and while holding to the idea of interconnected structures, she suggested that these structures or sets of relations are connected in different ways in particular circumstances and places. She moved from using the term patriarchy to that of a gender regime, also constituted by the same six sets of relations. Walby distinguished two main regimes in advanced industrial societies: what she terms a domestic regime distinguished by private patriarchal relations and a public regime dominated by public patriarchal relations. This is how she describes the two regimes:

> The domestic gender regime is based upon household production as the main structure and site of women's work activity and the exploitation of her labour and sexuality and upon the exclusion of women from the public. The public gender regime is based, not on excluding women from the public, but on the segregation and subordination of women within the structures of paid employment and the state, as well as within culture, sexuality and violence. The household does not cease to be a relevant structure in the public form, but it is no longer the chief one. In the domestic form the beneficiaries are primarily the individual husbands and fathers of the women in the household, while in the public form there is more collective appropriation. In the domestic form the principal patriarchal strategy is exclusionary, excluding women from the public arena; in the public it is segregationist and subordinating. In both forms all six structures are relevant, but they have a different relationship to each other. In order to understand any particular instance of gender regime it is always necessary to understand the mutual structuring of class and ethnic relations with gender. (Walby 1997: 6)

While these regimes may be analytically distinct, Walby recognizes that they often coexist and that women are differently involved in each structure.

> Different forms of gender regime coexist as a result of the diversity in gender relations consequent upon age, class, ethnicity and region. [In Britain] older women will be more likely than younger women to be involved in a more domestic gender regime. Women whose own occupations place them in higher socio-economic groups are more likely to be in a more public form. Women of Pakistani and Bangladeshi descent are more likely to be in a domestic form and Black Caribbean women more likely to be in a more public form than white women. (p. 6)

I find that this idea of different regimes composed of separate but inter-connected structures is a useful way analytically to distinguish changing gender relations, especially as Walby has shown how to include class and ethnic differences in her most recent formulation of regimes. In the chapters that follow I shall address many of the areas and social relations that Walby outlined, focusing, for example, on the home and the social relations within it and then on the ways in which gender relations are both constituted in and affected by the social relations of capitalist workplaces.

Walby's recent replacement of the notion of patriarchy by the more nuanced concept of gender regimes brings her work closer to that of another important theorist of gender relations. This is Robert Connell, who has been a key influence on gender scholarship, perhaps especially because he was one of the first analysts to focus on the social construction of masculinity (Connell 1987, 1995). He too finds the notion of a gender regime useful, and like Walby emphasizes change and variety in its structure. Connell writes from a Gramscian perspective (an Italian Marxist writer, Gramsci emphasized the non-coercive aspects of power, often operating through cultural forms, as opposed to the more brutal and direct forms of domination). Thus, in contrast to Walby, who theorizes the singular dominant and coercive male oppression of women in the same way as Marx theorized coercive class oppression, Connell is interested in forms of cultural consent and pleasure and in the multiple ways in which gender relations are constructed and maintained.

Although Connell argues that different societies are characterized by a dominant or hegemonic gender regime which is relatively stable over time, he also notes that a range of oppositional regimes may coexist with the dominant one, challenging the assumptions about sexuality and gender that maintain it, and that this may lead to change. Connell thus provides a way to escape from the criticism of patriarchy as all-encompassing and seemingly incapable of change. He also suggests that notions about sexuality and gendered positions are not only enforced by power and oppression but that people take pleasure in their subject position in a particular gender regime. This understanding moves Connell closer to the arguments of those feminists who began to recognize that the social construction of femininity brings pleasure and delight to individual women (see, for example, Coward, 1984).

Gender regimes according to Connell consist of three sets of structures, compared to Walby's six. He distinguishes 'relations of (a) power, (b) production and (c) cathexis (emotional attachment) (1995: 73-4). So we see that as well as the dominance produced through force that Walby emphasizes, if we adopt Connell's approach we are now more able to understand why people, and especially women, are bound into, even enjoy and cel-

18

ebrate their position in patriarchal relations – what earlier feminists used to rather disapprovingly refer to as women's 'collusion with patriarchy'. Let's look in more detail at Connell's threefold model in the extract below. This is how Connell distinguishes power, production and cathexis:

(a) *Power relations* The main axis of power in the contemporary European/ American gender order is the overall subordination of women and the dominance of men – the structure Women's Liberation named 'patriarchy'. This general structure exists despite many local reversals (e.g. woman-headed households, female teachers with male students). It persists despite resistance of many kinds, now articulated in feminism.

(b) *Production relations* Gender divisions of labour are familiar in the form of the allocation of tasks, sometimes reaching extraordinarily fine detail. . . . Equal attention should be paid to the economic consequences of gender divisions of labour, the dividend accruing to men from unequal shares of the product of social labour. This is most often discussed in terms of unequal wage rates, but the gendered character of capital should also be noted. A capitalist economy working through a gender division of labour is, necessarily, a gendered accumulation process. So it is not a statistical accident, but a part of the social construction of masculinity, that men and not women control the major corporations and the great private fortunes. Implausible as it sounds, the accumulation of wealth has become firmly linked to the reproductive arena, through the social relations of gender.

(We might note here that the significance of intermarriage and of legitimate births for inheritance purposes has long interested the capital-owning classes and was, indeed, the basis of Engels's arguments about women's domination in the family well over a century before Connell's work.)

(c) *Cathexis* Sexual desire is so often seen as natural that it is commonly excluded from social theory. Yet when we consider desire in Freudian terms, as emotional energy being attached to an object, its gendered character is clear. This is true both for heterosexual desire and homosexual desire. The practices that shape and realize desire are thus an aspect of the gender order. Accordingly we can ask political questions about the relationships involved: whether they are consensual or coercive, whether pleasure is equally given and received. In feminist analyses of sexuality these have become sharp questions about the connection of heterosexuality with men's position of social dominance. (Connell 1995: 74–5)

We can see that there are clear areas of overlap between Walby's and Connell's model. They both have their origins in Marxist theorizing and both emphasize the social relations of production and reproduction. We might map Walby's fifth and sixth structures – sexuality and culture – on to Connell's cathexis, but whereas Connell explicitly separates power out as a distinguishable structure, it also underpins his other structures; Walby assumes power in the arenas of production and reproduction, but chooses to identity its particular manifestation in male violence against women as a separate structure.

The main problem with Walby's analysis, in my view, is that she does not explain the reasons for women's attachment to individual men or to a particular gender order or regime order. Connell, through his emphasis on emotional attachment is able to grasp this but does, I feel, somewhat underplay the other ways in which women may feel they have no option but to 'buy into' the dominant gender order. I want, therefore to briefly introduce a third way of understanding gender regimes. Unlike Connell and Walby whose work is based on examples from advanced industrial societies, Deniz Kandiyoti in a paper published in 1988, explicitly focused on non-European societies. In this paper, Kandiyoti was anxious not only to differentiate patriarchal structures on a broad geographical basis (distinguishing African from Asian patriarchy, for example), but also to explore the reasons why women in the main accepted rather than rebelled against patriarchal structures. She drew attention to different family structures and the ways in which wives and widows were dependent on particular structures of patriarchal kinship relations, arguing that it was in women's self-interest to support a system that was essential for their long-term survival and living standards even while it was also oppressing them and their daughters.

In her work, Kandiyoti insisted on the recognition of women's agency; women in the two broad forms of patriarchy, may be subordinate but they are not necessarily subservient. They are able to work within and to some extent subvert partriarchal relations, and so like Connell, and Walby in her later work, Kandiyoti identifies the ways in which gender regimes may change. All three authors insist on complexity and variety: both in the ways in which gender relations result in unequal relations between women and men, and in the scope and reasons for change. They also all insist on the interconnections between gender, class position and ethnic origins. In his book *Masculinities* (1995), Connell shows, for example, how white men's sense of themselves is constructed in relation to an idealized notion of black masculinity as well as in opposition to white femininity (Lynn Segal (1990) in *Slow Motion* also argues the same point), and argues that acceptable notions of both manliness and femininity vary by class position and by 'race', as well as over time and between regions and nations.

Thus the idea of dominant and oppositional gender regimes, which are complex and variable, gives a useful and structured way of investigating the geographic diversity of gender relations. I shall draw on it in the later chapters. Like that of Walby and Connell, my own empirical work, together with the literatures I have read during its development, has been based on case studies of advanced industrial societies, and the focus of this book reflects this. In places, I do introduce ideas and case studies from scholars working in other societies, but I am afraid my knowledge here is too limited to provide comprehensive comparisons between the 'north' and the 'south'.

One final word about a structural approach before we move on in this voyage through the history of feminist theorizing: the belief that patriarchy or gender regimes are a structured set of inequalities has recently come under attack from deconstructive and postmodern arguments about the impermanence of the very categories 'woman' and 'man' (and I shall turn to these arguments in more detail in a moment) and the impossibility of understanding difference and diversity through 'grand theories'. I believe, however, like Walby, that it is not necessary to give up wide-ranging notions of structured relationships in order to theorize complexity. All three theorists whose work I have drawn on above recognize the complexity of the ways in which gender is intercut by class, age, ethnicity and by other factors such as sexuality; but in circumstances where women, as a group, are clearly subordinate to, unequal with and dominated by men as a group, then it seems to me that we must hold on to ways to theorize these differences which recognize structured inequities between social groups. However fluid and variable the social construction of versions of femininity and masculinity, it is still habitual practice to assume that the former constructions are inferior to the latter and so men as a group are implicated in the domination of women.

Diversity, difference and deconstruction

From the arguments that I have outlined above, it should now be clear to you that gender relations are 'at the base, relations of power, hierarchy and inequality, not simply dichotomous, symmetrical and complementary relations, as commonsense categories like to put it' (de Almeida 1996: 8). There are many different ways of 'doing gender' (West and Zimmerman 1987), of being a man and a woman. Multiple and oppositional as well as hegemonic versions of femininity and masculinity exist. They are geographically and historically specific and vary across the range of spatial scales. And gender itself is now theorized as one variable among others, or rather, and more correctly, as mutually constituted by class and by ethnicity (Brewer 1993; Davis 1981; Giddings 1984; Kobayashi and Peake 1994; Malson et al. 1990; Mirza 1997; Peake 1993).

21

Despite this recognition of multiplicity and differences between women, a range of critics, influenced in particular by poststructural and postcolonial theory, began, from the 1970s, to deconstruct the very notion that gender is a stable construct at all. Their critique built on earlier arguments from black feminists that most feminist scholarship and politics implicitly assumed a white subject. In the political struggle for women's right to control their own bodies, for example, freely available contraception and abortion was a key demand, whereas many women of colour argued that for them, often sterilized against their will, the right to be fertile and to give birth was more important. Similarly lesbians pointed to the implicit heterosexuality of a great deal of feminist writing and scholarship and demanded that questions about 'alternative' sexualities were put on the agenda. Their demands were reinforced by the rapid rise of gay and queer scholarship in the 1980s (Craig 1992; Fuss 1990; Herdt 1992; Kimmel 1988; Sedgwick 1990; Simpson 1994; Weeks 1986).

Feminists influenced by postmodern theory have argued that, despite the earlier feminist critique of Western Enlightenment knowledge as reflecting the world-view of bourgeois men, this feminist scholarship itself still held to Enlightenment notions of the centred subject and to an idealized view of social progress. As part of the general movement to include the voices of the dispossessed – a motley ban of 'Others' – within academic discourse the singular view of knowledge and of truth (what Haraway (1991) termed 'the view from nowhere'), was challenged. Postcolonial critics such as Gayatri Spivak (1988) and Chandra Talpade Mohanty (1991), and women of colour, including bell hooks (1982), were influential in forcing white women to re-examine the female subject in their work, to theorize the complexities of 'raced' identities and to write from their particular position as white women, not as 'Woman'. A new feminist scholarship that explores the racialization of white women is developing. Thus Vron Ware (1992), for example, has begun to explore the position of white women in imperial India, and Ruth Frankenberg (1993) has investigated her own and other white women's beliefs about racism while they were growing up white in the postwar period in the US.

This exploration of multiple standpoints was accompanied by a more challenging development as feminist scholars versed in the psychoanalytic literature, as well as influenced by the work of Michel Foucault, began to retheorize the subject as relational and contingent. The subject, it is argued, rather than being a fixed and stable entity which enters into social relations with its gender in place, is always fluid and provisional, in the process of becoming. Gender is constructed and maintained through discourse and everyday actions. There have been a number of directions in which this work has been taken by those that we might group together as deconstructionist feminists and I shall explore these in greater depth in the next chapter. Briefly, however, this work questions the dichotomous distinction of sexual difference as well as the mapping of gender attributes on to the bipolar division. Thus Donna Haraway has argued that 'there is nothing about being "female" that naturally binds women. There is not even such a state as "being" female, itself a highly complex category constructed in contested sexual scientific discourse and other social practices' (1991: 155).

A key theorist in the new feminist work on the body is Judith Butler. She argues, somewhat differently from Haraway, that sexed bodies are constructed as such, from the standpoint of already dichotomized gender – that is, it is taken for granted that there are two genders: male and female – and through scientific, medical and other discourses, bodies are identified in the same way. Butler (1990a, 1993) suggests that this identification and its maintenance over time is constructed through what she terms a gender performance, in which the regulatory fiction of heterosexuality constrains most of us to perform within the hegemonic norms that define bipolar feminine and masculine norms in specific societal contexts. She suggests, however, that the discursive or taken-for-granted construction of bipolar gender may be challenged through subversive performances, and identifies drag as a key subversive act. I discuss these arguments in more detail in the next chapter but I want to note here that they have raised important questions about the materiality or reality of the body. Commenting on these debates, Caroline New (1997) has recently attempted to reinsert the 'real' into the discursive construction of the sexed body.

> I maintain that sexual difference is real, though it is not merely dichotomous. However, it is no accident that human beings have been able to dichotomize it more or less successfully: sexual differences do have a bipolar distribution, explicable by evolutionary accounts of sexuality. There are real male and female capacities and liabilities, although whether and how these are instantiated in particular cases depends on the entire causal context. (New 1997: 179)

I agree with the spirit of New's comment. Indeed it has an affinity with realist notions of science which have been so important in our discipline, although I disagree with her attribution of causality to the context. It seems to me that the relationships between sex and gender are historically and spatially contingent, although as she notes, evolutionary biological changes affect 'real' sexual difference. What it means to be a woman or a man is, therefore, context-dependent, relational and variable, albeit constrained by the rules and regulations of the time which define permitted and transgressive acts. Thus gender, as Linda Alcoff, a feminist political theorist, argued, 'is not a point to start from in the sense of being a given thing but is, instead, a posit or construct, formalizable in a nonarbitrary way through a matrix of habits, practices and discourse' (1988: 431).

The retheorization of gender as a discursive construction and a performative fiction has been extremely exciting. In studies of the workplace, for example, it allowed a new set of questions to be asked about workplace cultures, how gender identities are constructed through daily interactions at work, and, importantly, offered the prospect of thinking through challenges to unequal gender relations in immediate ways. The recognition of diversity and possible oppositional strategies provided a more nuanced way to think about the domination of women in the workplace than the rather overarching concept of patriarchal domination. It also led to the introduction of new research questions about language, gestures, speaking styles and bodily presentation (Halford et al. 1997; McDowell 1997a; Tannen 1994).

A further impetus to conceptualizing gender as fluid has come through the impact of new technologies, in the spheres both of reproduction and reconstructive surgery. Gender seems nowadays to have escaped the constraints of the body, or more accurately the body has been redefined. Control over reproduction for example, in a wide range of ways from in vitro fertilization and fertility treatment to surrogacy, has led to gender and sexuality increasingly becoming fluid and malleable, almost something to be chosen as one further aspect of personal identity. Women are now 'free' to become mothers after the menopause, or to reshape their bodies as they wish, with, in most cases it seems, income level being the sole constraint. We seem to have arrived, in the words of the feminist anthropologist Marilyn Strathern (1992), at a time 'after nature' when conventional bonds of blood, kinship and marriage seem almost irrelevant to the process of reproduction and family life.

What the 'cultural' or deconstructive turn in feminism has achieved is the placing of arguments about specificity and particularity right at the centre of new comparative work. In this sense we might claim, not without some justice I think, that geographic questions are now central to feminist scholarship. This claim is made not only by other geographers (see for example Katz and Smith 1993) but also by scholars in other disciplines (see for example a book by Kirby 1996 who is a professor of English); they emphasize the importance of questions about place, about the location and positionality of the person making claims and about how to listen to and interpret voices from the margins that we too often ignore (McDowell 1992a, 1992b). New theories of the subject and the deconstruction of stable identities bring in their wake, however, new anxieties about the prospects

24

for a specifically feminist scholarship and politics. If there is no longer a stable category 'woman', how may we make claims on her behalf?

'Many feminists have pondered the implications of this dilemma (Fox-Genovese 1986; Grosz 1994; Mascia-Lees et al. 1989; McDowell 1991b). Here is Linda Alcoff as a representative voice: What can we demand in the name of women if "women" do not exist and demands in their name simply reinforce the myth that they do. How can we demand legal abortions, adequate childcare, or wages based on comparative worth without involving a concept of "woman"?' (1988: 420). These are clearly difficult issues but it seems to me not irresolvable. As social scientists our purpose is to uncover and explain the structures and processes that operate to distinguish between people and place them in social groups that are in an unequal relationship one to another. In contemporary capitalist societies – and at the end of the twentieth century capitalism seems to be triumphantly marching through ever-larger numbers of nations – people are divided into social classes with radically different life chances and opportunities. Similarly, racist attitudes and racial discrimination blight the lives of many people of colour. As I have argued in this introduction, and as the rest of the chapters will show in more detail, women as a group have fewer opportunities than men as a group. In many societies, women are often denied educational opportunities. In probably all societies, women earn less than men and have less control over the sources of wealth. While I am anxious not to construct women as victims, it must also be noted that they are subjected to particular forms of domination and violence. In these circumstances, while the differences that differentiate women should not be denied – differences of class and ethnicity, for example, and of place in different parts of the world – it remains important for women to speak as women and to proclaim a vision of a better future. As Nancy Fraser has suggested, 'feminists need both deconstruction and reconstruction, destabilization of meaning and projection of utopian hope' (1991: 175).

Geography and feminists

As I have just argued, people, knowledge and social institutions are subject to and defined by unequal gender divisions. Whatever the variation between men, and whatever the extent (often great) of the changes in women's status in the last few decades, men as a group continue to constitute the majority in the bases of power in contemporary societies. This is as true in the academy as in other institutions. Although the years beginning in the 1970s to end of 1990s have been a crucial period in feminist scholarship, and in human geography where there have been huge paradigm shifts affecting the nature of the discipline and the ways in which it is related to the 'real world', it is still men in the main who are the heads of departments and the chairs of key committees. The growing proportion of women as undergraduates (a majority in recent years in my own department) has not (yet?) been matched by a similar increase in the proportion in teaching and professional research, although there are growing numbers of women among the younger appointments in British geography departments. But at the senior level, women are relatively few and far between – in Britain chairs are held by women in only four departments – and the geographical agenda at this level continues to be set by men, few of whom (some, but too few) are as interested in questions about the geographical differentiation in masculinity and femininity as many women geographers seem to be. Not all women are interested in questions of gender, of course, and it would be a mistake to assume so, as it is equally mistaken to assume that gender issues are 'women's' issues. But it should be extremely clear from the previous pages that men are gendered too.

The origins of feminist organization within geography, in the English-speaking world at least, date from some time in the 1970s, and from the start included the dual focus of uncovering gendered geographies and acting, where possible, to implement alternatives. Thus, when a study group was formed in 1979 within the British professional association, the Institute of British Geographers (now amalgamated with the Royal Geographical Society), its dual aim included theoretical work on gender and a commitment to improve the position of women within academic institutions. A wider political commitment at that time would probably have frightened the geographic establishment – and was inhibited as well by our own recognition of its utopianism. And anyway, idealistic notions of international sisterhood were quickly dissipated in the growing recognition throughout the 1980s of the differences and distances between women. Divisions of class, ethnicity, age and sexual preference, among others, made it impossible to speak for all women geographers, let alone womankind as a whole.

The commitment to a political project, however, has remained a central aim. The feminist groups formed by geographers in universities in Canada and the United States also involved explicit statements about women's position in the academy, and for a number of years statistics have been collected to monitor women's movement into institutional positions (McDowell and Peake 1990; Momsen 1980; G. Rose 1993). There are now a small number of women who are self-identified feminists in positions of power, holding chairs of geography for example in Britain, Canada, the US and Australia, although the numbers remain tiny. Although at the undergraduate level, in Britain at least, as I noted above, the discipline is becoming female dominated, at the graduate level, women are still outnumbered two to one by men. It has been suggested that there is something particularly masculinist about the structure and practice of our discipline: perhaps this lies in its image as what Cosgrove, in another context, has termed 'a hairy chested discipline' (Cosgrove 1993). In its commitment as it developed to Enlightenment ideals of disembodied and rational knowledge (see G. Rose 1993), geography was, of course, not alone among the sciences and social sciences, although in its association with exploration and the Empire (Driver 1992, and see also Stoddart 1986 and Livingstone 1992 on geography's origins), which it shared with anthropology, it perhaps seemed particularly attractive to men.

There has been a marked growth in the impact of feminist scholarship on geography since the late 1970s – and lest the brief statements about male dominance above seem overly gloomy, I should emphasize that it has been rapid. New courses in many departments, a new journal – *Gender, Place and Culture* – and growing numbers of papers in existing journals (look at the changes in *Society and Space* for example), new books (Gregson and Lowe 1994; Hanson and Pratt 1995; Massey 1994; G. Rose 1993), readers (McDowell and Sharp 1997) and collections (Jones III et al. 1997; Women and Geography Study Group 1984, 1997; and the growing series of *International Studies of Women and Place* (the general editors of this series are Janice Momsen and Janet Monk) dealing with feminist geographical scholarship are now available. The growth in membership of the different feminist caucuses in the professional associations in different countries has also been rapid, especially among younger women. In their foundation, however, it seemed to be those women, in Britain at least, who had been teenagers or who had entered higher education during the 1960s who were particularly influential in the early years. This, of course, is not surprising given the associations between the rise of the women's movement and other radical political struggles and movements in the 1960s. Feminism, anti-racism, anti-war and student movements were all important in the late sixties.

Some brief glimpses into the lives of these women and why they became interested in feminist geography are available in scattered places. I interviewed Susan Hanson for the *Journal of Geography in Higher Education* in 1993 (McDowell 1994a) and both Susan Hanson and Janice Monk, who were co-authors of one of the earliest feminist papers published in a US journal (Hanson and Monk 1982), have provided introductions, especially personal in Monk's case, to parts of the new US-oriented collection *Thresholds in Feminist Geography* (Jones III et al. 1997). Reflecting on their lives and summaries of changes in geography, I began to ponder my own commitment to feminist scholarship. I came to the conclusion that I think I have

27

been a feminist for most of my life, although for the first twenty years or so it was unthinking, and for several years after that my political beliefs and academic work were not coincident. I grew up as one of three sisters in a household where both my parents 'worked', both cooked and cleaned. How much of an exception to the rule this was I did not fully realize, although I was puzzled that my best friend at school seemed to be treated rather differently by her parents from her elder brother.

Ann Oakley (1985) has noted the importance of single-sex siblings and single-sex secondary education for many of the women involved in the late 1960s and 1970s in what has now become known as the second wave feminist movement and I am no exception. Indeed my single-sex secondary education was followed by three years at Newnham, an all-women's college in Cambridge where the dominance of women muted the then singularly masculine atmosphere of the geography department in that university at that time (late 1960s and early 1970s), when there were no women among the lecturing staff. It wasn't until I became a graduate student in London that I noticed and was affected by male dominance. There were fewer women students and very few women teachers at University College London at that time. Luckily, in my own academic career, however, I have never been the sole woman in any of the departments that I have worked in (although I was one of only two women for my first three years teaching in Cambridge), and I have also had the support of being a member of the Women and Geography Study Group from 1979 onwards.

This group has recently published a second edited book about feminist geography (1997). I was involved in the first (1984) when the sort of self-reflexive writing that is now much more common barely affected the discipline at all. We chose deliberate anonymity among the group who produced the first published statements about feminist geography, not, I hasten to add, because we wished to hide from the establishment but rather because we wished to assert a collective voice rather than assert our authority. The second set of feminist scholars – with some overlap with that first group – also chose this collective strategy, although very sensibly, I think, they also identified themselves more clearly. In a fascinating chapter in their book *Feminist Geographies: Explorations in Diversity and Difference* (and the title reflects, of course, some of the changing emphases in feminist scholarship that I have outlined in this chapter), called 'Writing personally', ten feminist geographers of the Women and Geography Study Group provide insights into their histories as feminists. I hope you will read these. Indeed, I hope that you will read this present book – my contribution to understanding feminist geography – in conjunction with *Feminist Geographies* and with *Thresholds in Feminist Geography* (Jones III et al. 1997). There are many similarities and also many differences between the three, although they are aimed at the same group of readers: those of you beginning your careers as geographers, and I hope many others just curious about what feminist geography might be.

This book is also a companion to Gillian Rose's book *Feminism and Geography*, (1993). Whereas Gillian's concern was predominantly with the theoretical status of geographical knowledge and the ways in which it is gendered, my focus here is primarily on social and cultural changes in gender relations, although the two are of course not as separate as this division seems to imply. For both of us a major concern in our academic work is to think through feminist ways of seeing and knowing the world. The issues I discuss here and the approaches I develop also reflect and complement the focus of *Space, Place and Gender* (1994) a collection of Doreen Massey's papers written over almost twenty years, which reveal the fascinating path of her changing interest in and approach to gender relations. I had the privilege of working with Doreen for over a decade and, indeed, I am joint author of one of the papers in her collection. So there is a personal association between the two of us as well. Finally, I have recently collaborated with Jo Sharp in the production of a collection of feminist readings, *Space, Gender, Knowledge* (McDowell and Sharp 1997). That collection aims to introduce some of the 'classic' work about space, place and identity by geographers and other scholars to undergraduate readers and I hope you will also find it a useful guide.

These recent books have made it plain that there is a hungry audience out there of people who want to know what constitutes femininity and masculinity in different places and how this has changed, or may be changed, at the end of the millennium.

Structure of the book: grounded places, flows and scales

In the chapters that follow I explore the extent of changes in women's and men's everyday lives, and in their sense of their connections to a particular place or places, at the end of the twentieth century. As I suggested earlier, it is often argued that the consequences of increasing mobility have been a reduction of the extent to which women and men are members of relatively stable place-based communities and networks throughout their lives. While mobility cannot be denied (both of people and money flows), like Massey, I want to argue that places – local attachments – remain significant. For most of the time, many of us live spatially restricted, geographically bounded lives, in a home, in a neighbourhood, in a city, in a workplace, all of which are within a nation-state. Of course, all these sites or places are constructed through sets of complex, intersecting social relationships that operate at a variety of levels and which are affected by beliefs and attitudes, images and symbols that are themselves increasingly variable and complex. Television, video, the Internet have made accessible to growing numbers of people (but still restricted, in the main, to the affluent urban dweller in the world's 'north') an almost infinite variety of text and images about every conceivable issue. But even so this material is received and processed by people who are members of different sorts of communities – some of which are spatially fixed and territorially restricted – in which they are divided by social distinctions such as class, race, age and gender.

These communities themselves may be 'real' – in the sense that members know each other and engage in regular face-to-face interactions. Thus at home, in the local streets and in the workplace we often know many of the other people whose 'place' of locality overlaps with ours. In other cases the community is 'imagined' in the sense that Benedict Anderson (1991) has suggested for members of a nation-state. We belong to the same 'place' but we are strangers: our 'community' in the sense of communal belonging is constructed through myths and imagery, through customs and rituals that reinforce our sense of being, say, British or French, Kenyan or Japanese. In the chapters that follow I want to examine the range of places in which our sense of ourselves as a man or as a woman is constituted. I want to argue that both people and places are gendered and so social and spatial relationships are mutually constituted.

The chapters are organized somewhat approximately on an ascending spatial scale, considering the most local relationships first. I have identified a range of the sites and places where gender relations are differentially constituted, both affecting and reflecting the nature of the sites and common expectations about acceptable ways of being masculine or feminine. As I have explained, I have conceptualized place as constituted by sets of relations which cut across spatial scales; but in order to analyse these interconnections there must be a local or locality focus. Places, in other words, touch the ground as spatially located patterns and behaviours. And remember too that I have also suggested that for all but the most affluent members of any society, everyday life is indeed a local affair. However, to understand these local relationships in places, where, for example, Chilean migrants reconstruct their sense of 'home' in Glasgow, or Tamil refugees in London, combining cultures and habits from 'there' and 'here' to create a new sense of place, requires not just an analysis 'in place' but the unpicking of relationships and spatial practices across space and over time. It is at the nodes in these networks, and through the cultural meanings associated with them, that places are constituted.

This conceptualization is challenging, however, for the scrivener. As

30

Marcus has also recognized, representing interconnections may require a new form of writing. He asks:

> if ethnographic description can no longer be circumscribed by the situated locale or community, the place where cultural process manifests itself and can be captured in the ethnographic present, what then? How to render a description of cultural process that occurs in transcultural space, in different locales at once, in parallel, separate but simultaneous worlds? (1994: 40)

He suggests the possibilities of adopting a montage technique to move away from a linear realist mode. I am less ambitious though and in what follows I have adopted a traditional way of writing. Perhaps montage lends itself more to the representation of original fieldwork than the task of the reviewer which faces me here. A conventional narrative structure seems to be more appropriate. But in a sense, montage, or at least simultaneity, is increasingly evident in geographic work the more the position or identity both of the subjects and of the author is the focus of the analytical gaze. And certainly, as a glance at many journals will show, geographers lately seem to have developed a greater reliance on visual material as well as text in their published work.

I have divided my material into chapters focusing in the main on particular arenas and locales, distinguishing, for example, the shopping mall from the workplace, the street from the home, the familiar local neighbourhood from the more anonymous arena of the city streets and public spaces. It might be argued that some of these distinctions are artificial, and indeed they are. For places as territorially bounded spaces at different spatial scales are social constructions too. Like ideas about gender, ideas about place, boundaries and membership are social constructs. I have chosen the particular sites and places that I discuss here because they are significant locations for alternative constructions of gender and gendered behaviours and images in contemporary industrial (in the main) societies. For young women and men, or older women and men, for straight or gay people, different spaces have particular significances and different relations of power that vary over time. For women with small children, for example, the home may be simultaneously a place of safety and a trap; for waged workers at the end of the day it may be a longed-for haven or a place where complex relations of age and gender have to be negotiated and renegotiated. The urban street and park, which for some are spaces for liberation and exploratory behaviours, are for others inaccessible, or places of fear and danger.

As I shall show, these divisions, especially that between the public and the private, have long been associated with gender divisions, each assumed to be the 'natural' sphere of one or the other sex. One of the major achievements of feminist scholarship over the last two decades or so has been to deconstruct and denaturalize these divisions. In what follows I too shall challenge these naturalized assumptions and show the connections between the different arenas of social activities. But, as I shall also show, the divisions remain significant, embodied within the legal and institutional structure of many societies as well as in the constitution of gender divisions. They also remain an influential way of dividing the subject matter of our discipline: economic from social geography, urban from retail, for example. Here, however, despite seeming to parallel these divisions in my chapter structure, I shall emphasize the interconnections. It is, after all, unusual to see all these topics discussed together within the covers of a single geographical text.

I have tried to weave together here something about gender relations and feminism as a social movement, as a set of theoretical shifts and as a material subject for analysis. The major emphasis however is on the latter aspect. My aim is to illuminate theoretical shifts through detailed empirical examples and case studies which I have drawn from a wide range of sources. I have used my own work where it is relevant, but I have also tried to introduce the work of a considerable number of others from inside and outside the boundaries of the discipline of geography. I have included a large number of references to other work in the hope that this short introduction might also act as a stimulus to and a source for further exploration of the growing literatures about gender differentiation in the social sciences and the humanities. All I can hope is that you find the chapters that follow both interesting and provocative and that they lead you into further explorations of feminist scholarship.

Further reading

There are many good introductions to feminist theory and research, both in geography and other disciplines. I have referenced these in the text, but I might mention just one or two again here. The geographical story is told in *Geography and Gender* (Women and Geography Study Group 1984), *Feminism and Geography* (G. Rose 1993), in *Feminist Geographies* (Women and Geography Study Group 1997), *Thresholds in Feminist Geography* (Jones III et al. 1997) and in *Space, Gender, Knowledge* (McDowell and Sharp 1997). I also provided a summary of research in the 1970s and 1980s in a pair of articles in *Progress in Human Geography* (McDowell 1992a, 1992b). All these books and articles, however, have a dominantly Anglo-centric emphasis. There are a number of reviews of the development of feminist geographical scholarship in other societies. Lynn Brydon and Sylvia Chant (1989), for example, Janice Monk (1994) and Janet Momsen, alone (1991) and writing with Janet Townsend (1987) and later with Vivian Kinnaird (1993), have begun to tell this story but the details remain to be filled in. The journal *Gender, Place and Culture* encourages feminists working in institutions outside the West to publish in its pages, and the International Geographic Union's Commission on Gender publishes a useful newsletter that includes lists of new books and papers by the international community of feminist geographers. *Progress in Human Geography* also includes excellent annual surveys of recently published feminist geographical research.

For more general views of feminist scholarship you might turn to Terry Lovell's reader *British Feminist Thought* (1990), Sneja Gunew's *Feminist Knowledge: Critique and Construct* (1990) and *A Reader in Feminist Knowledge* (Gunew 1991), Heidi Safia Mirza's *Black British Feminism* (1997) or Mary Evans's recent excellent text *An Introduction to Contemporary Feminist Thought* (1997), of which the last has the advantage of brevity. For two excellent reviews of feminist anthropology, which after all is very close to feminist geography, look for *Feminism and Anthropology* by Henrietta Moore (1988) and *Gender at the Crossroads of Knowledge* by Maria De Leonardo (1991). Finally, for assistance with terms there is a useful *Glossary of Feminist Theory* edited by Sonya Andermahr et al. (1997), which by the time you read this should have been joined by a specialist companion *A Glossary of Feminist Geography* (McDowell and Sharp 1999).

2

In and Out of Place: Bodies and Embodiment

Introduction

In the last chapter I suggested that a useful way to order the variety of questions and issues that absorb feminist geographers is through a focus on different kinds of places, distinguished each from the other through the operation of the relations of power that construct boundaries between them. I want to start with the most immediate place: that is the body. Although geographers might not readily think of the body as a place, it is one. The body is the place, the location or site, if you like, of the individual, with more or less impermeable boundaries between one body and another. While bodies are undoubtedly material, possessing a range of characteristics such as shape and size and so inevitably taking up space, the ways in which bodies are presented to and seen by others vary according to the spaces and places in which they find themselves. In a club, for example, you might find that your gestures, bodily adornment and the freedom with which you take up space are all quite different from when you appear in the lecture theatre on a Monday morning. It is these attributes of flexibility, presentation and the occupation of space that I want to focus on in this chapter, suggesting that, contrary to common sense or first impressions, our bodies are more fluid and flexible than we often realize. Because this mutability is related to place and position, many of the issues that we first meet in this chapter will be readdressed elsewhere; bodies at work will be re-encountered in chapter 5 and on holiday, on the beach for example, in chapter 6. But it is in this chapter that I lay the groundwork for an understanding of embodied geographies.

The chapter is divided into five parts. In it I shall introduce you to some of what I think has been the most exciting research by feminist scholars in the last few years. Recently there has been a remarkable flowering of feminist scholarship about the body which has challenged not only many taken-for-granted notions about the nature of our bodies but has also forced feminist and other scholars to rethink their ideas about biology, about bodies and about the distinction between sex and gender: that key distinction through which feminists first dealt with questions about the sexed body.

But we shall come to this in a moment. The issues and questions that I shall focus on in each of the five sections are as follows. First, why have questions about the body become particularly important for social scientists at present? Secondly, what do we know about how bodies occupy space and what, as social scientists, can we discover from this? Thirdly, I want to look at how the body has been understood as something natural and as something that is distinguishable from the mind. I shall argue that this mind/body dichotomy has been a crucial factor in the construction of women as different from and inferior to men. In this section I shall also suggest that bodily differences – in size, shape and so on – are a basis of social discrimination and disadvantage and assess the implications of this for notions of social justice. Fourthly, I turn to ways of rethinking and so challenging the mind/body distinction, asking questions about how bodies are related to gender and how variable are the possible relationships. Why do bodies matter? Are bodies social scripts and performances? How have these been theorized? And then finally, as in all the chapters in this book, I shall introduce some geographical research about the subject.

Questions about the body are not usually – or immediately – seen as part of geographical research. Traditionally the discipline has focused on the public arena to the exclusion of the private, and the body, with its attributes and performances and its sexuality, has been firmly identified as exactly that: as fundamentally a private concern. But, as I shall show here, this assumption has been challenged and rethought in recent feminist work which shows how the body itself is constructed through public discourse and practices that occur at a variety of spatial scales. Work on the body has also altered understandings of space, as it has become clear that spatial divisions – whether in the home or in the workplace, at the level of the city or the nation-state – are also affected by and reflected in embodied practices and lived social relations. As the new work about the body is expanding rapidly and is also theoretically complex and challenging, I shall provide little more than a basic introduction here. The suggested reading at the end should help you to explore some of this work in greater detail.

Why has research on the body grown so rapidly in the last few years?

As the many good introductions to feminist thought make clear, the spatial division of everyday life into a so-called public arena and a private sphere, the former associated in the main with men and the latter with women, has been a central theme in feminist discussions for many decades (see for example Jones III et al. 1997; Lovell 1990; Pateman and Grosz 1987; Phillips 1987; Massey 1994; McDowell 1992a; G. Rose 1993; Women and Geography Study Group 1984, 1997). In these discussions, however, the body has often been under-privileged. Indeed, this neglect of the body – its physical attributes and its feelings and desires – is partly because it has long been the most troublesome site for feminist theorists as thinking about bodies raises awkward questions about the significance of physical differences between women and men. In the last few years, though, a vast social science literature on the body, not necessarily but often focusing on gender differences, has been published (Butler 1993; Bordo 1993; Diprose and Ferrell 1991; Falk 1994; Featherstone et al. 1991; Grosz 1994; Jacobus et al. 1990; Jagger and Bordo 1989; Martin 1987; Synnott 1993; Tseelon 1995; Turner 1996; Young 1990a, 1990b). It seems that, as we move towards the end of the twentieth century, the body has become a major theoretical preoccupation across the social sciences, as well as an object for scrutiny and regulation by society as a whole.

For most people, the body is certainly a central object of personal concern, as well as a key social issue. At the end of the twentieth century fascination and fear seem to jockey for position in common attitudes to the body. Thus the cult of the body – in sport, diet and surgical intervention – and its celebration coexists with the development of AIDS, that twentieth-century syndrome which ravages the body. And as fears about this disease make clear, the body is intimately associated with sexuality and sexual behaviour. In the tabloid press this association is also linked to notions of sexual excess, 'perversity' or abnormality. Thus questions about the body, its form, meaning and its practices are associated with complicated issues about subjectivity and identity and with social practices often defined both as deeply personal and as subjects of public comment. I want to argue here that the body and sexual practices are socially constructed and variable, involving changing assumptions about what is or is not 'natural' or 'normal'. They have, in other words, a history and a geography.

The centrality of the body in recent social theory is, in part at least, a consequence of the profound material changes that have taken place in late twentieth-century advanced industrial countries. Rapid economic change has transformed the nature of work and leisure and placed the body at the centre of concern for individuals and for society. It is both a motor of economic development, and a source of individual pleasure and pain. As Bryan Turner has argued,

> the emphases on pleasure, desire, difference and playfulness which are features of contemporary consumerism are part of a cultural environment which has been brought about by a number of related processes, namely postindustrialism, postfordism and postmodernism. The moral apparatus of bourgeois industrial capitalism with its religious and ethical condemnation of sexual enjoyment has largely disappeared with the erosion of Christian puritanical orthodoxy and the spread of mass consumerism. (1996: 2)

I have suggested elsewhere that the shift from a manufacturing to a service-based economy has transformed the embodied worker from muscle power to part of a product for exchange (McDowell 1997a). Particular bodily performances in service occupations become part of the exchange process, and, as Turner astutely remarks 'the labouring body has become a desiring body' (1996: 2).

In leisure activities, too, the body has moved centre-stage. The idealized desiring and desired body of late capitalism needs work on it to produce a sleek and acceptable performance in an era that has seen the triumph of the cult of the fit body. Thinness and fitness, for men and for women, are dominant desires, achieved not only through exercise, but also general improvements in healthcare and in dietary practices (despite recent scares in the UK about, for example, red meat). Desirable body shapes are also achievable through advances in surgery, which enable people to trim, tuck, reshape and excise unwanted aspects of their bodies. In these senses, then, the body has become a more malleable and changeable object for growing numbers of people. Perhaps the most radical change now possible is gender reassignment, in which the association between sexed identity and embodiment is altered. Indeed, some critics have identified the body as the last frontier in postmodernity, the most challenging arena in which to achieve variation.

The late twentieth-century issues about the body mark the end of a long period in which the body, sexuality, fertility, property and ownership were connected in particular ways. In the feudal period and in the development of industrial capitalism, traditional views of sexual mores involving purity and faithfulness for women were crucial because of the role of inheritance for the transmission of wealth and private property. Indeed Friedrich Engels argued that the origins of women's oppression were found in industrial capitalism with male control of women's bodies. (See Evans and Redclift

37

(1987) and Coward (1983) for excellent summaries and criticisms of Engels's argument.) Economic and social changes in the twentieth century, including reliable contraception, divorce legislation, greater economic independence for women with their entry into waged labour in large numbers, the rise of the service industries, mass consumption and advertising, have all altered ways of living and attitudes to monogamy and relationships between men and women. Indeed, it is suggested in some quarters that the pursuit of happiness, hedonism and desire has replaced fidelity: a replacement that some see as not entirely positive.

So great have been the changes that the sociologist Anthony Giddens (1992) has suggested that a 'transformation of intimacy' has been the result. For many women, as Giddens recognizes, the changes have been beneficial, freeing them from fear of pregnancy and from male control of their fertility (although medical treatment of infertility remains firmly in male hands). Giddens argues that a new form of social contract between men and women is now possible, based on emotional expression and bodily intimacy, creating a different concept of sexuality, termed by Giddens 'plastic sexuality', in which negotiation rather than imposed power and struggle is the basis of new relationships between men and women. But for some women and for many men the effects of these changes are not positive. Men who fear women's greater economic and emotional independence seem to be turning in increasing numbers to violence against women, and many women suffer as negotiated (and enforced) serial relationships leave them to live alone for periods. These arguments are interesting but in his book Giddens provides only thought-provoking examples rather than a thorough evaluation of empirical evidence of the extent of changes and their variability between the social classes, age groups, or regions of the country, for example. He also ignores the growing economic disparities between those at the top and the bottom of the income distribution. For many women, the end of a relationship still brings poverty in its wake. What is incontestable, however, is that the body and sexuality have a key dominance in contemporary cultures in industrial societies in ways previously unparalleled.

These material changes are accompanied by the theoretical shifts that have occurred in the 'postmodern' period. Feminist scholarship has been particularly influential in rethinking and retheorizing the body in the late twentieth century, although other theorists, from Freud in the late nineteenth century to contemporary French poststructuralists, have also placed the analysis of the sexed body at the centre of their work. The deconstruction of the centrality of the opposition between the mind and the body established in Enlightenment thought has been a key element of this work. As Lois McNay noted:

a main concern has been to unpack the concept of the stable and unified subject by demonstrating how the ideas of rationality and self-reflection, which underlie it, are based on the exclusion and repression of the bodily realm and all that which, by analogy, it is held to represent – desire, materiality, need and so on. The category of the body, then, has a tactical value in so far as it is used to counter the ideophilia of humanist culture. (1992: 13)

Further, as I indicated in the previous chapter, the body has become a crucial site of feminist theorizing and retheorizing as the old way of side-stepping the importance of embodiment – that useful feminist distinction between sex and gender – also had to be deconstructed in the face of these new ways of thinking about the self (Gatens 1991).

Definitions

Before we begin our examination of bodies and spatial questions, it might be useful to clarify some of the terms used in this chapter. Although the terms body and embodiment tend to be used interchangeably by many writers, I think that the latter term is more useful as it captures the sense of fluidity, of becoming and of performance that is a key element in the recent theoretical approaches that question the relationship between anatomy and social identities. In this work, as we shall see below, the body is not taken for granted as a fixed entity but is instead seen as having a plasticity or malleability which means that it can take different forms and shapes at different times, and so also have a geography.

Although I will not be discussing sexuality alone – bodily questions about weight and health for example will also arise – it is important to define this term too. Sexuality consists of a set of sexual desires, identities and social practices which are affected by the beliefs and ideologies which sanction or regulate specific sexual activities. Sexuality is therefore, as the French philosopher Michel Foucault (1979) argued, concerned with 'the body and its pleasures'. It is now widely recognized that sexuality is as much a matter of custom and practice as it is of 'natural' instinct. Indeed, it has been suggested that, in sexual behaviour the most important organ in humans is that between the ears. And as these behaviours and practices are socially and historically defined, they take place within sets of power relations, the most common of which within heterosexual activity is the definition and control of female sexuality by men. This is not to deny power relations within same-sex relations, nor to ignore the ways in which individual women exert power over men in some circumstances. It will be useful to hold on to this definition of sexuality because recent work in, for example, gender discrimination in the workplace draws on feminist arguments that organizations themselves are imbued with attributes of desire and pleasure as well as constructing certain bodies – usually but not only women's – as primarily sexual and so out of place at work. Let us turn then to some of these issues about bodies being in or out of place.

Bodies in space – bodies as places

For the moment, in this second section, I want to concentrate on what we might term Western bodies, people living in contemporary Western industrial societies. There are, of course, huge variations in understandings of and attitudes towards the body in different societies and these will be considered before the chapter ends. Let's start this section with the words of the geographer Neil Smith. The extract below is from his paper on scale that I referred to in chapter 1. This is how he describes the body as a scale (and remember his definition of scale as a boundary between different kinds of places):

> The primary physical site of personal identity, the scale of the body is socially constructed. The place of the body marks the boundary between self and other in a social as much as a physical sense, and involves the construction of a 'personal space' in addition to a literally defined physiological space. The body is also a 'cultural locus of gender meanings', according to Judith Butler. . . . Indeed, Simone de Beauvoir argued that masculine culture identifies women with the sphere of the body while reserving for men the privilege of disembodiment, a non-corporeal identity. Not just gender, obviously, but other forms of social differences are constructed around the identity of the body. Young, in particular, argues that the 'scaling of bodies', as she puts it, appropriates a variety of corporeal differences in addition to sex – most obviously race, but also age and ability – as the putative bases for social oppression and 'cultural imperialism'. (Smith 1993: 102)

So, as Smith recognizes, bodies in space raise all sorts of questions about the space and place they occupy. I want to explore this aspect of spatial location first. Notice that Smith also refers to three feminist theorists – Judith Butler, Simone de Beauvoir and Iris Marion Young. I shall introduce you to their ideas in this and a later section. First, though, bodies positioned in space. The science of ergonomics – which is perhaps the single subject that is solely concerned with bodies in space – considers not only questions about the design and shape of furniture and machinery to fit the 'standard' (or indeed non-standard) human body but also looks at questions about how bodies fit into certain spaces. This part of the subject is known as proxemics, reflecting its focus on questions of proximity between strangers in public or semipublic spaces. It includes investigations of 'packing' factors in public transport (in the underground systems of both London and Tokyo, for example, a 'crush factor' is added to calculations of how many passengers can be squeezed into train carriages during rush hour), how people choose where to stand or sit in public spaces, such as libraries or on public transport, even the space occupied by cinema queues (apparently people waiting to be admitted to a sexy film stand closer together than audiences for other types of films). Social scientists – especially psychologists, anthropologists and sociologists – are also interested in questions about bodies in space but their focus is more commonly on issues of class and status, ethnicity and sexuality, and group acceptance and exclusion, than on practical issues of crowds and crush factors.

Hexis

The work of Pierre Bourdieu, a French anthropologist, has been important in developing an understanding of the social significance of bodies and their physical placing in space. He studied the class distinctions that operate through bodily posture, gestures, facial expressions and speaking voice, summarizing these effects in his concept 'hexis'. This is the term which describes the relationship between the social world and its inscription on bodies. Thus hexis includes the different ways individuals and groups have of bearing their bodies, presenting them to others, moving or making space for their bodies. Bourdieu argued that 'social distinctions and practices are embedded in the most automatic gestures or the apparently most insignificant techniques of the body – ways of walking or blowing one's nose, ways of eating and talking' (1984: 466). As he recognized:

> one's relationship to the social world and to one's proper place in it is never more clearly expressed than in the space and time one feels entitled to take from others; more precisely, in the space one claims with one's body in physical space, through a bearing and gestures that are self-assured or reserved, expansive or constricted ('presence' or 'insignificance'). (1984: 474)

As most women know, especially if they have recently made a plane journey in economy class, seated next to almost any man, men seem to feel that they are entitled to occupy more of the available space than women. In Bourdieu's terms, men are presence in space and women are insignificance.

Bourdieu also suggested that the body might be theorized as a memory which is not easily obliterated by conscious thought or action. He suggested that:

41

There is no better image of the logic of socialization, which treats the body as a 'memory-jogger', than those complexes of gestures, postures and words – simple interjections or favourite clichés – which only have to be slipped into, like a theatrical costume, to awaken, by the evocative power of bodily nemesis, a universe of readily made feelings and experiences. The elementary actions of bodily gymnastics, especially the specifically sexual, biologically preconstructed aspect of it, charged with social meanings and values, function as the most basic of metaphors, capable of evoking a whole relationship to the world and through it a whole world. (1984: 474)

In this passage, we see that Bourdieu understands the sexed body as 'natural', a 'biologically preconstructed' object, an argument that feminists, and later poststructuralist theorists of the body have been at pains to deconstruct. Before turning to the arguments of some of these theorists, however, let us pursue the questions of bodies, their gestures, words, their clothes, hair and decoration, and their occupation of space, shifting the emphasis from Bourdieu's focus on class to look at gender differences.

The politics of the body

Questions of bodily style, gestures and presentation and the ways in which these are constructed and enforced have long been the preoccupation of feminist politics. The women's liberation movement, associated with second wave feminist theorizing, emerged in the West in the late 1960s at the same time as student activism around anti-war, anti-racism, anti-consumer and workers' movements, and these movements had certain issues and strategies in common. A woman's right to control her own body, including the right to abortion and contraception, was one of the main demands of the movement from its inception in the 1960s. It is probably difficult for many readers to imagine the climate that existed in Britain in the 1950s and early 1960s when contraceptive advice was not easily available for unmarried women (I remember sending off for a *Sunday Times* publication 'Living with the Pill' when I was an undergraduate in the late 1960s and hoping it would come in an unobtrusive brown envelope) and before abortion was legalized in 1967. The medicalization of 'female complaints' was also challenged through a network of self-help movements, assisted by the publication of a manual from the Boston Women's Health Collective, *Our Bodies Ourselves*, which was published in a British edition in 1976, and the development of Well Women clinics in many towns and cities.

The commodification and 'normalization' of women's bodies through diet and make-up, and especially in beauty pageants were also directly challenged. One of the earliest actions in the US, for example, was the 'No

More Miss America' demonstration in August 1968. In these early years, Andrea Dworkin, a feminist activist and author, wrote passionately of the ways in which women are constructed as artifice and their physical freedom controlled from their early years. More recently, Naomi Wolf (1991) has resurrected these arguments, although with a more positive attitude to 'artifice'. The quote below is from Dworkin:

> Standards of beauty describe in precise terms the relationship that an individual will have to her own body. They describe her motility, spontaneity, posture, gait, the uses to which she can put her own body. They define precisely the dimensions to her physical freedom. And of course, the relationship between physical freedom and psychological development, intellectual possibility, and creative potential is an umbilical one.
>
> In our culture not one part of a woman's body is left untouched, unaltered. . . . From head to toe, every feature of a woman's face, every section of her body is subject to modification, alteration. This alteration is an ongoing, repetitive process. It is vital to the economy, the major substance of male–female differentiation, the most immediate physical and psychological reality of being a woman. From the age of 11 or 12 until she dies, a woman will spend a large part of her time, money and energy on binding, plucking, painting and deodorizing herself. It is commonly and wrongly said that male transvestites through the use of makeup and costuming caricature the women they would become, but any real knowledge of the romantic ethos makes clear that these men have penetrated to the core experience of being a woman, a romanticized construct. (1974: 113–14)

In these early years, physical pleasure was also a political issue and women asserted their rights to the sexual freedom that the invention of reliable contraception had made more possible. In retrospect, however, many feminists active in the women's movement in the 1960s have argued that the 'free love' of the era played into many men's desire for sex without commitment (Rowbotham 1989; Greer 1997). But it was in these years that the sexual hypocrisy of the 1950s and earlier decades was seriously challenged and greater freedom enabled women to explore a wide variety of both bodily images and sexual desires. In more recent decades, feminists have begun to reclaim fashion and artifice as more than the commodification of women's bodies and to celebrate looks, style and fitness.

This has led to disagreements about the extent to which intervention to alter the shape and arrangement of the body might be seen as an issue of choice. Susan Bordo, for example, quotes with shocked disapproval from an article in a US feminist journal *Hypatia*, which defends cosmetic surgery as being '*first and foremost* . . . about taking one's life into one's own hands' (Davis 1991: 23, quoted Bordo 1993: 20, Bordo's emphasis). Bordo suggests that this is irresponsible at a time when the dangers of silicone breast implants, to take one example, were becoming known, let alone the issues that are raised yet again about the dangers inherent in trying to conform to a particular classed and racialized image of feminine beauty.

Women and nature – women as nature

In the extract from Smith (1993), it was noted that Simone de Beauvoir argued that women are seen as restricted to their bodies while men are non-corporeal or disembodied, mind to women's body. As I showed in the last chapter, the mapping of binary categories on to the social attributes of masculinity and femininity is a key feature of Western Enlightenment thought. In its development, it was taken as self-evident that women's particular biological attributes, especially menstruation, childbirth and lactation, were the source both of their difference from and inferiority to men. Because these features were regarded as natural, it was hard for women to escape their entrapment in their bodies. Indeed, the body has been so problematic for feminist theory because this binary distinction between male and female bodies seems so clear and 'natural'. The original decision in feminist theory to separate sex from gender – the former apparently natural and unchanging, the latter socially constructed and so amenable to change – created a problem, as Sheila Rowbotham recognized: 'It was easy for the anti-feminist to determine a woman by her anatomy because the feminists persisted in ignoring that her anatomy existed at all' (1973: 11). And even now, as this sex/gender distinction is being undermined by new understandings of the body, anxieties remain. Henrietta Moore is not alone in her reaction to feminist theoretical work on the body: 'Is it really the case that our similarities are grounded in our bodies? I find that my antipathy even to simply posing this question is so great that I have to remind myself not to grind my teeth' (1994: 17).

But the question remains: what is the significance of embodiment? Does the body matter? How far is it a basis for patterns of power and domination between men and women? As anthropologists have noted, in many societies and at many different times the apparently natural biological distinction between women and men has been mapped on to a distinction of worth or social quality. Women are seen as closer to nature, as irrational, as polluters, as sacred but as inferior because they menstruate and because of their ability to bear children. Men, on the other hand, are seen as civilized, rational and superior, mind to women's body, even, indeed, unbodied or disembodied. So pervasive is the association of naturalness with 'Woman'

Plate 2.1   Urban art: depicting the male body

that nature and/or the Earth has often been symbolically represented as female.

In her splendid book *The Death of Nature* (1980), Carolyn Merchant has traced the historical path of this relationship, in myth, legend, art, scientific texts and in other forms of representation in a wide range of different societies. In the myths of the Hopi Indians, for example, the earth is regarded as female, to be treasured and protected from rape, just as in English pastoral poetry of the eighteenth and nineteenth centuries the countryside is bountifully female. The reverse imagery of nature as red in tooth and claw and women as threatening, or witches, is also a common association between nature and women. The image of the earth as mother drawn on by ecological movements is a more recent example. Geographers are not immune to this link and in less than thoughtful moments have produced book covers or illustrations in which hills and valleys may be read as naked women's bodies (see for example the frontispiece to Porteous's book *Landscapes of the Mind* (1990)). In a challenging reversal of these stereotypical associations between femininity and nature, Diane Baylis, a photographer, has represented the landscape as a male body (see Nash 1996b). Because men's bodies are so seldom the subject of urban art or graffiti, the mural in plate 2.1 is arresting.

45

The association between woman and nature, or nature's representation as female, is so widespread that the anthropologist Sherry Ortner suggested in 1974 that the separation of nature from culture and its association with women and men respectively might be the basis of a cross-cultural or universal distinction between women and men. She argued that despite the extraordinarily diverse cultural conceptions and symbolizations of women and femininity, women's secondary status appeared to be universal. In searching for an explanation for this subordination, Ortner argued that women must therefore be associated with something which every culture devalues. There is, she argued, only 'one thing that would fit that description, and that is "nature", in the most generalized sense' (Ortner 1974: 72). So long as men are symbolically identified with culture, which attempts to control and transcend nature, then women, because of their close associations with nature, must also be controlled and contained. It is important to emphasize, however, that Ortner was not arguing that women are 'nature' or 'natural', but rather that in a wide range of societies they are symbolically associated with nature. While there have been criticisms of Ortner's universal assumption and of her taken-for-granted binary division between men and women, her work provided an extremely useful way of discussing the social construction of gender, which, as Ortner herself took care to emphasize, is extremely diverse, culturally constructed and maintained through social practices.

In later anthropological work, however, the apparent universality of a binary distinction between women and men was questioned. Olivia Harris (1980), for example, found that the Indians in the Bolivian Highlands associated single people with nature and married couples with culture. Ten years later Anna Meigs (1990), on the basis of research in the Eastern Highlands of Papua New Guinea, argued that individuals there are classified not only by anatomical sex but also by the different amounts of certain male and female substances they have in their bodies, which may be altered and transferred through activities such as eating and casual contacts. Indeed, Thomas Lacquer has argued that in Western societies the 'two-sex' view of the body was not dominant until the eighteenth century. Based on a study of medical texts from the Greeks onwards, he shows that a 'one-sex' view was common. In the outline of a 'generic corporeal economy of fluids and organs' (Lacquer 1990: 35–6), women were distinguished from men only by their possession of less developed versions of the same organs. The modern Western understanding of 'two-sex' bodies emerged in relationship to other social and cultural changes in modern societies, especially new views of the self and the growing division between domestic and non-domestic life.

46

The association between sex and genitals in the West in general precludes men from being defined as women and vice versa, other than in specific cases of transsexualism, in ways that are not the case elsewhere. Thus in certain African societies, someone with female genitalia is able to occupy the social position of 'husband' in ways that are impossible in Britain (Amadiume, 1987). And among certain Native American peoples the reverse example is found. As identity is bound up with spiritual values as well as corporeal identity, 'men' – those with male genitals – are able to be identified as half man/half woman (Williams 1986).

Many women anthropologists working in the field have also noted that their authority confuses their gender attribution (see Okely and Callaway 1992). Deborah Gewertz, for example, found during her work on Tchambuli views of gender difference, embodiment and identity that her participation in meetings with men meant that her respondents thought she was 'probably not a woman at all, but a strange creature who grew male genitals upon donning trousers' (Gewertz 1984: 618). And, as Linda Nicholson has noted, women in the academy challenge some of the associations between female embodiment and femininity: 'beings whose genitals should have made us completely feminine but whose actual political skills and/or presence in such previously male-dominated institutions as the academy must indicate some masculine socialisation' (Nicholson 1995: 57).

The development of an explicitly feminist anthropology in the last two decades has also challenged what seems a self-evident assumption in the 'West' that the self and the body are congruent, fixed and bounded. As Henrietta Moore has argued, anthropological studies of indigenous concepts of the self and identity 'cast doubt on the assumption that persons are necessarily conceived as bounded entities with fixed essences, and question the assumption that the body is always the source and locus of identity' (1994: 36).

I think this is a difficult argument for us to grasp because the notion of a rational, bounded self is so dominant in Western thought. However, the ideas that bodies are surfaces that may be differentially affected by social practices and that they may be transformed and differentially presented to particular audiences are easier for us to understand. In the next section I want to examine both notions – of the body as an inscribed surface and bodily performances – as they are central to recent feminist theorizing. First I want to conclude this section by briefly returning to the opening contention, that the association with or confinement to the body and its physicality of certain groups – women in particular but also a set of diverse others – is the basis of inequality and oppression.

Scaling bodies and cultural imperialism

The notion of 'scaling bodies' – distinguishing social worth on the basis of bodily distinctions – was developed by a feminist political scientist, Iris Marion Young, who has argued in *Justice and the Politics of Difference* that 'the situation of any woman within a given sociohistorical set of circumstances, despite the individual variation in each woman's experience, opportunities and possibilities, has a unity that can be described and made intelligible' (1990b: 142). This unity, she suggests, is based in their female embodiment. In this book, which is a remarkable challenge to liberal theories of social justice (we shall meet it again, and in more detail, in chapter 7), Young outlines the operation of what she terms the mechanism of 'cultural imperialism' that constructs dominant and inferior groups. Bodily distinctions are crucially important in the production of inferiority as dominated groups are defined as nothing but their bodies, and seen as imprisoned in an undesirable body, whereas the dominant groups occupy an unmarked neutral, universal and disembodied position, which is white and masculine by default. Women, trapped in their bodies and marked by inappropriate gestures, are defined as 'Other'. Their confinement is exacerbated through the construction of an idealized female body (currently young, slim and white) that most women fail to measure up to anyway. As Young explains, 'while a certain cultural space is reserved for revering feminine beauty and desirability, in part that very cameo idea renders most women drab, ugly, loathsome or fearful bodies' (p. 123).

Tseelon has extended this argument in suggesting that women are trapped within and punished for five paradoxes that construct female embodiment. These are the modesty paradox – the woman is constructed as seduction to be punished for it; the duplicity paradox – the woman is constructed as artifice, and so marginalized for lacking essence and authenticity; the visibility paradox – the woman is constructed as a spectacle while being culturally invisible; the beauty paradox – the woman embodies ugliness while signifying beauty; and finally, the death paradox – the woman signifies death as well as the defence against it (1995: 5–6). Through the mechanism of cultural imperialism, women are constructed as inappropriate bodies in the rational spaces of the mind – especially in bureaucratic, academic, scientific and high-tech workplaces. In my own work on embodiment in the labour market, I have tried to show how women's imprisonment in their bodies defines them as Other in workplaces where the disembodied (for which read masculine) attributes of the rational intellect are highly valued (McDowell 1997a) and Doreen Massey (1995) has undertaken similar work in the high-tech laboratories of Cambridge's science parks. I shall come back to questions about gender and embodiment at work in chapter 5.

Challenging the mind/body split: bodies as surfaces and performances

Michel Foucault, a French historian of ideas who died in the mid-1980s, was one of the most influential postwar social theorists writing about the body and sexuality. His work has become well known to geographers, as one of the areas he was interested in was the social construction of space and time. Through his highly-influential three-volume study of the history of sexuality in post-Enlightenment Europe, Foucault (1979, 1987, 1988) has been particularly significant in challenging the separation of the mind and the body in Cartesian secular rationalism. He argued that the Enlightenment view of the body as already existing before it entered into social relations was incorrect. Instead he showed through detailed historical analysis how moral attitudes, legal and institutional structures and personal and interpersonal attitudes and actions produce the forms of sexed embodiment that they regulate. In simple terms, therefore, Foucault argued that a 'natural' body does not exist. Even its biological attributes are socially constructed through scientific and other discourses.

Foucault suggested that there is nothing 'natural' or 'normal' about bodily pleasures and sexual practices. Unlike many histories of sexuality which have argued that sexual practices are secret and unspoken, Foucault argued the reverse, suggesting instead that at different periods there was common agreement about what was 'normal', about which sexual practices were permissible and which were transgressive, offensive to accepted standards of 'decency' and so prohibited. He termed the dominant set of ideas about sexuality that was in force at any particular time a discursive regime and linked different discursive regimes to the development of capitalist social relations and the rise of modern societies.

In modern capitalism new forms of social regulation were introduced to control the newly urbanizing population. In the rise of what Foucault termed disciplinary societies, he suggested that this regulation relied on the social control of the body through new mechanisms of surveillance. In *Discipline and Punish* (1977) Foucault argues that power in the modern period should be seen not as force from above based on negative prohibitions, but rather as a force operating from the bottom up as it were. Foucault called this form of power biopower to indicate the significance of bodily controls. He suggested that rather than citizens being subjugated by

49

the imposition of power from above by the state and its institutions, power is also a fine network of micro-scale or capillary relations that links objects, events and different levels of society, through positive regulations concerned with, for example, improving living standards and health. Thus the regulation of sexuality operates not only through state controls but also by what he termed the self-surveillance of individual behaviour. As Angela Carter once memorably remarked, even in the bedroom when we imagine we are engaging in the most private and 'natural' of activities, we drag in with us 'the baggage of our society' which influences who puts what where.

According to Foucault, the regulation of the body and sexuality are central in modern societies. Biopower operates through the control of the sexuality of women and children, the regulation of procreative behaviour and the identification of sexual perversions as problems of individual pathology. The long history of sexual politics throughout the twentieth century has been an attempt to dislodge the power of these dominant discourses and to challenge the views of what is 'normal'.

Returning to the body *per se* rather than the regulation of sexuality, Foucault theorized the body as a surface to be inscribed by social practices, suggesting that bodies are acted upon in discursively constructed institutional settings. These result in taken-for-granted practices in which bodies are disciplined and normalized, and social reproduction is facilitated. The disciplining occurs in a wide range of social settings, from the home and the school to the workplace. Although Foucault was particularly interested in institutions such as prisons and asylums, and in criminal and 'abnormal' individuals, he noted that the economic use of the body also involved relations both of power and subjection:

> it is largely as a force of production that the body is invested with relations of power and domination; but on the other hand, its constitution as labour power is possible only if it is caught up in a system of subjection; the body becomes a useful force only if it is both a productive body and a subjected body. (Foucault: 1977: 26)

The balance of these forces, and the ways in which they are regulated, may vary between men and women, although Foucault did not address the specific sexed differences in the production of masculine and feminine bodies. Geographers have begun to investigate the different ways in which biopower produces appropriate and docile bodies at different sites and locations. Philo, for example, has followed Foucault's interest in the 'abnormal' by investigating lunatic asylums in the nineteenth century (Philo 1989; and see Philo and Parr 1995), and geographers interested in the production of 'docile' bodies in the workplace have also drawn on Foucault, as we shall see later.

50

Bodies as surfaces

For feminist scholars Foucault's notion of the body as a map, as a surface for social inscription, has been particularly productive, and, of course, the geographical analogy is provocative for geographers. Elizabeth Grosz (1990) has suggested, however, that this notion leaves open major questions. If the body is a blank surface, it is not clear how different messages are inscribed on it and whether and how they might be resisted. Foucault seems to suggest that there are bodies and pleasures that exist outside power/knowledge discourses, but he does not specify what these are or their origins. Despite these absences, Grosz argues that the metaphor of corporeal inscription is useful for feminists interested in writing the history of women's bodies in which their effacement by patriarchal scholarship and institutions is revealed. Grosz insists that feminists recognize that biopower is not always perceived as negative. As well as being inscribed by repressive and violent practices to produce productive and subjected bodies, she notes that the body is also marked by a range of 'voluntary practices, habits and lifestyles that distinguish female from male bodies: make-up, stilettos, bras, hairspray, clothing, underclothing mark women's bodies in ways in which hairstyles, professional training, personal grooming, gait, posture, body-building, and sports may mark men's' (Grosz 1994: 142).

Here then we can see the parallels with the work of Bourdieu and Foucault, as well as links back to the feminist analyses and political campaigns that I mentioned earlier in the chapter. However, what distinguishes Grosz's claim from the previous feminist claims, by Dworkin and others, is its emphasis on male as well as female bodily inscription. Feminists now recognize that both women *and men* are subject to disciplinary power and regimes of corporeal production, albeit to different degrees and in different ways. As Grosz notes, women 'are no more cultural, no more natural than men. Patriarchal power relations do not function to make women the objects of disciplinary control while men remain outside disciplinary surveillance. It is a question of not more or less, but of differential production' (1994: 144). Furthermore, both men and women are capable of resistance to as well as compliance with disciplinary power, capable of taking pleasure in bodily inscription and in subverting dominant discourses.

The idea that the body is a surface for decoration is, of course, not a new one. Surface inscription has a long history in which the most obvious examples are tattooing and body piercing, which, as decorative and also as transgressive acts, may be traced across space and over time from prehistoric peoples to twentieth-century punks (Maffesoli 1995).

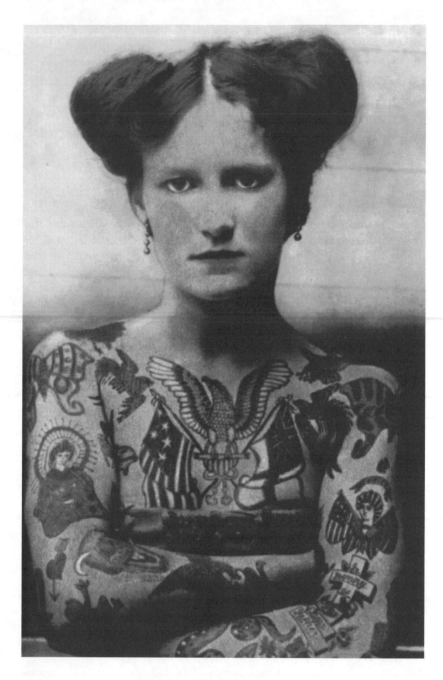

Plate 2.2   The Tattooed Woman

In her recent work, Grosz begins to theorize the possibility of multiple female bodies, to think through ways of being female that are not reduced to a maternal body. In this way she mounts a further challenge to some of the early work by radical feminist theorists who locate gender differences in the maternal body. While, like Foucault, Grosz believes that the body is a surface to be inscribed, she goes further than he does in her argument that the body itself is also culturally produced rather than existing prior to its inscription, as an inert slab of meat, if you will. Thus Grosz argues that

the body, or rather bodies, cannot be adequately understood as ahistorical, precultural, or natural objects in any simple way; they are not only in- scribed, marked, engraved, by social pressures external to them but are the products, the direct effects, of the very social constitution of nature itself. It is not simply that the body is represented in a variety of ways according to historical, social and cultural exigencies while it remains basically the same; these factors actively *produce* the body as a body of a determinate type. (1994: x, emphasis added)

Grosz suggests that 'representations and cultural inscriptions quite literally constitute bodies and help to produce them as such'. Bodies are objects like no others, 'they are the centres of perspective, insight, reflection, desire, agency. . . . Bodies are not inert; they function interactively and productively. They act and react. They generate what is new, surprising, unpredictable' (1994: x–xi).

But even so, the question of how sexed differences are produced re- mains to be answered. Here Grosz's own clear posing of the set of interre- lated issues is helpful. She asks:

Are sexually neutral, indeterminate, or hermaphroditic bodies inscribed to produce the sexually specific forms with which we are familiar? Or do bodies, all bodies, have a specifically sexual dimension (whether it be male, female or hermaphroditic) which is psychically and culturally inscribed according to its morphology? In other words, is sexual difference primary and sexual inscrip- tion a cultural overlay or rewriting of an ontologically prior differentiation? Or is sexual differentiation a product of the various forms of inscription of culturally specific bodies? Do inscriptions produce sexual differentiation? Or does sexual difference imply a differential mode of inscription? (1994: 189)

Answering these questions would, I think, demand a long examination of the complex relations between bodies and their inscriptions across time and space, constructing comparative geographies of embodiment, but clearly there does seem to be a materiality to bodies, and a binary distinction between the sexes is common in many societies: Grosz suggests that 'the bifurcation of sexed bodies is, in my opinion, an irreducible cultural universal' (1994: 160). (But remember Lacquer's suggestion that this bifurcation was not accepted in the 'West' until the eighteenth century, as well as anthropological work in some societies today which makes us question this assertion.) Even if we do accept the bifurcation, there is still an almost infinite pliability to the body, to the forms, processes and activities it is able to undertake. What is possible or permitted in some cultures, at certain times, is impossible or forbidden elsewhere and at other times. While Butler, to whose work we shall now turn, agrees with Grosz about the irreducible materiality of bodies, she is less certain that sexed bifurcation is either pre-existing or universal. As I show below, Butler argues that the binary distinction itself is a product of social practices.

Bodily performances

Theorizing the body and the self as fluid and changeable has led to an understanding that physical characteristics of the body and its gender performance need not necessarily be congruent. Although the social constructionists, from Goffman's work in the 1960s onwards, have long recognized that social behaviour consists of a variable performance at different sites, in the 1990s the complex theoretical work of the feminist theorist, Judith Butler has been extremely influential. Butler's central notion is the idea of 'performative gender'. In contemporary societies, Butler argues, gender identities are a performance, constituted by the 'stylized repetition of acts' (1990a: 140) in a regime that attempts to enforce compulsory heterosexuality. (Remember the earlier discussion of gender regimes in chapter 1.) Butler argues that what we assume to be 'natural' about our gender identity is almost non-existent and so gender identities may be disrupted or overturned by transgressive acts that reveal 'the regulatory fiction of heterosexual coherence' (1990b: 338).

Butler argues that in contemporary advanced industrial societies an epistemic regime of compulsory heterosexuality produces and reifies that ontological binary gender division – the constructs of man and woman – that enforces women's inferiority. But she suggests that gender, rather than being a binary division located in biological difference, is instead a persistent impersonation that passes as real. Being female is not a 'natural fact' but 'a cultural performance [in which] "naturalness" [is] constituted through discursively constrained performative acts that produce the body through and within the categories of sex' (1990a: viii). The aim of this fabrication is the production of a coherent identity, which, for the majority of the population, is based on that heterosexual regulatory fiction. Through acts, gestures and clothes we construct or fabricate an identity that is manufactured, manifested and sustained through corporeal signs and other discursive means. Thus, Butler believes that

> gender ought not to be constructed as a stable identity or locus of agency from which various acts follow; rather, gender is an identity tenuously constituted in time, instituted in an exterior space through a *stylized repetition of acts*. The effect of gender is produced through the stylization of the body and, hence, must be understood as the mundane way in which bodily gestures, movements, and styles of various kinds constitute *the illusion* of an abiding gendered self. (1990a, 140–1, original emphases)

So here we have a statement rather close to the earlier work of Bourdieu, but with the extremely significant difference that whereas Bourdieu took sexed difference for granted, Butler does not. Instead she theorizes the body itself not as a sexed, pre-existing surface for cultural inscription but as bounded and constituted by the political forces which constitute systems of compulsory heterosexuality. This vision of 'the body' contrasts with the Cartesian view of the body as inert matter. Butler argues that even bodily boundaries are established by hegemonic practice, by the social limits of acceptability which defines 'fixed sites of corporeal permeability and impermeability' (1990a: 132).

If gender is defined as a construct that is congruent with the dominant discourses and practices of a particular location, rather than as a fixed or stable category, it prises open a space to examine not only the ways in which a particular heterosexual performance becomes hegemonic but also the prospect of resistance to it. Butler's work is particularly provocative, however, because, as she identifies possibilities of the transgression of binary genders through cultural practices that 'trouble' the binary categories, she forces us to turn our attention to other ways of constructing bodily performances. A whole range of acts, she argues, may produce subversive discontinuities and dissonance among the categories of sex, gender and desire, calling into question their alleged relations. The possibility of 'subverting and displacing the naturalized and reified notions of gender that support masculine hegemony and heterosexual power . . . [arise] not through strategies that figure a utopian beyond, but through the mobilization, subversive confusion, and proliferation of precisely those constitutive categories that seek to keep gender in its place by posturing as the foundational illusions of identity' (Butler 1990a 33–4).

Butler herself investigates these dissonances through an examination of homosexuality and the incest taboo. Her work has been particularly influential among geographers: in, for example, understandings of lesbian and gay acts of resistance in the city, as well as analyses of how 'perverse' sexualities are 'out of place' in different arenas in the city (Bell and Valentine 1995). In the final section of this chapter, I shall look at some of this work on 'perverse' sexualities and parodic performances, as well as work that geographers interested in the body are beginning to undertake focusing on pregnant and on sick bodies.

I hope by now that it is clear to you that the question of the sexed body, the reasons for its development and its distinction and the connections between the body, sexuality and gender lie at the base of all analyses of gender relations. As I shall show in the succeeding chapters, assumptions about the correct place for embodied women are drawn on to justify and to challenge systems of patriarchal domination in which women are excluded from particular spatial arenas and restricted to others. In this sense to 'know their place' has a literal as well as a metaphorical meaning for women, and sexed embodiment is deeply intertwined with geographical location. Social relations and spatial processes are mutually reinforcing (in different ways at different times and places, of course, which is what makes a geographical analysis of gender relations so pertinent and exciting) in the construction of gender regimes with particular patterns of the segregation of the sexes and gendered hierarchies of power.

So as we move through the chapters that follow, sexed bodies, performing gender in different ways in different sites – in the home, at work and on holiday, for example – will be encountered again and again. In the final section of this chapter, I begin this exploration of sexed bodies with a small number of empirical case studies undertaken by geographers and other feminists. The first two sets of examples are related to the discussions in the middle sections of this chapter – about bodies and boundaries and distasteful bodies – whereas the later examples draw on geographical work that has developed the ideas of Judith Butler about bodily performances. In the final example we turn to the metaphorical associations between bodies and cities.

Case studies of bodies in space and place

1   *Bodies at school*

I want to pursue the differences between women's and men's occupation of space through a number of empirical studies, by political theorists, anthropologists and a cultural theorist as well as by geographers. Let's start with a straightforward account of how girls are brought up to occupy space in gender-specific ways.

In her book *Own or Other Culture*, Judith Okely turned her anthropologist's eye on her own childhood and education in an all-girls boarding school in England in the 1950s. Here is Okely reflecting on the different ways in which male and female adolescent bodies are allowed to occupy space:

> Sport is the body's playground. Whereas the games favoured in the girls' boarding curriculum impose artificial limits on the girls' potential, those in boys' schools tend to develop potential. This gender bias is also found in state schools and is continuous. Sports exclusively for males include rugby, football and boxing. [Okely's footnote: Since the mid-1980s some women's rugby and football teams have emerged. But these and many other sports are still male dominated, as any TV sports programme or newspaper section demonstrates.] Those mainly for females include netball, lacrosse and hockey. Tennis and occasionally cricket are played by both sexes.
>
> Differences between male and female sports indicate different bodily experience. Certain characteristics of male sports are absent from the sports permitted for females. Rugby demands physical contact between the players. The arms and whole body are used as weapons. Players are expected to throw themselves and their opponents to the ground. Neither physical contact nor such use of the body is permitted in girls' sports. . . .
>
> Both rugby and football require vigorous kicking of the ball, and thus the opening and the raising of the legs. Females must never kick balls, lest they kick the other kind. Females who raise and kick the leg are seen, in the dominant male ideology, to be metaphorically exposing their genitals. This movement, without a target, is institutionalised in the titillating can-can. (1996: 144)

Okely recalled the control of the girls' bodies in her school, from rules forbidding them to leave the grounds to smaller-scale regulations.

> The girls' bodily posture was constantly reviewed. At all times the pupils were to sit, stand or walk erect, chin up, back straight and shoulders well back. The games mistresses, as guardians of the girls' bearing and movement, wielded considerable power. Girls were scrutinised at meals, in chapel and at 'roll call'. The fear was to be poked unexpectedly in the back by a bayonet finger, when a girl lolled forward . . . Uniform was checked, fingernails inspected. Hair which touched the back of the collar had to be cut, because longer hair hinted at sexuality. (1996: 140)

A decade later at the all-girls' state school I attended, the same rule about hair was in force, as well as one forbidding us to roll up our sleeves. To do so, according to the headmistress, made us 'look like washerwomen'. Clearly, class as well as gender boundaries had to be policed. I would be interested to know whether these rules and regulations were still in force when you, the readers, were at school or whether Okely's experience seems like another world to you.

2   Bodies 'out of place': pregnant bodies and sick bodies

Pregnant bodies   The first example here is from the work of Iris Marion Young, and it is about the pregnant body. Her focus is explicitly spatial, in the sense that she is interested in how the changing form and boundaries of the pregnant body, an essential part of the subjective experience of pregnancy, raise questions about the body's place.

It is perhaps surprising that the subjectivity of pregnant women has been so little studied by the philosophers of bodily existence, as there is no clearer example of the limitations of the Cartesian assumptions of a singular unified subject. As Young argues 'pregnancy reveals a paradigm of bodily experience in which the transparent unity of self dissolves and the body attends positively to itself at the same time as it enacts its projects.' Instead of being a unified subject,

> the pregnant subject is decentred, split, or doubled in several ways. She experiences her body as herself, and not herself. Its inner movements belong to another being, yet they are not other, because her body boundaries shift and because her bodily self-location is focused on her trunk as well as her head. . . . Pregnant existence [also] entails a unique temporality of process and growth in which the woman can experience herself as a split between past and future. (1990a: 161)

And it is pregnancy, of course, that radically alters the notion of an individual as a bounded body, separated by space from another. 'Pregnancy . . . renders fluid the boundary between what is within, myself, and what is outside, separate. I experience my insides as the space of another, yet my own body'; giving birth is perhaps 'the most extreme suspension of the bodily distinction between inner and outer' (Young 1990a: 163) (see plate 2.3). Just as Freud and Lacan have argued that the infant has no initial sense of the boundaries between the mother and itself, Young suggests that pregnant women and new mothers have the same experience.

> The integrity of my body is undermined in pregnancy not only by this externality of the inside, but also by the fact that the boundaries of my body are themselves in flux. In pregnancy I literally do not have a firm sense of where my body ends and the world begins. My automatic body habits be-

Plate 2.3   A celebration of birth: an urban mural

come dislodged; the continuity between my customary body and my body at this moment is broken. . . . I move as if I could squeeze around chairs and through crowds as I could seven months before, only to find my way blocked by my own body sticking out in front of me – but yet not me, since I did not expect it to block my passage. As I lean over in my chair to tie my shoe, I am surprised by the graze of this hard belly on my thigh. I did not anticipate my body touching itself, for my habits retain the old sense of my boundaries'. (Young 1990a: 164)

Young suggests that for some women, the experience of pregnancy, its weight and materiality, 'produces a sense of power, solidity and validity' and self-respect in a society which tends to devalue and trivialize women and which defines feminine beauty as slight and shapely. She argues that pregnant women often feel a form of satisfaction or self-love for their bodies, a sort of primordial sexual continuity with the maternal body that the French feminist theorist Julia Kristeva has called 'jouissance'. 'The culture's separation of pregnancy and sexuality can liberate her from the sexually objectifying gaze that alienates and instrumentalizes her when in her non-pregnant state' (Young 1990a: 167). Young writes less optimistically, however, of women's treatment by the medical profession and the resulting alienation from the experience of pregnancy, and more particu-

59

larly of the birth, which is often treated as a 'disorder' or dysfunctional condition needing medical intervention.

Robyn Longhurst, a geographer working in New Zealand, made the pregnant body in space the subject of her doctoral work, examining the response of pregnant women to their changing bodies and the reasons why they feel uncomfortable in certain, mainly public, spaces. She found that rather than the self-love and confidence expressed by Young, many pregnant women felt extremely awkward as the relationship between their bodies and the space they occupied changed (Longhurst 1996, 1997). A common response was to withdraw into an increasingly private and localized arena, as women progressively stopped socializing in public spaces, and even began to feel out of place in the street, in shops and, to Longhurst's surprise, even in the hospital or a doctor's clinic, although this may correspond to Young's finding of women's distaste for the medicalization of pregnancy as a 'condition'.

Transformations of the body also occur in illness, with weight gain and in old age, often turning the body into a burden in ways that are perhaps not so marked in pregnancy. The physicality of pregnancy is a dual one: both burden and delight as the body purposively changes. Further, it is a shift in bodily boundaries and weight that is impermanent, marked by the specific temporal boundaries of pregnancy. Eventually, the old boundaries are (almost) re-established. Illness, though, may be experienced differently, as an alienation from the body and as a permanent renegotiation of an individual sense of herself or himself as a woman or a man. In the next section, I examine some recent work by geographers about disability.

'Sick' bodies   In recent work in the geography of illness, disability, health and healthcare, similar issues about bodies being 'out of place' recur (Dyck 1995, 1996). As has been widely argued, the 'environment' in the widest sense of the physical buildings and infrastructure and the relations between people, is designed with an able-bodied individual, without dependants, in mind. In an interesting paper, Pamela Moss and Isabel Dyck argue that embodiment is brought to the fore in extremely clear ways for people suffering from chronic illnesses (Moss and Dyck 1996). Through a study of older women with arthritis, carried out by Moss and of women with multiple sclerosis, by Dyck, they show how material and discursive practices (biomedical and general representations of the body and of gender) construct these women as 'deviant' bodies. Moss and Dyck argue, however, that the women whom they interviewed resist their attribution and through diverse strategies not only resolve physical problems of access and movement within their homes and workplaces, but also construct a different understanding of themselves as embodied sexed and feminine subjects.

In some cases the strategies of resistance had the positive connotations we associate, perhaps too often, with the word 'resistance'. For example, some women who had 'invisible' disabilities, such as chronic fatigue, attempted to maintain an 'able performance' in the workplace. As Moss and Dyck noted:

> concealment of symptoms and non-disclosure of a diagnosis were important strategies. Using stairs because co-workers did so, although the elevator would be easier; walking behind others on the way back from lunch so that an unsteady gait would not be noticed; or taking work home that involved fine hand coordination were instances of attempts to maintain an able identity. Such women resisted the stigmatising consequences of a biomedical representation of their diseased body. (1996: 744)

I want to suggest, however, that their resistance in these cases may arise as much from fear as from a positive strategy that we should celebrate. Other women took an opposite course and fought to have their deviant body recognized through special treatment and provision. In particular ways in different locations, therefore, Moss and Dyck argue that the body is both a site of oppression and a site of resistance, and they suggest that 'coming to terms with the disjuncture between one's own body and its representations is important in defining the boundaries of individual identities: boundaries that are continually adjusting' (1996: 474). I find this an interesting way to think about the fluidity not only of a subject's identity but also of her or his body, and one that is as applicable to the 'well' body or the able body as to 'deviant' bodies. As many theorists have pointed out few women's or men's bodies fit idealized representations of desired bodies at different life stages and this 'coming to terms' is a widespread phenomenon that affects our sense of ourselves.

3   Embodied performances: challenging compulsory heterosexuality

Some of the most interesting geographical work in the last few years has addressed the relationships between 'perverse' sexualities and the transgression of normalizing assumptions about places. A growing number of geographers (Adler and Brenner 1992; Bell et al. 1994; Bell 1995; Bell and Valentine 1995; Forest 1995; Geltmaker 1992; Knopp 1992, 1995; Valentine 1993a, 1993b) have studied the ways in which gay men and lesbian women feel out of place in 'straight' spaces. As I shall argue in greater detail in later chapters, the built environment both affects and reflects dominant assumptions about social relations. In a society in which heterosexual and familial relations are assumed to be 'normal', those who do not conform often feel uneasy in spaces structured through heterosexual norms. In restaurants and pubs, in hotels and in open spaces, public displays of heterosexual affection may go unmarked or be tolerated where displays of affection between same-sex people may not.

In their paper 'All hyped up and no place to go' (1994), David Bell, John Binnie, Julia Cream and Gill Valentine drew on the arguments of Judith Butler to think about the performance of sexual identities in space. They explore Butler's argument that queer identities are oppositional, transgressing and parodying the dominant heterosexual regime, through 'a long hard look at two current dissident sexual identities – the hypermasculine "gay skinhead" and the hyperfeminine "lipstick lesbian" (p. 31). As the authors note, 'the mimicry of heterosexuality by gay men and lesbians has the potential to transform radically the stability of masculinity and femininity, undermining its claim to originality and naturalness. Heterosexuality is a performance, just as constructed as homosexuality, but is often presumed and privileged as the original' (p. 33). And, as they go on to argue,

> the excessive performance of masculinity and femininity within homosexual frames exposes not just the fabricated nature of heterosexuality but also its claim to authenticity. The 'macho' man and 'femme' woman are not just tautologies, but work to disrupt conventional assumptions surrounding the straight mapping of man/masculine and woman/feminine within heterosexual and homosexual constructs. The gay skinhead, with his Doctor Marten boots, his drainpipe jeans held up by braces, bomber jacket and shaven head; and the lipstick lesbian with her make-up and high heels, have different historical legacies and have intervened in different debates, from neofascism to feminism, but what unites them is their parodying of heterosexuality. (p. 33)

In their paper the authors explore a range of issues that trouble them – about 'passing' in straight spaces, about attitude and visibility and its consequences (an important issue for hypermasculine skinhead gay men in particular), about how performances may be read by those 'in the know' in different spaces, both straight and queer, and whether transgressive gender performances are successful in challenging the heterosexual construction and coding of space. In their discussion of gay skinhead styles, for example, they suggest that the visibility of these men has a challenging and empowering effect: 'the last thing any straight person expects skinheads to do is to hold hands in public, or gently kiss. When this happens, people notice. By behaving in this way the gay skinhead can disrupt or destabilise not only a masculine identity but heterosexual space' (p. 36). Further it enables gay men to recognize each other: 'the visibility means that through the mutually-constituting exchange of glances on the street, gay skinheads create a queer space in a heterosexual world, which is itself empowering' (p. 37).

Around the same time that a skinhead style became important for gay men (in the early 1990s), lesbians began to 're-engage with the feminine on new terms' (p. 42) in a parody of hyperfemininity that both mirrored and challenged heterosexual femininity. The authors explain this seeming paradox:

> the hyperfemininity of the lipstick lesbian has theoretically broken the last link in the chain which joined man/woman and masculine/feminine together as binary opposites in a heterosexual matrix for whilst the notion of inverts – 'real woman' and butch-femme – broke the assumption that gender identity (masculinity or femininity) necessarily mapped neatly onto binary sexed bodies (male, female), these notions still maintained the link between gender identity and sexual desire, because the masculine woman (invert/butch) still desired the 'feminine' real woman. The lipstick lesbian is the feminine desiring the feminine, breaking the last stable construct of heterosexuality. While butch/femme seemed to outsiders to reinforce the validity of the heterosexual original, the lipstick lesbian, with her subtle mixing of heterosexual signifiers within a feminine disguise, reveals that the heterosexual 'original' was, as Butler [1990a] argues, only an imitation after all. (p. 42)

As this feminine performance is common to most women, it has a transgressive and disrupting affect, as it

> has the potential to make heterosexual women question how their own appearance is read, to challenge how they see other women and hence to undermine the production of heterosexual space. Similarly the disruption of space in this way means that heterosexual men may be unable to distinguish the object of their desire. (p. 42)

Through the selection of extracts to indicate the main arguments of this paper I may unwittingly have given a more definite feel than the authors intend. As they conclude, their aim was to raise a series of questions: 'Does the performance of gay skinhead and lipstick lesbian identities disrupt the "heterosexuality" of "straight space"? . . . What is transgression? What is parody? Who wins, and who loses, when "in jokes" get told?' (p. 44). They note the criticism of Butler's work by Susan Bordo (1992), who points out that Butler does not consider the cultural context of transgressive performances and the importance of the responses of different audiences. As Bordo argues, Butler 'does not consider the possibly different responses of different "readers" (male/female, black/white, young/old, gay/straight, etc.) or the various anxieties that might complicate their readings . . . When we attempt to give [Butler's] abstract text some "body", we immediately run into difficulties' (Bordo 1992, 171; and quoted in Bell et al. 1994).

While I agree with this comment, I hope that, through empirical work, different 'audience responses' might be uncovered. Indeed, I have tried to do just this in merchant banks in my own research work and I shall come back to this effort in chapter 5. Rather surprisingly perhaps in a paper by geographers, Bell et al. pay little attention to particular spaces. These gay men and lesbians, and especially the latter group, never actually go out anywhere much at all.

In a later issue of *Gender, Place and Culture* (where the paper by Bell et al. appeared), four interesting responses to it were published (Kirby 1995; Knopp 1995; Probyn 1995; Walker 1995). Probyn and Knopp both suggest ways in which work about sexuality and space might move from the abstract level. As Probyn explains, 'I want to seek out the singularities of a lesbian body in space, posed in relation to other lesbians in space'. She is interested in 'thinking about lesbian desire and how it may change structures of spatiality, and be changed within different spatial structures' (Probyn 1995: 79). In a vivid description of a scene in a hypothetical pub, Probyn suggests what happens when different women enter such a masculine space. She urges geographers to remember 'that the conditions of the production of space as gendered or as sexed are historically, materially and strategically different', noting that the lesbian subject is always a doubled subject, caught up in the doubling of being a woman and a lesbian.

As Probyn suggests, 'she is at once an instance in the doubling of spaces and an instigator of the production, the folding of one kind of space upon another' (1995: 81). In such abstract terms this idea is rather hard to grasp, but I think Probyn's idea of a doubling of space is rather similar to the geographical argument about spaces both being affected by and affecting social relations. In this particular instance, then, to return to Probyn's example of the pub, a lipstick lesbian and her partner initially enter a space which men, through their interplay of glances, reinforce as a heterosocial space. If the women are openly affectionate, they then fissure both the space of the pub and men's perception of them as women, creating, albeit momentarily, a sexed lesbian space. In this way we can see that sexing of spaces may be challenged, even if the dominant construction of a space as masculinized and heterosexual is barely disturbed.

I shall return to some of these themes through other case studies in later chapters, looking, for example, at sexuality as the basis for local identity in chapter 4 and sexuality at work in chapter 5.

4 Bodies/cities

In the final case study, I want to turn not to another empirical example but to a theoretical and speculative paper in which Elizabeth Grosz (1992) began to document the links between the ways in which bodies are inscribed as sociocultural artefacts and the ways they simultaneously 'reinscribe and project themselves onto their sociocultural environment so that this environment both produces and reflects the form and interests of the body' (1992: 242). Here I think Grosz's aim is close to that of Probyn, who argued in the paper we have just considered that space is sexed through bodies, 'through the relational movement of one . . . body to another' (Probyn 1995: 81). As I noted above, too, the idea that the built form both affects and reflects social relationships is now widely accepted by geographers: as I shall demonstrate over and over again, space and place are gendered and sexed, and gender relations and sexuality are 'spaced'. But Grosz challenges the assumption that the body and the city are separate forms:

> neither the body nor its environment can be assumed to form an organically unified ecosystem. The body and its environment, rather, produce each other as forms of the hyperreal, as modes of simulation which have overtaken and transformed whatever reality each may have had into the image of the other: the city is made and made over into the simulacrum of the body, and the body, in its turn, is transformed, 'citified', urbanized as a distinctively metropolitan body. (1992: 242)

In ways that provide a link between the subject matter of this chapter and the next, Grosz speculatively links bodies and cities in a number of ways. Thus she argues,

> the form, structure and norms of the city seep into and affect all the other elements that go into the constitution of corporeality and/as subjectivity. It affects the way the subject sees others (domestic architecture and the division of the home into the conjugal bedroom, separated off from other living and sleeping spaces, and the specialization of rooms are as significant in this regard as smaller family size), as well as the subject's understanding of alignment with, and positioning in space. Different forms of lived spatiality (the verticality of the city, as opposed to the horizontality of the landscape – at least in the 'West') affect the ways in which we live space, and thus our comportment and corporeal orientations and the subject's form of corporeal exertion – the kind of terrain it must negotiate day by day, the effect this has on its muscular structure, its nutritional context, providing the most elementary forms of material support and sustenance for the body. Moreover,

the city is, of course, also the site for the body's cultural saturation, its takeover and transformation by images, representational systems, the mass media, and the arts – the place where the body is representationally re-explored, transformed, contested, reinscribed. In turn, the body (as cultural product) transforms, reinscribes the urban landscape according to its changing (demographic, economic and psychological) needs, extending the limits of the city, of the sub-urban, ever towards the countryside which borders it. (1992: 248–9)

While this passage seems complex at first sight, on a second reading I think it becomes both clear and uncontentious, and yet Grosz's argument links the body and the city in a way which geographers have tended to ignore so far. But as Grosz suggests, and as feminist geographers have also recognized, 'the city organizes and orients family, sexual and social relations insofar as the city divides cultural life into public and private domains, geographically dividing and defining the particular social positions and locations occupied by individuals and groups.' To see a social theorist so clearly lay out the claims of geography as a key social science discipline is delightful.

Grosz ends her essay with some speculations about the effects that the 'implosion of space into time, the transmutation of distance into speed, the instantaneousness of communication, the collapsing of the workspace into the home computer system' will have on the 'specifically sexual and racial bodies of the city's inhabitants as well as on the form and structure of the city'. She believes that the city and the body will become part of electronic networks, 'forming part of an information machine in which the body's limbs and organs will become interchangeable parts with the computer' (1992: 251). Thus the era of the cyborg, about which Donna Haraway (1991) has written so perceptively, may be close, and we (as enhanced bodies/cyborgs) may move more and more into and between Augé's non-places. Whatever happens, Grosz believes that new technologies 'will fundamentally transform the ways in which we conceive both cities and bodies, and their interrelations' (1992: 252).

This is an enjoyable essay and the parallels between the body and the city are provocative, but I think Grosz stretches the analogy too far. Bodies and cities are both 'things' but they also have differences. Indeed David Harvey has argued that 'it makes no sense to talk about the city as the same kind of "thing" as a body (its boundaries are, for example, far more diffuse and while it typically has institutions it has no psyche or even agency of the sort that human beings possess)' (1996: 278). And Grosz also, in my view, underplays the significance of dominant institutions. Social, economic and political structures are crucial in defining and maintaining not only a particular urban form but also particular versions of acceptable bodies.

Drawing analogies between bodies and cities, however, has a long history in architecture and urban planning. In a fascinating analysis of the history of the city in Western civilization from ancient Athens to contemporary New York, Richard Sennett (1994) has traced the connections between medical knowledge of the body, its images and representations and urban form and layout. Sennett shows, for example, how Roman ideas about the geometrical perfection of the body in the time of the Emperor Hadrian were translated into urban designs. He also explores the Christian city and shows how developing notions of impure bodies led both to the creation of urban sanctuaries and to the Jewish ghetto. In modern cities, medical advances such as the discovery of the circulation of the blood became analogies for urban design to improve traffic circulation, for example, through the arteries of the city, as well as to civic improvements to facilitate the growth of 'healthy' cities.

Sue Best, an Australian art historian, extends the parallel between bodies and cities and suggests that cities are often literally conceived of and written about as if they were feminine or female. In her essay on sexualized space, Best develops the links between women's bodies and space through an examination of metaphors as well as social practices. I include a short extract:

> Paris, the 'capital of the nineteenth century', is described by Marina Warner as quintessentially feminine, a city of ladies. The whole public space of Paris is cushioned by accommodating feminine flesh, the buildings are even described as having 'bosomy and vaginal contours . . . pillowy roofs and open-mouthed entrances' (1985: 36–7).
>
> New York, 'capital of the twentieth century', is not quite so accommodating, offering a much more speedy twentieth-century style of romance. Scott Fitzgerald has but one nocturnal affair with New York. She was, as he put it, 'essentially cynical and heartless – save for the one night when she made luminous the Ritz roof' (1971: 143). As befits a twentieth-century woman, New York has an active libido – unlike Oedipalized, vaginal Paris – and hence she has a clitoris at the entrance to her harbour, or, rather, a 'clitoral appendage', as Rem Koolhaas refers to Coney Island (1978: 23).
>
> Thoroughly modern Los Angeles, the capital-to-be of the twenty-first century, predictably perhaps is a simulacrum of woman. According to Lyotard [in *Le Mur du Pacifique*] she is just a stretch of white skin, a surface without openings or depth. . . . An erotic encounter with this city of highways is an arid affair, mediated, of course, by the car. The car becomes a hand seeking out the remaining erogenous zones of this vast, stitched, patchwork body: 'The blindness of the car in the labyrinth of LA is none other than the blindness of the palm as it traverses the length of the thighs, the span of shoulder, of groins' (Lyotard 1989: 64). (Best 1995: 182)

67

Best began her essay with quotes from the writings of the French feminist theorists Kristeva (1986) and Irigaray (1987) asserting the association of space with femininity. Time, by contrast, they suggest, tends to be associated with masculinity. Doreen Massey (1992) has challenged these associations in an interesting essay about the ways in which space and place might be theorized as active rather than passive. As I have begun to suggest here, space is not inert, not merely a container for social action, but is a significant element in the constitution of identity. Massey's and Best's essays are well worth reading in full and I hope you might turn to them to pursue some of these interesting new ways to think about the connections between sex and gender, space and cities.

Conclusions

The placing of the body right at the centre of social theory has perhaps been one of the most exciting moves in contemporary theoretical endeavours. As I shall argue again and again, questions of the sexed body – its differential construction, regulation and representation – are absolutely central to an understanding of gender relations at every spatial scale. Attitudes about the body and its place run through the meaning of the nation as much as the meaning of the home, as well as ideas about community and open spaces such as the street and the city. All these issues will be discussed at greater length in the chapters that follow. Here I hope I have shown through the theoretical summaries and the empirical examples both how our understanding of the body has changed over time and how it has allowed a deeper understanding of the construction of both female and male bodies in all their variety.

Western Enlightenment theorists, in general, ignored women's bodies either by naturalizing them or by theorizing them as lack or as absence. Feminist theorists, in response to this absence, reclaimed women's bodies as an object for theoretical explanation, but ironically, at least initially, paralleled conventional thought by ignoring men's bodies and so leaving them in place as the norm. More recent approaches that theorize the body as a surface inscribed by institutional practices allow both men's and women's bodies to be problematized as spatially and temporally variable objects, and so open up a rich field for geographical exploration and interdisciplinary effort. Ideas about embodiment and its significance, about thinking through and speaking from the body in both its material and symbolic relationship to the world, are, in my view, close to ideas about positionality and location. These are nicely geographic concepts and seem to be an increasingly common way in which a wide range of other feminist theorists not directly concerned with issues of embodiment have begun to describe the particularity of gender differences. For geographers, of course, the growing emphasis on rethinking questions of position and location in feminist theory has led to an invigorating cross-disciplinary debate and some magnificent theoretical and empirical work by the growing number of feminist geographers.

Further reading

For those interested in a more thorough comparison between different theories of the sexed body, Jane Flax's splendid assessment of feminism and psychoanalysis, *Thinking Fragments* (1990), is extremely clear and insightful. Elizabeth Grosz's book *Volatile Bodies* (1994) is also an excellent critical introduction both to a wide range of approaches and to recent feminist work on the body. Caroline Ramazanoglu's edited collection *Up against Foucault* (1993) is worth reading for a discussion of how feminists have reacted to and developed the work of Michel Foucault, while Michael Bristow's short introductory text *Sexuality* (1997) is a useful introduction to some key theories and (male) theorists. The collection edited by David Bell and Gill Valentine, *Mapping Desire* (1995), includes some work by geographers on the body and sexuality, while Beatriz Colomina's edited volume *Sexuality and Space* (1992) includes a multidisciplinary look at issues about representations of a range of spaces.

Steve Pile, in *The Body and the City* (1996), with Nigel Thrift in *Mapping the Subject* (1995), and with Heidi Nast in *Places through the Body* (1998) has explored the relationship between bodies, subjectivity and space. *Gender, Place and Culture* often has papers about the geographies of bodies in different places. Keep an eye on this journal. The paper by Catherine Nash (1996b), for example, challenges arguments about the feminization of landscape and the significance of the male gaze in her assessment of female pleasure in looking at a series of images of the male body as landscape. In this paper she builds on work by feminist film theorists as well as the work by the geographer Gillian Rose (1993), who showed how ideas about the masculine gaze have influenced landscape analyses in geography.

Rose herself is doing interesting work about photographic records of women as bodies in place. See, for example, her recent article about 1930s photographs of East London (Rose 1997) and her paper in the *Mapping the Subject* volume (Rose 1995a) where she looks at the links between spatiality and subjectivity in a range of images produced by feminist artists. Feminist geographers have begun to examine bodily performances in different arenas. Lynda Johnston (1996) shows how the sculpted bodies of women body builders challenge binary notions of femininity and masculinity; and with Robyn Longhurst (Johnston and Longhurst 1998) she has compared their bodily form with that of pregnant women. Clare Lewis and Steve Pile (1996) examine the eroticism of performing bodies in the Rio de Janeiro carnival. There is also an expanding focus on less able bodies in, for example, the papers in a special issue of *Environment and Planning D: Society and Space* (1997) and in a useful survey (Park et al. 1998) with an excellent bibliography in *Progress in Human Geography*.

One of the absences in this chapter is skin colour but to date there is little explicit work by geographers, although some recent studies are outlined in chapter 4. There is, however, a large social science literature about black bodies, examining the ways in which black bodies are both desired and reviled by the non-black population. The stereotypical association of black masculinity with rampant heterosexuality, for example, is a common feature in media representations, parodied in the blaxploitation films of the 1970s such as *Shaft*, but with horrifying consequences when accusations of rape led to lynchings in parts of the US South. Lynne Segal (1990) has examined ways in which the myths about the 'white man's black man' are constructed and reinforced. Geographers have unpacked associations between place and colour in, for example, representations of Africa as the 'dark' continent in literary and geographic texts (Barnett 1996; Jarosz 1992) and Pieterse (1995) has examined images of Africa in Western popular culture.

In a challenge to negative connotations, the phrase Black is Beautiful became a symbol of black pride, but there are dangers in reversing and celebrating characteristics imposed by what bell hooks (1991c, 1994) terms white heteropatriarchal society. Ann DuCille (1996) notes that with its commodification in advertising, 'capitalism has appropriated what it sees as certain signifiers of *blackness* and made them marketable' (p. 27) but still fails to employ black models in significant numbers. Debbie Weekes (1997) listens to how young black British women define beauty, faced by contradictory images of blackness.

3

Home, Place and Identity

Introduction

I argued in the previous two chapters that the social construction of gender
and embodiment combines both material social relations and symbolic representations of difference in ways that distinguish the masculine from the
feminine, the revered from the abhorred, the desirable from the undesirable. In a similar way, the 'reality' and the symbolic meaning of the home
combine to produce the construction of a particular version of a home in
different ways in different societies.

The term 'the home' must be one of the most loaded words in the
English language – indeed in many languages. The geographer David Harvey,
for example, is constantly drawn back to the work of the German national
socialist, Heidegger, and his argument that the dwelling, or home, is the
key location in which a spiritual unity is found between humans and things.
Here, for example, is Heidegger's lyrical description of a Black Forest
farmhouse – his ideal home:

> Here the self-sufficiency of the power to let earth and heaven, divinities
> and mortals enter in simple oneness into things ordered the house. It
> places the farm on a wind-sheltered mountain slope looking south, among
> the meadows close to the spring. It gave it the wide overhanging shingle
> roof whose proper slope bears up under the burden of snow, and which,
> reaching deep down, shields the chambers against the storms of the long
> winter nights. It did not forget the altar corner behind the community
> table; it made room in its chamber for the hallowed places of childbed and
> the 'tree of the dead' – for that is what they call a coffin there – and in this
> way it designed for the different generations under one roof the character
> of their journey through time. A craft which, itself sprung from dwelling,
> still uses its tools and frames as things, built the farmhouse. (Quoted by
> Harvey 1996: 300)

71

For the French theorist Gaston Bachelard, too (who is also quoted by Harvey), dwelling and the home are a key element in the development of people's sense of themselves as belonging to a place.

> All really inhabited space bears the essence of the notion of home. [Here] memory and imagination remain associated, each one working for their mutual deepening. In order of values, they both constitute a community of memory and image. Thus the house is not experienced from day to day only, on the thread of a narrative, or in the telling of our own story. Through dreams the dwelling places in our lives co-penetrate and retain the treasures of former days. [Thus] the house is one of the greatest powers of integration for the thoughts memories and dreams of mankind . . . Without it, man [sic] would be a dispersed being. (Bachelard 1969)

Here we see an interesting parallel between the home and the body as memory stores. Bachelard's view of the home is particularly influential. For example, both Nancy Mairs (1989) in her moving memoirs about her childhood and growing disablement from multiple sclerosis and French anthropologist Joelle Bahloul (1992) in an anthropology of her Jewish ancestors' house in French Algeria, have used the following quotation from Bachelard at the beginning of their books: 'Not only our memories, but the things we have forgotten are "housed". Our soul is an abode. And by remembering "houses" and "rooms", we learn to abide within ourselves' (Bachelard 1969).

So we see here, in these lyrical descriptions, the power attributed by theorists to the house and dwelling, with its connotations of shelter and security, of pleasure, and as a storehouse of memories. In some senses, both male theorists, Bachelard and especially Heidegger, seem to be harking back to a pre-industrial idyll and both, of course, deny the labour, of men as well as women, that goes into constructing and maintaining a dwelling, turning a house into a home. In the Heidegger quotation, for example, the farmhouse seems to build itself, a phenomenon that seems almost as 'natural' as the landscape itself. Yet the work of Bachelard clearly 'speaks to' women in his recognition of how important the home is in the social construction of meaning and subjectivity. Domestic space is 'the material representation of the social order' and 'social reproduction is achieved through the symbolic perpetuation of the social order represented in the habitat' (Bahloul 1992: 129).

This *representation* in domestic space and order is what Pierre Bourdieu termed a *habitus* (Bourdieu 1977). So for Bahloul, the recollections of home that she drew from the inhabitants of a single house in Algeria between 1937 and 1962 were representations of a whole social order in colonial Algeria and the place of Jews and Muslims within it. Thus a focus on the social relations within a domestic space crosses the boundary between the private and the public, between the particular and the general, and is not, as is often incorrectly asserted, a focus on the 'merely' domestic or the private sphere.

The origins of domesticity and its spatial separation in industrial societies

Unpicking and making visible the assumptions that lie behind the sort of spiritual reification of the home as an arena of security and of respite from the cruel world of work, found not only in Heidegger's work but more widely, was the focus of some of the earliest work by post-1968 feminists, building on the remarkable critiques by feminist theorists in earlier decades. What these women writing from the late 1960s onwards pointed out was that the division of urban space into worlds of home and waged work – a so-called private arena associated with women, and a public world of men – that developed with industrial capitalism in the West had a huge impact on women's lives and status (Allen and Crow 1989; Mackenzie and Rose 1983; Madigan and Munro 1991). For women, who were encouraged (and forced in some circumstances) to identify with and restrict themselves to the home, the home 'is alternatively a site of disenfranchisement, abuse and fulfilment. Just as men have traditionally been encouraged to "earn a good living", women are still expected to "keep house"' (Mertes 1992: 58). And because this housekeeping was seen to rely on women's 'natural' skills and was financially unrewarded, it was correspondingly devalued and long left untheorized.

Individual women, however, were well aware of the reality of housework, its tedium and repetitiveness and, in many places, the extremely hard labour involved in housework and in childcare. From the late nineteenth century on, campaigns in Britain and North America were organized to recognize women's contribution to the family and the economy by some form of state-provided family allowance. As part of her campaign to improve the health of working-class women in the 1930s, for example, Margery Spring Rice undertook a questionnaire survey of 1,250 poor women to reveal the drudgery involved in their domestic work and the struggle to survive on an inadequate income. As Spring Rice demonstrated, the work of the women, undertaken 'for love',

is more unremitting than that of any man, and it is only the strongest of them that are able to keep level with it and to prevent the tragic slipping back in health, in happiness, and in cultural if not in moral standards, which

73

is too often seen. The last thing that can be expected of them is quiet thought and any action other than the minimum demanded by the immediate job in hand. They lead private and often very solitary lives; their work is unpaid and unorganised. Its inevitability is taken for granted not only by themselves but also by the other half of the public, who themselves have grown up and thrived upon it. Members of Parliament, for whom now women can cast their vote, do not see what is going on in the small dark unorganised workshop of the home. (Spring Rice 1981: 18)

This is a powerful plea to recognize that housework is, indeed, work like any other form and that the conditions in which it takes place are often much worse than in other workplaces. As Spring Rice described, being at home is an isolating experience:

The very large majority of men work away from their homes and return there for rest and recreation. In nearly all families all children except the very youngest spend a great deal of time away from home, either in school, or, if they have left school, in their own wage-earning jobs. For them too the home is a place of play or rest. For fathers and children alike, these hours away from home bring new contacts, recreational, such as clubs, camps and games, as well as more serious interests. But in general the mother stays at home. (1981: 13–14)

In the United States at the end of the nineteenth century a number of utopian thinkers suggested ways of reorganizing domestic provision. Dolores Hayden in her book *Seven American Utopias* (1976) has documented some of the plans for kitchenless houses and shared facilities developed by communitarian socialists between 1790 and 1935, similar to the suggestions of the Owenite socialists in mid nineteenth-century Britain (for a brief outline of their proposals see Barbara Taylor's *Eve and the New Jerusalem* (1983)). Sadly most of these experiments either failed to get off the ground or were short-lived. US writer and novelist Charlotte Perkins Gilman (then Charlotte Stetson) published *Women and Economics* in 1898, in which she also criticized the domestic slavery of women and argued for their participation in the public sphere. She not only believed this was essential to ensure women's equality, but she also passionately believed that female qualities of cooperation and nurturance were needed to restore 'balance' to a public world of men that was too assertive and combative. She suggested that women as well as men should leave the home to undertake 'world-work' (her phrase).

Gilman dealt with feminist issues in her fiction too, some of which is interesting to read a century after its original publication. *The Yellow Wallpaper* (from 1892) is a story of a young mother driven mad by her well-meaning husband and it was apparently reprinted as a horror story until its feminist reinterpretation in the 1970s. In a series of other novels, including her most famous, *Herland* (from 1915), Gilman described a mythical socialist society in which women held power, household chores were removed from the family house and childcare was a collective responsibility. These still seem radical, even utopian, ideas almost a century later.

The division of home from work that developed in industrial societies in the West in the nineteenth century, and women's seclusion in the former sphere, was never complete, however – over a third of all women were involved in some form of waged labour in Britain for the hundred years between 1850 and 1950. But during the nineteenth century, women were increasingly excluded from the better-paying industrial occupations, as men recognized the dangers of competition from lower-paid female labour. It is also undeniable that appalling conditions and high child mortality among the offspring of wage-earning women led philanthropists to support claims that women should not be permitted in certain jobs (C. Hall 1992). It is important to remember, too, that for working-class women the domestic work needed to ensure that their families had anything approaching a reasonable standard of living, and that their menfolk went to work each day fed and clothed, was hard and time-consuming. Imagine the work involved for a miner's wife in the nineteenth century when there were neither pithead baths nor running hot water in the home (McDowell and Massey 1984).

Angels of the home

The significance of the labour undertaken in the home and its importance in reproducing the industrial labour force tended, however, despite the exceptions I have discussed above, to be ignored, at least in theoretical and ideological terms. Instead the home became associated, particularly during the nineteenth century but also from an earlier date in Britain, with characteristics that were constructed in *opposition* to the developing capitalist economy. Thus in Britain, as in other Western European societies during industrialization, the home was invested with a spiritual quality (reminiscent of the Heidegger quote at the beginning of this chapter), and the idealization of the home took on religious characteristics. Housework and childcare in particular were seen as women's 'sacred' duty, they and the 'master' of the house being protected in this sphere from the harsh competitive world of capitalism. The home became an idealized centre for emotional life, where feelings that might be disguised elsewhere were allowed full rein. Thus the home was constructed as the locus of love, emotion and empathy, and the burdens of nurturing and caring for others were placed on the shoulders of women, who were, however, constructed as 'angels' rather than workers. The home also became a status symbol of a man's worth and women were encouraged not only to reach ever higher standards of cleanliness but also to decorate and embellish their homes. Mertes quotes from a US labour leader's speech in 1906 which nicely encapsulates the prevailing ideology:

> I contend that the wife or mother, attending to the duties of the home, makes the greatest contribution to the support of the family . . . I entertain no doubt but that . . . the wife will, apart from performing her natural household duties, perform that work which is most pleasurable for her, contributing to the beautifying of her home and surroundings. (Gompers quoted in Mertes 1992: 66)

Notice not only Gompers's assumption that doing housework is natural for women, but also that it is pleasurable!

The complete separation of working lives from home life and women's exclusion was most prevalent among the middle class in Britain and in the US. Catherine Hall, for example, has traced the history of the Cadbury family and shown how the wives and sisters of the male Cadburys were slowly but completely excluded from the commercial life of the firm (Hall 1982). And by the late nineteenth century, all married women, not just the family, were banned from working in the Cadbury factory at Bournville. Middle-class women's lives of idle luxury or 'good works' depended, however, on the efforts of their working-class sisters to keep their labour-intensive Victorian homes running smoothly. At the end of the nineteenth century in Britain almost a million women were working for wages in other women's houses and other women were forced to do waged work in their own homes, such as taking in laundry or boarders. Somehow the fact that both these types of work were 'domestic' employment in the home, albeit in the former case in another family's home, meant that this form of female employment was ignored and left unregulated. It did not lead to demands for women's exclusion from the labour market as in the factories and mines of Victorian England.

Catherine Hall was one of the early historians of women's domestic labour and her essays on this and other themes are collected in *White, Male and Middle Class*. Here she argued that

> housewives have rarely thought of themselves as having a history – and historians have not thought of the housewife as worthy of academic study [but] the history of women in the home – of the changing nature of marriage, childcare and domestic labour, for example – is an area which badly needs exploration . . . being a housewife is a condition which is socially defined and its definition changes at different historical moments. (1992: 43).

Hall herself, in work with Leonore Davidoff (Davidoff and Hall 1987) as well as in the study of the Cadbury family I mentioned above, has been influential in uncovering the history of women's domestic work in the late eighteenth and nineteenth centuries, noting the gradual withdrawal of middle-class women into the seclusion of their homes and the exclusion of working-class women from many trades and service activities. She argues that limitations on domestic activity took place because of the developing capitalist organization of many trades that had previously been part of an extended household:

> Brewing is a classic example: it was an entrepreneurial area which had been particularly popular with women but by the end of the seventeenth century brewing had become an organized trade and was no longer open to women. The skills which could be acquired domestically were not enough to establish women's position in trade – women could still, of course, brew for their own families if they wanted to, but that became a privatized activity which could not easily be extended into the social sphere . . . it became more important for men to organize their trades protectively once the separation of capital and labour and of the home from the workplace took place: the separation of commodity production from domestic labour was an inevitable result, male workers were gathered together and employees began to form associations in addition to the employers' guilds which existed. For journeymen in their new position as waged labourers to be able to bargain well, they had to maintain their exclusive position by long apprenticeships and many restrictions on entry: the easiest group to exclude were women. (Hall 1992: 52)

As well as men uniting to exclude women from trades, the philanthropist movement that grew throughout the nineteenth century also contributed to women's increasing restriction to the home, as for the benefit of women's own health they were excluded from what were perceived to be rough and dangerous trades. Coal mining is a classic example (see John 1980). The third strand that completed the ideological exclusion, if not the complete actual exclusion, of women in Britain was religion. From the time of the Puritan revolution and through the later rise of middle-class Nonconformism, women were constructed as secondary beings, as domestic helpmeets for their husbands. Catherine Hall (1992: 58) quotes Adam from Milton's *Paradise Lost*:

> For nothing lovelier can be found
> in woman, than to study household good
> and good works in her husband to promote.

Leonore Davidoff and Catherine Hall (1987) have also argued that the development of evangelical movements through the late eighteenth and the nineteenth century was important in the emergence of a particular view of domesticated femininity. The movements drew on a rational and scientific view of the world and a moral order in which myth, superstition and nature were associated with inferiors – women, children, rural dwellers and the working class – and so regarded as in need of control.

> Sexuality, regarded as one of the most irrational forces, was relegated to the inner core of marriage and sexual play became the ultimate antithesis of rational work. Women, particularly when pregnant and thus incontrovertibly sexual beings, were associated with animalistic nature, incompatible with the serious work of the world. Categories of purity and pollution, the separating of the useful from waste, weeds and rubbish, were invoked by scientific and sanitary movements to control noxious materials, sights, sounds, smell – and people. (Davidoff and Hall 1987: 26–7)

Here again we see parallels between women's bodies and the social construction of femininity and the home. So women, or rather married women, were thus constructed as in need of control, and somewhat ironically, given the associations between sexuality and pollution, as pure and sacred, as the angels of the domestic arena whose duty it was to bring order to the homes. As the Victorian era progressed, the home was portrayed as the source of the virtues and emotions that could not be found elsewhere – in the busy worlds of industry and commerce, for example, among men. As Ruskin notes in his essay *Sesame and Lilies*:

> This is the very true nature of home – it is the place of peace – the shelter not only from all injury, but from all terror, doubt and division. In so far as it is not this, it is not home; in so far as the anxieties of the outer life penetrate into it, and the inconsistently minded, unknown, unloved, or hostile society of the outer world is allowed by either husband or wife to cross the threshold, it ceases to become home'. (Quoted in Hall 1992: 61)

Ruskin himself did not manage to create a happy home life because he was so shocked by the reality as opposed to his imaginary notions of his wife's body and sexuality. But even at the time, as this ideology of the home was created and purveyed, some commentators were not seduced by this rhetoric. In an *Appeal on behalf of one half of the human race*, published in 1825, William Thompson instead described home as 'the eternal prison house of the wife; her husband painted it as the abode of calm bliss, but took care to find outside its doors a species of bliss not quite so calm, but of a more varied and stimulating description' (quoted by Hall 1992: 61). One hun-

dred and sixty years later, feminist author Beatrix Campbell wrote in almost exactly similar terms: 'the Englishman's home may be his castle, but
he takes care not to spend much time there' (Campbell 1984). Clearly, the
critique of domestic labour and the home as a prison in the twentieth
century had an early forerunner.

The ideology that 'women's place was in the home', however, became
dominant across all the social classes in Britain in the nineteenth century
and exercised a vital hold on the lives and minds of all women. It meant
that for working-class women who went 'out to work', it was still their lot
in life to do the housework as well. Recognizing the burden of domestic
work for many working-class women in the nineteenth century, feminist
economist Jane Humphries (1977) has argued against the feminist ortho-
doxy that restriction to the home is necessarily oppressive for women. She
suggested that the payment of a family wage for men which would allow
women to stay at home would increase the overall standard of living for
many working-class households. In her oral histories of working-class women
living in Lancaster at the beginning of the twentieth century, Elizabeth
Roberts (1988) also found that for many working-class households gender
relations were largely based on cooperation rather than antagonism. Both
men and women were fully aware of the inequalities and injustices which
produced their poverty and were anxious to find a way to 'get by' and raise
their children as best they might within their means. Thus their common
class interests outweighed gender differences.

In the early decades of the twentieth century, the naturalized association
of domestic work with women became institutionalized in all sorts of ways,
despite the 'blips' of the two world wars when women neglected their domestic work and left the home in large numbers in response to labour
shortages (see plate 3.1). It is interesting to note, too, that in these wars
industrial labour was compared with a range of domestic tasks in government propaganda to encourage women's participation. Welding was compared to knitting, for example! Despite gradually expanding numbers of
women entering waged labour throughout the twentieth century, especially
in Britain as part-time workers so that they might combine their 'dual roles',
it was not until the significant rise of service sector employment associated
with industrial restructuring in the early 1970s that the ideology of domesticity was seriously challenged. In the interwar and postwar periods, housework was established even more securely as a woman's lot in life. Domestic
science was invented as a school and then a college subject, for example, and
taught, in the main, only to girls. Domestic work in the home was presented, especially by the growing professionalized advertising industry, as a
rational and systematic set of tasks requiring specialized instruments and
other goods. One of the major early tasks that feminist theorists turned to,

79

Plate 3.1   Rosie the Riveter: a familiar image of a woman worker in the
Second World War

then, was to think through the role of women in the domestic sphere and the
contribution of their labours to reproducing the capitalist system as well as
maintaining the structures of women's oppression.

80

Domestic labour and capitalism

Despite Charlotte Perkins Gilman's pioneering work, the theorization of domestic labour floundered until the reflowering of the women's movement and the development of feminism as a theoretical subject from the late 1960s onwards. Influenced by the then-dominant socialist feminist perspective, economists and sociologists fiercely debated the significance of domestic labour as a category in the social relations of capitalism. Drawing on the earlier work of Engels on the role of the family and private property in nineteenth-century industrial capitalism, contemporary feminists argued that the division of labour between productive work in the factories and offices and reproductive labour by women in the home was necessary for the functioning of capitalism. Women's domestic labour, in the language of this perspective, reproduced labour on a daily and generational basis. Women kept men clean, clothed and fed and so ready to go out to work each day, as well as bearing and caring for children who would be the labour force of the future. Thus women, too, were exploited by capitalism, but, it was argued, they were also exploited by individual men who appropriated their labours in the home. As Sylvia Walby has explained:

> The work performed by the woman may range from cooking and cleaning for the husband to caring for their children. Women as housewives perform this work for husbands. In these relations of production the housewife is engaged in labour for her husband who expropriates it. She is not rewarded with money for this labour, merely her maintenance (sometimes). The product of a wife's labour is labour power: that of herself, her husband and her children. The husband is able to appropriate the wife's labour power because he has possession of the labour power which she has produced. He is able to sell this labour power as if it were his own. (1989: 221)

The family also increasingly became a market for the mass-produced goods of the capitalist system, many of which had previously been made by individual women in their own homes. Goods like tinned food and jams for example, as well commercially brewed beer, replaced home produce, and, along with cheap factory-made clothing, soaps and so forth, became consumer items. The family increasingly became a unit of consumption rather than one of production.

Zillah Eisenstein (1979), in one of the earliest and most influential papers defining the links between capitalism and patriarchy (the system of male power which produces women's inferiority) suggests that women fulfil four major functions in capitalist societies. First, they stabilize patriarchal structures, especially the family, by fulfilling socially defined roles such as a wife and a mother; secondly, they reproduce new workers for both the paid and unpaid labour forces; thirdly, they stabilize the economy in their role as producers; and finally, they themselves work in the labour market for lower wages than men. I shall discuss this fourth function in the next chapter, and as you will remember from the first chapter, Sylvia Walby (1990) identified domestic labour and waged work as two of the six structures of patriarchal relations in contemporary industrial societies.

Counting (and paying for) women's domestic work?

As well as theoretical discussions about domestic labour, second wave feminists also made practical contributions to the debate about the recognition of and reward for women's work in the home. For a time in the late 1960s and 1970s, wages for housework was one of the demands made by the British women's movement. However, there was never full support for this demand as some people argued that paying women for work in the home would reinforce women's responsibility for domestic work and so their secondary status. It might make it even more difficult for them to challenge existing gender divisions and enter well-paid occupations in the waged labour market. What these feminists argued for instead was for men to accept their responsibilities in the home and to share domestic work.

Unfortunately, as time budget surveys from the 1960s until the present day have illustrated, men have shown a marked reluctance to shoulder a fair share of tasks in the home. Figures produced by the Office of National Statistics for men's and women's use of time in Great Britain in 1995 showed that women spent an average of 68 minutes a day cooking, 86 minutes looking after children, 25 minutes doing the washing, 70 minutes cleaning and 46 minutes shopping. Men, by comparison, spent only 28 minutes in the kitchen, 55 minutes with their children, 3 minutes doing laundry, 43 minutes cleaning or doing other household chores, and 26 minutes shopping. Other research has shown that when women are also in paid work, their contribution to domestic work declines, although not substantially. The time their male partners put into housework and childcare does rise somewhat, interestingly in direct proportion to the woman's earning capacity (Morris 1992).

When domestic work is done by women in other women's homes (I shall examine paid domestic work in more detail in the next section), its value enters national economic estimates of the gross domestic product. Unpaid labour is, however, excluded. For many years, feminist economists and others have argued that this is a patent disparity and that estimates of women's unpaid labour should be included in national accounting systems

(Waring 1989). Finally in 1997, after more than thirty years of pressure, the British government acknowledged that the value of domestic labour, if counted, might more than double the size of the economy. The time budget survey just outlined revealed that people spent one and a half times as long doing domestic tasks as they spent at work. The Office of National Statistics calculated that if the time spent on unwaged work was valued at the same average rate as paid employment, its worth would be a huge £739 billion per annum. If the imputed value is calculated by disaggregating tasks and applying the average wage rate for nannies and childminders to looking after children, the rate for cleaners to housework, for painters and decorators to DIY, and so forth, the overall figure declines to £341 billion, because these jobs are among the lowest paid in the labour market. But even so, the figure is 56 per cent of current GDP and its value is greater than the whole of the UK manufacturing sector.

While there is little prospect of actual monetary reward for these tasks, it is a step forward to see them included in national accounts and for the government to recognize feminist arguments that, unpaid or not, domestic tasks that are undertaken primarily by women within the confines of the home are work nevertheless. In the next section, I want to look at domestic work that is paid for – work which is also, but not solely, undertaken by women.

Paid domestic labour

Paid domestic work within the home not only challenges the socially accepted meaning of the home and its association with the private and the familial, but also makes plain the complex intersections of domesticity, class position and racial difference that distinguish women and create divisions between them. It is also important to note that waged domestic labour was ignored in the theorizations of patriarchy outlined above and in chapter 1, which assumed that all domestic labour was undertaken 'for love' by women in a relationship of dependency with an individual man.

Paid labour in the home – cleaning and childcare in the main – is performed for middle-class women by working-class women, and commonly in the US and Canada by women of colour who work for white women. Thus the common cult of domesticity – the idea of the woman as the angel of the hearth that developed both in industrial Britain and the US – took different social and geographical forms between these two nations and indeed within them, depending on the way in which working-class women and women of colour were drawn into domestic service.

In Britain, geographers Nicky Gregson and Michelle Lowe (1994) have investigated the geographic patterns of different forms of domestic work. They found that whereas daily cleaning jobs were filled from a predominantly local labour market, childcare, especially live-in nannying jobs, attracted young working-class women from a wider catchment area. They noted in particular the movement of young women from the northern areas of Britain to work in middle-class households in London and the south east. As they argue in the introduction to their book,

> Waged domestic labour in contemporary Britain, and particularly that relating to childcare, is an emotive issue. It is a phenomenon which appears to challenge the associations between all women and domestic labour and the assumption that domestic labour is an unwaged activity, carried out for love not money. In addition it appears to be generative and reflective of some of the major differences and divisions between women. (Gregson and Lowe 1994: 5)

They suggest that the assumptions about gender, love and caring that structure childcare as an activity are the basis for the construction of what they term 'false kinship' relations between employees and employers, constructing childcare as a personal and emotional task rather than a straightforward wage relation. Consequently, the notion of kinship often leads to difficulties between the women involved on both sides of the relationship and dissatisfaction by nannies and other domestic workers with their terms and conditions of employment.

Gregson and Lowe found few examples of ethnic differences between employers and domestic employees, but in the United States there are ethnic as well as class divisions in domestic employment. In the southern states, black domestic service is a relict of the patterns established, in slavery, and as Haug (1992) argues, the 'mammy figure' has become a cultural stereotype. In the northern cities of the US and in Canada, poor white immigrant women originally dominated domestic service (the recent novel by Margaret Atwood, *Alias Grace* (1996), is an absorbing assessment of the life and conditions of one such woman in Canada in the 1840s). From the 1940s onwards, however, in the US there was increasing employment of black women who had moved north in large numbers with the men who were recruited to the new industries. In the southwestern states, Mexican immigrants and the native population were originally recruited for domestic work. It was only on the west coast that the association between gender and domestic labour was broken by the recruitment of Chinese men, whose masculinity was thus impugned.

84

Table 3.1   Share of employed women working in private household service by racial-ethnic group 1900–1980, USA

	1900	1930	1960	1980
African American	43.5	53.5	39.3	5.0
European American	29.8	12.0	4.4	0.8
American Indian	13.4	22.5	16.8	1.4
Chinese American	35.6	12.1	1.7	0.8
Japanese American	28.6	29.9	8.2	1.4
Filipina American	n.a.	34.4	3.7	0.9
Chicana	n.a.	33.1	11.5	2.4
US Puerto Rican	n.a.	n.a.	1.2	0.7
Island Puerto Rican	78.4	27.5	13.7	1.4

Source: T. Amott and J. Matthaei, *Race, Gender and Work*, Montreal and New York: Black Rose Books, 1991 p. 325, table 10.3

Table 3.1 shows the ethnic breakdown of domestic employment in the United States between 1900 and 1980. For black women, especially black women of the South, there was little option of any other form of work, especially before the Second World War. In the same way in which women in general are constructed as inferior to men through a set of dichotomous comparisons, a set of polarities that had developed during slavery and continued in domestic service counterposed white and black women. In this way other relational categories were mapped on to the black/white dichotomy, such as sexual/frigid, impure/pure, dirty/clean, animal/human, loose/moral. Thus the dirty work of the household was done by women who themselves were constructed as inferior and dirty.

In Britain a similar set of polarities were used to distinguish working-class middle-class women, exhibited perhaps in its most extreme form in the drawing and photographs of Alfred Munby, a Victorian academic and lawyer who fetishized 'dirty' working-class women, these connections between dirt, race and class are further explored in the context of imperialism by Anne McClintock in her stimulating book, *Imperial Leather* (1994).

Historical assessment of the changing nature of the waged work undertaken by women of African and African-Caribbean origin in the US, reveals that recent economic changes and the shift to a service-based economy have opened up opportunities other than domestic service for women of colour. However, considerable numbers have moved from cooking, catering, cleaning and childcare in the domestic arena into the same sort of work in commercial organizations, such as laundries, nursing homes, canteens and fast food outlets (Amott and Matthaei 1991; Glenn 1992). And many women of colour still work within other women's homes.

In South Africa, gender and race are similarly connected and millions of Black women have, over the century, left their own children in rural areas to move to the city to care for white children. In her moving book *The Women of Phokeng* (1991), Belinda Bozzoli, with the assistance of Mmantho Nkotsoe, has documented the life stories of a group of elderly Black women born in Phokeng, in rural South Africa, before the First World War. During the apartheid era their settlement was in the 'homeland' of Bophuthatswana. As Bozzoli notes, the lives of such women have been largely hidden from history and relatively little is known about their early lives as peasant daughters or about their coping strategies during periods of intense hardship as adults. Most of the sixteen women included in the project became urban workers in their twenties, many of them as domestics. Their migration took a common pattern, with moves over gradually increasing distances – first to Rustenburg, a nearby town, and later to Johannesburg.

Here is Bozzoli describing the reasons why these women entered domestic service, and their views of it. Her warning against automatically regarding these women as oppressed or disempowered is important.

> We should not assume that the choice of domestic service as an occupation was entirely accidental or a result only of the economics of the labour market. Important as larger structural forces were in steering women towards this type of work, from the point of view of their own consciousness of the situation, domestic service was a relatively good deal. . . . It was a choice between one working-class occupation or another, and as one woman said, 'firms' (meaning companies) were clearly 'not for women'. A number of factors reinforced domestic service as an occupational choice, ranging from their preparation for such work by missionaries to their acceptance of its paternalistic ideology. Domestic service, was, according to Nthana Mokale (one of the interviewees), far better than farm work – and indeed it was perceived as offering a good income, a means to the end of earning enough for the needs of the family, and for accumulating the protodowry that had come to be necessary to make a good marriage. The women's own instrumentalism was also at play here, and it served to retain their sense that they were coming to the city for their own reasons, and raiding it for the resources they needed for their own dreams to be fulfilled. (Bozzoli 1991: 96–7)

This is an important corrective to analyses that construct women as victims, failing to credit their own agency and the ways in which they made the best of limited opportunities. Remember from chapter 1 that Deniz Kandiyoti (1988) argued that women 'bargain' with patriarchy and paternalism, struggling against circumstances but also making the best choices possible in existing circumstances. And the sixteen women whose lives were so vividly recorded by Bozzoli and Nkotsoe certainly struggled. Many of them were politically active throughout their lives in the struggles against racism and apartheid, especially in the campaigns against the pass laws. These women relied on networks of their kin and the women Bozzoli calls the 'homegirls'. They used these networks to build up a good position in the labour market in the better-paying suburbs, where in some cases they were not the only domestic worker in a household. Here are two of the women in Bozzoli's study reflecting on their position in the 1920s:

> 'Women only cleaned and looked after children,' says Mrs Mekgwe. Male domestics, who had in earlier times monopolized domestic service and were still preponderant in the occupation, often performed such jobs as gardening and cooking. Nthana Mokale says in one household in which she was employed, for example, 'I was literally a monkey from Phokeng, I could only cook pap and not casseroles.' A Mosotho male did the cooking, serving and gardening, while 'I only cleaned house and looked after the kids, you know, like a nanny'. In the evenings 'he cooked the supper, set the table and dished out, while I would bathe the kids and put them to bed.' (Bozzoli 1991: 99)

So within domestic service at that time in South Africa there was an internal gender division of labour and men as well as women were servants. This same division is found in, for example, present-day Californian cities, as Latina women do childcare and housework and Latino men are employed as casual handymen and gardeners (Romero 1992). In Britain, where domestic work is overwhelmingly undertaken by women, there is a status hierarchy in which cleaning is regarded as less skilled and correspondingly is often more poorly paid than childcare (Gregson and Lowe 1994). And for many women domestic workers, especially those who are migrants from rural areas to the city or who move across national borders, taking such employment often means leaving their own children in order to care for those of more affluent women, thus disrupting the links between motherhood and home in their own lives (Hondagneu-Sotelo and Avila 1997).

Domestic work in Canada: constructing stereotypes and differences

It is often argued that the focus of feminist scholarship has altered as its practitioners age. Perhaps then it is reflection of the growing maturity of Canadian feminist geography that in a recent volume of *Gender, Place and Culture* two articles were published focusing on constructions of ethnicity and difference, and their effects on the employment of women from different backgrounds as nannies and other domestic workers in Canadian cities. In the first paper, by Geraldine Pratt, the author begins by clarifying her own very real interest in the subject: 'Even before my baby was born I was worrying about day care' (1997: 159). One of the worries that interested Pratt, both as a mother and as a geographer, was the way in which nanny agencies, government policy and individual practices construct racial stereotypes. The second paper, by Bernadette Stiell and Kim England (1997), dealt with similar issues, showing how, through a complex set of institutional practices, a hierarchy of nannies is created in which white European nannies are placed above women of colour, affecting both the power and pay of domestic workers and their relations with potential and actual employers. Pratt shows, however, that these relationships, albeit ones of power, are not straightforward but are riven by inconsistencies and ambivalences that are related to 'anxieties about maternal substitution, colonial pasts, racial differences and working mothers'.

These two studies of Canadian cities bring together the two major themes that are emerging in the growing geographic literature about paid domestic work. The first emphasizes the growing importance of national and international migration for low-income women and the significance of ideas about nationality or national stereotypes (England and Stiell 1997; Mattingly 1996; Radcliffe 1990) whereas the second focuses on the ways in which economic and social restructuring in 'core' economies alters the relationships between home and waged work both for high-income women in high-status jobs and for the growing numbers of low-paid women who enter low-status 'servicing' work (Gregson and Lowe 1994; Moss 1995a).

Home as haven and/or prison

As well as the socialist feminist emphasis on the theorization of domestic labour and its relationship to capitalism, feminists interested in questions about the structure of the family and male power began to construct an argument from the late 1960s onwards about the home as a cage or a trap, a prison (Gavron 1968; Oakley 1974) and, for some women, a site of fear and abuse (Campbell 1988). The dual focus here was male violence against women and child abuse. It was argued that the assumption that 'an Englishman's home is his castle' in combination with the idea of the home as a private place for personal relations led to official tolerance by the state of unacceptable forms of male power over women. Domestic violence, for example, was not defined as grievous bodily harm like other forms of interpersonal violence, and police were reluctant to intervene in what they saw as private disputes between 'man and wife'. Many women were also reluctant to complain as they were often financially dependent on their male partners, as well as often not being joint owners or tenants of the home. In Britain Erin Pizzey, among others, was instrumental in establishing the women's refuge movement, which set up a series of refuges in many cities in Britain.

On some occasions, however, certain authorities have a right of access to the home and women's behaviour and housekeeping standards were, or still are in some cases, policed (Donzelot 1979). Local authority housing managers for example, used to not merely hand out patronizing advice about standards of cleanliness but also used to visit unannounced. And in housing transfer requests it was usual for the standard of care to be considered when discussing a new allocation (Sarre et al. 1988). Social workers, school attendance officers, health visitors and community nurses still have a right of access to the home.

In the theoretical literature of this time, there was, however, a perhaps too easy assumption that both the family and the institutional structures of the state – the welfare state and the medical profession, for example – were automatically instruments of patriarchal oppression. Elizabeth Wilson's 1977 book *Women and the Welfare State* is a good example of this approach. Gradually a more nuanced argument began to be heard, as it was realized that institutions often reflect and operate more contradictory aims and policies. For many women, the family is not only the site of oppressive social relations and (too much) domestic labour, but also an arena of personal fulfilment through romantic love and relationships with children and other dependants. Similarly, while the institutions of the welfare state may reflect assumptions of women's dependency on men, they also support women and their children in a range of policies and programmes as well as provide the opportunity for waged work for many women (Pateman 1989).

The assertion that the home is a locus of oppression has been particularly criticized by black feminist scholars and writers, who have argued that for them the home has long been one of the only places of escape from the oppressive relations of first slavery and later racist society: what the US feminist writer bell hooks has termed 'white supremacist capitalist patriarchy'. In a widely quoted paper called 'Homeplace: a site of resistance', she argues that 'black women resisted by making homes where all black people . . . could be affirmed in our minds and hearts despite poverty, hardship and deprivation, and where we could restore to ourselves the dignity denied outside in the public world' (1991b: 42).

The contradictory nature of the home has been more widely recognized in recent feminist work, as have the struggles by women to transform adverse housing environments (Breitbart and Pader 1995).

Homelessness

Growing numbers of people in Britain and the US are, however, without a home at all. Poverty and economic restructuring, male unemployment, and cuts in state benefits, where there are any, in many industrial societies have affected the size and nature of the homeless population and have led to growing numbers of young people living on the streets (Sassen 1990; Venness 1992). At one time, the stereotypical homeless person was a rather romanticized version of the hobo or the tramp: a masculine figure who was unable to settle down and shoulder the responsibilities of home and work. In the 1950s a particular version of this figure appeared in the form of the Beats – young men who periodically took to the road. Their quintessential representative is Jack Kerouac who fictionalized a version of his own life in *On the Road* (1957), a book which has come to symbolize rebellion for generations of young people. Kerouac and his companions, however, were only periodically on the road: they had families to return to, and also participated in various forms of waged work (Cassady 1990; McDowell 1996). For other men, as the number of beds in hostels declined in the postwar period, being homeless led to increasing hardship and a severely reduced life expectancy. In Britain in the mid-1990s it has been estimated that the average life expectancy for a homeless man is about forty years.

Homelessness for women challenges every assumption about a woman's place and, for that reason, many women themselves often try to disguise or deny their predicament. In Los Angeles, homeless women were found living in cars, changing in department stores and in some cases still holding down a job. It has also been argued by Sophie Watson (Watson with Austerberry 1986), April Venness (1992) and others that merely having a roof over one's head does not constitute having a home. Watson, for example, undertook research among women who were housed as part of their employment or who lived in hostel or temporary accommodation. She argued that these women in insecure accommodation should also be counted among the homeless.

In the 1980s the election of right-wing governments in the US and the UK, combined with an economic recession at the beginning and end of that decade, resulted in a growing shortage of affordable housing for low-income households to rent or purchase and an increasingly visible problem of homelessness on city streets. In her comparative analysis of London, New York and Tokyo, Saskia Sassen (1990) found a change in the nature of homelessness in these cities. Growing numbers of women and children as well as men were on the streets. One 'solution' in New York has been the invasion of subway tunnels by homeless people. In a remarkable photo essay (1995) Margaret Morton has recorded the efforts of people with the very minimum of income and possessions to construct some version of 'home life' in the most adverse circumstances in these tunnels.

A team of geographers at the University of Southern California have for some years now being doing a mixture of academic and practical work with homeless people in downtown Los Angeles. In 1990, Stacey Rowe and Jennifer Wolch published an interesting paper in which they mapped the everyday activities of a small number of homeless men and women. They found that complex, although spatially restricted, networks were established between women and men, as lovers or spouses, which played an important part in the maintenance of relative security and self-esteem for some women and in the temporary achievement of some sort of 'homebase' on the streets. Although conventional patriarchal divisions of labour were re-established on the streets, with women undertaking what cooking was possible, for example, Rowe and Wolch suggested that these networks may be an important route out of chronic homelessness, providing some support and sense of personal worth.

In a comparable study of the socio-spatial networks of a much younger group of homeless people, street kids in Newcastle in Australia, Hilary Winchester and Lauren Costello (1995) found no parallel set of networks, nor routes out of homelessness. Instead these children were an outside group whose networks reinforced their difference from their settled peers and whose behaviour appeared to encourage them into long-term and chronic homelessness. Interestingly, Winchester and Costello found relatively little evidence of traditional patriarchal relations between the young men and women. Girls became gang leaders and they 'were not confined to the domestic sphere nor expected to undertake domestic duties any more than the boys', although, as the authors remind us,

> this is because the domestic sphere barely existed. . . . The squats used by the kids were utterly squalid, with no attempt at order and cleanliness made by either the girls or the boys . . . there was no washing and tidying up, and relatively little cooking and shopping to be done. There was therefore no sense in which the squats were made to resemble 'home'. (1995: 340)

Winchester and Costello also found that the

> girls did not conform to any accepted standard of conventional beauty or fashion. Many of the group, both girls and boys, undertook forms of tattooing and personal mutilation such as the ritual slashing of parts of their bodies to make, for example, parallel scars along their forearms. This self-mutilation, seen by the group as an indication of personal bravery, may also be interpreted by outsiders as a form of group identification and an indication of low self-esteem. (1995: 341)

91

But the net result for the girls was an important one: a denial or at least disguise of their femininity and inferiority. As Winchester and Costello noted, it was important for these girls' safety that they did not present a conventionally attractive bodily appearance. As has been shown to be the case with 'bag ladies' (Merves 1992), anonymity and eccentricity make women less obvious targets for sexual harassment.

Conclusion: the meaning of home

In Third World cities, the scale of homelessness far outweighs that in many cities in the 'West'. Indeed, the distinction between being housed or homeless is less useful in parts of the world where so many urban dwellers live in insecure circumstances in squatter camps, favellas or bidonvilles. In all societies, however, the home is much more than a physical structure. The house is the site of lived relationships, especially those of kinship and sexuality, and is a key link in the relationship between material culture and sociality: a concrete marker of social position and status. In an interesting collection of essays entitled *About the House*, a number of social anthropologists have examined the interrelationships between people, their buildings and ideas through ethnographic case studies in different parts of Latin America and South-East Asia (Carsten and Hugh-Jones, 1995). The editors start their introduction with what is beginning to seem to be obligatory, a quotation from Bachelard: 'House images move in two directions: they are in us as much as we are in them' (Bachelard 1969).

The contributions in this volume provide a fascinating insight into the diversity of house types and social relationships in a range of different places. They are too varied to summarize here (but social geographers will find them well worth exploring despite their location in an unfamiliar theoretical debate). The starting point for all the papers is an evaluation of the utility of Lévi-Strauss's (1983, 1987) notion of a 'house society', although in his focus on the links with kinship, Lévi-Strauss virtually ignores the house as a material artefact, as a building. What I want briefly to comment on here, however, is the editors' introductory remarks about the relationship between the house and the body, which parallel those of Elizabeth Grosz's paper which I discussed in chapter 2. Carsten and Hugh-Jones also emphasis the links between material culture and the body, and show how a focus on the house might bring together areas of anthropological inquiry that are often seen as separate. For geographers, concerned as we are (as I outlined in chapter 1) to draw links across the spatial scales, their remarks are thought-provoking. They argue:

The house and the body are intimately linked. The house is an extension of the person; like an extra skin, carapace or second layer of clothes, it serves as much to reveal and display as it does to hide and protect. House, body and mind are in continuous interaction, the physical structure, furnishing, social conventions and mental images of the house at once enabling, moulding, informing and constraining the activities and ideas which unfold within its bounds. A ready-made environment fashioned by a previous generation and lived in long before it becomes an object of thought, the house is a prime agent of socialisation. . . . Moving in ordered space, the body 'reads' the house which serves as a mnemonic for the embodied person. Through habit and inhabiting, each person builds up a practical mastery of the fundamental schemes of their culture. (Carsten and Hugh-Jones 1995: 2)

Just like cities (see Sennett 1994), houses are often thought of as bodies, sharing common features and fates which affect the sense of self. 'If people construct houses and make them in their own image, so also do they use these houses and house-images to construct themselves as individuals and as groups' (Carsten and Hugh-Jones 1995: 3). Carsten and Hugh-Jones suggest, however, as I have for domestic labour, that houses, especially in non-Western societies, have been neglected as a site of study by anthropologists because they are ubiquitous, 'so commonplace, so familiar, so much a part of the way things are, that we hardly ever seem to notice them' (1995: 3–4). Add to this feminists' tart reminder that as the home is associated with 'woman' it is doubly taken for granted, and the neglect is partially explicable. Further, the study of the links between house forms and structures, and the different social relationships contained within, has been split across disciplines, studied in architecture and sociology, for example. The production of housing is seen as an aspect of economic analysis, and variations in patterns of childrearing as a sociological question.

Feminist scholars, however, have challenged these taken-for-granted divisions that fragment the house or the home as an area of analysis. Recent feminist work is producing exciting and more holistic analyses to which geographers are beginning to contribute. The meaning of the home, the nature of a house and the consequences of homelessness across space and time in different societies and regions are now growing areas of cross-disciplinary investigation. And although the house and the home is one of the most strongly gendered spatial locations, it is important not to take the associations for granted, nor to see them as permanent and unchanging. What Henrietta Moore (1986) terms 'spatial texts' may be rewritten over time as men and women challenge and contest conventional associations between, for example, inside and outside, the public and the private.

Indeed the anthropological studies in Carsten and Hugh-Jones's collection show that these spatial divisions may not be associated with gender at all in some places, but rather mark class or status divisions, descent or affinity, marriage or siblingship. Comparative research is one of the most efficient ways of challenging relationships that may seem 'natural' or taken for granted from the perspective of a particular society and there is scope for a great deal more cross-cultural work.

Migrants, of course, cross cultures themselves. Leaving home and recreating it elsewhere is an increasingly common experience for huge numbers of people. I shall return to questions of the meaning of home for people who have left one nation to move to another, and the associated issues of national identity and territorial attachment, in chapter 8. I want to end this chapter by quoting from bell hooks again, as she reflects on what moving away from home to fight poverty and oppression has meant for her:

> I had to leave that space I called home to move beyond boundaries, yet I also needed to return there. . . . Indeed, the very meaning of home changes with decolonization, with radicalization. At times, home is nowhere. At times, one knows only extreme estrangement and alienation. Then home is no longer just one place. It is many locations. Home is that place which enables and promotes varied and ever-changing perspectives, a place where one discovers new ways of seeing reality, frontiers of difference. (hooks 1991b)

Further reading

Perhaps the classic article by geographers in which the origin of the spatial division between the public and private spheres was addressed is by Suzanne Mackenzie and Damaris Rose (1983) in Anderson et al. (eds), *Redundant Spaces*. Leonore Davidoff and Catherine Hall's *Family Fortunes* (1987) is a splendid study of domesticity among the mid eighteenth- to mid nineteenth-century middle classes which provides a careful historical analysis of the idea of the home as haven in England. *Maternity: Letters from Working Class Wives* (Davies 1978) provides a moving insight into the lives of working-class women in Britain before the First World War and the consequences of becoming a mother.

More recent work on gender and the home includes a series of papers by Ruth Madigan and Moira Munro ('Gender, house and "home" ' (1991): is a good one to start with, and they also have a chapter in the useful collection by T. Putnam and C. Newton, *Household Choices* (1992)). Recent summaries of the significance of the public/private distinction may be found in Nancy Duncan's chapter (1996a) in her edited collection *BodySpace* and in a paper by Liz Bondi (1998). Mona Domosh's (1998) paper in *Progress in Human Geography* provides a summary of recent work on the home. April Venness includes a useful discussion about the meaning of the home in her paper 'Home and homeless in the United States' (1992), and Susan Ruddick's *Young and Homeless in Hollywood* (1995) is a fascinating look at the lives of young people in Los Angeles. Bahloul's ethnographic study *The Architecture of Memory* (1992) is a moving case study of social relations among Jewish and Muslim households occupying a communal building in Algeria between 1937 and 1962.

The recent collection edited by Roger Silverstone, *Visions of Suburbia* (1997) discusses the production and consumption of middle-class suburban environments in a range of locations, and Silverstone's earlier collection *Consuming Technologies* (1992) also includes papers about home making. Kim England's edited collection *Who Will Mind the Baby?* (1997) is another excellent book in the Routledge series International Studies of Women and Place edited by Jan Monk and Janet Momsen. As well as the work on waged domestic labour cited earlier, Pamela Moss (1997) has studied franchise housekeepers whose workplace practices straddle the boundaries between 'public' and 'private' spaces as they move between customers' homes in company-owned cars. Here the journey and the housework are both remunerated labour. While the home is the site of waged domestic labour, other forms of work are commonly undertaken there as well. Ann Oberhauser (1995, 1997) has examined the home-based production of craft and other goods by women in rural Appalachia. The home is also a locus of political struggles. Women have played an important role, for example, in a range of struggles over the provision, condition, cost and access to housing, especially public sector housing. Jackie Leavitt and Susan Saegert (1990) have documented struggles by African-American women in Harlem, New York, and Myrna Margulies Breitbart and Ellen-J. Pader (1995) have described issues of gender and race in Boston's public housing projects. Finally, I included a number of papers about the meaning of home in my edited collection *Undoing Place?* (McDowell 1997b), as well as in *Space, Gender, Knowledge* (McDowell and Sharp 1997).

4

Community, City and Locality

Introduction

In the preceding chapter I argued that the development of a spatial division between the private arena of the home and the public arena of the worlds of waged work, politics and power in industrial societies was crucial in the social construction of accepted attributes of femininity and masculinity. Not only is this division made visible in the symbolic meaning and material structure of the home, but it is also writ large in the spatial layout of urban areas: in the separation of residential from industrial areas (what British town planners term 'non-conforming uses'), in the notions of community planning and healthy living, and in ideas about social balance and 'the family' reflected in new towns, village developments and housing estates where three bedroomed houses are the major form of provision.

Assumptions about the places of the sexes also thread through the design of public buildings, where spaces for men's use and for women's use are often distinguishable by evident signs of status (think of the average head of department's office and that of his – it usually is a man – secretary), or are segregated, in sports arenas and facilities, for example. Certain buildings – monasteries and convents are the most obvious example, but also some schools and clubs – are strictly for one sex only. Other buildings, because of their grandeur and their long association with masculine forms of power, may be intimidating to enter, not only for many women but also for men in less powerful class positions – here the Houses of Parliament or the grander Oxbridge colleges are good examples. Yet other buildings, because of their association with one sex, are off-putting to the other: pool halls or certain pubs (ponder that combination – the public house – which seems such a contradiction in terms) for women, and for most men perhaps the child health clinic and the maternity ward.

The social and cultural construction of gender relations and their expression in the built environment have become a key area of feminist research (Bondi 1991; Booth et al. 1996; Boys 1984, 1990; Greed 1994; Hayden 1981, 1984; Little 1994; Little et al. 1988; Matrix 1984; McDowell 1983; Roberts 1991; Spain 1993; Watson with Austerberry 1986) in the last two decades or so. It is also important to look at the lives and intentional actions of individuals as they negotiate and change these structures. In this chapter, therefore, I shall examine some of this work, focusing on the level of the community, rather than on particular buildings. By community I mean places at an intermediate scale: a locality or residential area within a city, for example, or rural and single-industry villages. I want to explore the question of whether different versions of masculinity and femininity are associated with, reflect and affect socio-spatial relations in these different places.

In this chapter, too, questions about the ways in which class and ethnic divisions are part of the social construction of particular versions of gendered identities in different places will be raised. There is a long geographic tradition, deriving from the work of the Chicago School of urban sociologists in the first decades of the twentieth century, of analyses of the spatial segregation of different populations in cities. More recently gender and sexuality have become a focus, as well as the more traditional foci of race and class. It is perhaps not surprising that the social construction of gender and gender divisions were long ignored by geographers, because not only was gender considered 'natural' but men and women are spread throughout the urban area rather than confined to particular localities – unlike groups distinguished by social class or by ethnicity. For many years, therefore, it seemed as if there was no question to investigate; now, however, the relationships between the built form, urban symbolism and sexed and gendered subjectivities have become important issues for geographical treatment.

As always, distinguishing a place by its scale – community is an intermediate sort of level, as I said above – does not quite capture the way in which contemporary geographers define places. As I suggested in chapter 1, places are no longer defined as bounded or categorical but instead as the combination and coincidence of a set of socio-spatial relations. Thus, as Massey (1991) reminds us, a locality may be global. Just as Massey showed that in her own locality or community – Kilburn in West London – the particular sense of place that local inhabitants feel attached to is the result of a combination of its specific history and the impact of all sorts of contemporary changes, so too might other localities be defined by how they affect and reflect histories and geographies that construct particular ways of being a man or a woman in that area.

I want, in this chapter, to try and capture the difference it makes for

97

women and men, at different stages in the life cycle, to grow up and live their everyday lives in different localities – in the inner city, perhaps, or in declining agricultural or industrial rural villages. Here I am interested in everyday social relations in a general sense, rather than the specific experiences of the workplace or of leisure activities. I shall address the gendering of these activities later. So while I am aware that any spatial distinction cannot be watertight, as it were, this chapter is about localities, a version of what sociologists used to call community studies. My examples are drawn from Western industrial societies.

The difference that place makes

Almost thirty years ago now, David Harvey published *Social Justice and the City* (1971) in which he argued that the spatial distribution and location of urban goods and resources – work, housing, schools, polluting uses, and health-giving resources like parks – and their consequent differential access for the population that lived in that city or area were mechanisms for the redistribution of real income in a negative direction. While well-off residents can afford to live in the areas which bring them open space, clean air and access to good schools, as well as able to pay to overcome the costs of travelling to other parts of the city, poor and deprived people are forced through lack of choice to live in areas often marked by noise and pollution, and where the schools and the housing stock may be old and of poor quality. In this way the inequalities between the standards of living of the better-off and the worse-off are exacerbated by the structure of the city itself. This is what Harvey meant by the redistribution of real income.

Despite being open to the criticism that he concentrated on distributional questions to the exclusion of questions of power, control and the production of the built form (a criticism made by Harvey of his own work in the second part of the book), his work in my view remains a powerful way of examining the consequences of location in the city. This is so especially if a consideration of issues of the safety and freedom to express alternative identities is added to Harvey's discussion of access to desired material goods and resources. These are the issues that are at the centre of this chapter.

Gender relations in working-class communities

One of the main foci of work on residential segregation has been social class divisions and there are many fine studies of single-class communities, both in the inner areas of cities and in industrial or agricultural rural villages.

Despite not having an intentional or explicit interest in questions about gender, many of these studies describe the development of a particular version of masculinity, constructed through the shared male camaraderie that is created while engaging in heavy physical work which is often dangerous. Men who do this sort of work come to rely on each other in the workplace, and also often develop close personal links outside the workplace as well. It is in these sorts of communities, where the inhabitants often know each other personally in almost all spheres of their life, that what the cultural critic Raymond Williams has termed a 'structure of feeling' grows up.

A strong sense of belonging to the place, which is passed on from generation to generation, and pride in the tradition of hardship and hard work go hand in hand with a particular form of labour politics. While it may be a source of communal strength and pride, the feminist writer Beatrix Campbell (1984) has suggested that this politics may be off-putting for women. The working man's club, the pub and the Labour Party committee rooms are sites of a masculinist solidarity, which is only occasionally breached by women – the miners' strike in 1984 is a classic example when women's support was crucial and visible. In many of the early community studies, such as *Coal is Our Life* (Dennis et al. 1956), women's daily lives are virtually invisible, although in the work done at much the same time at the Institute of Community Studies in Bethnal Green (Young and Willmott 1957; Willmott and Young 1960), close ties between mothers and daughters were identified as characteristic of the inner city and an important part of the sense of communal belonging. Young and Willmott showed how these female cross-generational links were often broken when inner areas were redeveloped and the inhabitants rehoused elsewhere.

In this early tradition of community studies, however, gender divisions of labour were neither problematized nor explained. Instead the association of men with waged labour and women with the home was taken for granted. In a schematic paper written in the early 1980s, Doreen Massey and I tried to counter this neglect in our examination of the changing nature of gender divisions during successive rounds of spatial restructuring in different parts of England over about a century (McDowell and Massey 1984). We showed how in traditional working–class communities, as industrial work for men declined, branch plants were attracted by the 'green' female labour in these areas, changing the balance of men's and women's labour force participation rates. There is also a growing number of excellent feminist case studies of women's lives in working-class communities in other parts of the world. Meg Luxton (1980), for example, has compared three generations of women's lives in Flin Flon, an aluminium smelting town in northern Canada, and Kathie Gibson (1991) has studied gendered relations in an Australian mining community.

Defining community

Before I draw on some of these studies to illustrate the links between spatial divisions and gender identities, however, a brief word about the term 'community', which I have used above in a 'taken for granted' sense, is appropriate. Like the term place or locality, community is one of those rather unsatisfactory words that have been used in a wide range of ways and have many definitions. It is usually, although not always, used to designate a small-scale and spatially bounded area within which it is assumed that the population, or part of it, has certain characteristics in common that ties it together. Thus 'working-class communities' or 'the Asian community' are common phrases which are often linked to 'inner areas'.

The origins of the term community lie in the evolutionary sociology of Tönnies, who at the end of the nineteenth century distinguished a community united by common association, *gemeinschaft*, social life in its entirety, from those, particularly affected by industrialization, where associations are based on restricted areas of life, which Tönnies termed *gesellschaft* (Tönnies 1967). The implicit anti-urban bias in Tönnies's work has been the focus of a great deal of criticism and has stimulated empirical case studies that attempt to demonstrate the close ties that bind residents in industrial villages and urban communities. Indeed, the studies I have just mentioned fall into this category.

Community is also a term that carries with it connotations of warmth and solidarity, with the implicit assumption that a lack of community is a bad thing. More recently, however, it has been accepted that the term also has negative connotations, especially when it is applied as a euphemism for ethnic minority groups and more widely for conservative or backward-looking attitudes. Despite these problems it continues to be a commonly used term. I use it here in a specific sense: like the terms place and locality, to refer to a fluid network of social relations that may be but are not necessarily tied to territory. Thus a community is a relational rather than a categorical concept, defined both by material social relations and by symbolic meanings. Communities are context dependent, contingent, and defined by power relations; their boundaries are created by mechanisms of inclusion and exclusion. Although these mechanisms may change and so boundaries alter over time, communities are necessarily bounded entities. Whatever the criteria or characteristics of exclusion, certain groups or individuals are inevitably left outside. While the social commentator Michael Ignatieff (1992) has argued that the term is a 'pious fraud', and that 'ethnic minorities are called "com-

100

munities" either because it makes them feel better, or because it makes the white majority feel more secure', I want to suggest that it remains a useful term as long as its construction through unequal relations of power is remembered. The term 'community' should neither be rejected out of hand, nor automatically seen as either a good or a bad thing, but the complexity of its construction and its purpose should be the subject for analysis.

Bearing in mind these comments about relationships of power, I want to turn to a set of empirical examinations of the links between gender, identity and place. As I argued in chapter 1, gendered identities are fundamentally connected to and intertwined with race, ethnicity, class and sexuality, and in my selection of case studies I have attempted to illustrate some of these links. Thus the first case study draws on the work of Patricia Fernandez Kelly, an urban anthropologist who has done field work both in Latin America and the US. The case study I want to look at in more detail here is about the relationships between gender, adolescence and community in Baltimore in the United States. I shall then outline the growing interest in the role of gay men and single women in gentrification, and finally turn to a less familiar literature about suburban identity, gender and ethnicity. The suburbs are an under-studied location – by urban geographers and anthropologists seem to be seduced by the supposed dangers of inner city areas.

Growing up in an urban ghetto

In the early 1990s, Kelly undertook fieldwork in three inner area neighbourhoods in West Baltimore in the US. Her aim was to examine the ways in which people who live in impoverished neighbourhoods, especially African Americans, talk about their values and how their actions may or may not reflect this talk. Kelly recognizes that 'people derive their knowledge from the locations where they live' (1994: 89), and so urban space is a crucial aspect of identity construction, knowledge acquisition and social action. The areas of Kelly's interviews had been badly affected by economic restructuring and especially by the closure of a large steel plant and the consequent loss of employment opportunities for men. Widespread drug abuse and teenage pregnancies, as well as endemic poverty, were key social issues in the areas.

Kelly was particularly interested in the attitudes of teenage girls, the options they saw facing them and their decisions, especially to do with motherhood. As she emphasizes, white and black teenagers are faced with different options in US cities:

A 17-year-old white woman about to graduate from high school, living in a middle-class neighbourhood and contemplating college, even with ambivalence, is likely to defer motherhood in order not to jeopardize other opportunities. In this case, the young woman perceives giving birth to a child out of marriage not only as a breach of norms but also as an impediment to realistically perceived and desirable options.

A 17-year-old black woman about to graduate from high school in an urban ghetto faces a different set of choices. It is less likely, for example, that her social network will include a significant number of individuals who have pursued educations in 'good' colleges and gone on to secure 'good' jobs. As a result, many adults and adolescents in her circle may see graduating from high school as the culmination of a stage that should bring about mature responsibilities. Moreover, the young woman may share with men in her peer group the impression, fostered by mainstream values, that parenting qualifies individuals for membership in the adult community. In this case motherhood has a distinct meaning: it is not a deviation from, but a path to, approximate dominant norms. (1994: 100)

Thus location and class, as well as 'race', construct differences between women, and their significance varies over space and time. In a study of both black and white young single mothers in London, Ann Phoenix (1988, 1991) challenged the assumption that black British women have distinct 'cultural' attitudes to pregnancy and childrearing that differentiate them from white women. For both groups of women, motherhood provided a path to responsibility and maturity denied to these unqualified young women in the labour market. Living within a working-class community in Britain, or a ghetto in the US, means that access to a range of opportunities and social contacts in other parts of the city is restricted by poverty and discrimination. Behaviours and attitudes that are learned in the locality, and reflected in style and language, what Bourdieu termed 'embodied knowledge' (Bourdieu 1989; and see chapter 2), distinguish these young women from their more affluent peers. As Kelly concludes, 'none of the markers that account for success in better neighbourhoods exist in the Baltimore ghetto' (1994: 108). (In the next but one section, I shall discuss some remarkable research about ethnic identity in white suburbs, where the impact of location seems to counter ethnicity in the social construction of identity.)

In the ghetto, as Kelly argues, the passage into adulthood is particularly marked by gender differentiation. This is not only because motherhood is a key transition for young women but also because of the gender-specific policies and actions of state agencies.

The presence of the state in impoverished neighbourhoods, a key component in the experience of children, is not neutral; it too bifurcates along

102

gender lines. Public assistance touches the majority of single women and their children. The corrections and criminal justice system deals primarily with boys and men. That split has repercussions for the lives of children growing up in the Baltimore ghetto. (Kelly 1994: 106)

Many young black people in Baltimore live in areas where the state and its agencies construct them as problems to be resolved or contained. Thus their sense of identity is mutually constituted in the combination of spatial location, their class and their gender in an environment where these adolescents lack 'bridges to other social networks that control access to a larger set of opportunities and meanings' (1994: 109). In circumstances such as these, motherhood, and even participation in criminal activities, may be seen as attempts to conform to mainstream values and achieve maturity rather than as defiance or 'problem behaviour'.

Gender, sexuality and gentrification in inner city areas

I want to look now at another thread of recent geographical scholarship about inner city areas. Although there has been a long tradition of analysing the 'problems' of the inner city, residential turnover and social change in these areas has also been a key focus for many decades. At the beginning of the twentieth century that remarkable group of men who founded a school of urban sociology in Chicago realized that the population characteristics of inner urban areas changed over time. Chicago in those years was a city that grew extremely fast as huge numbers of in-migrants were drawn to work in the stock yards and meat processing plants (Upton Sinclair's remarkable novel *The Jungle*, first published in 1936, is a fascinating portrait of these years and enough to make any reader a vegetarian), and later into the automobile industry. First from East and West Europe and then from the southern states, men, women and children moved into the cheapest housing available, then located in the inner city. Although the Social Darwinism that informed the explanations of the early Chicago urban sociologists has long been discredited, residential turnover in the inner city has remained one of the most important areas of research for urban geographers.

In the postwar period, as British and US cities expanded and middle-class employees living in the suburbs but working in the city centre faced increasingly long journeys to work, a new demand for inner area housing became significant. Anticipated and encouraged by city planners who saw the potential of a changing residential base for improving inner areas and attracting new commercial and cultural facilities (Zukin 1988, 1995), and

103

by real estate developers and builders who smelled profits, gentrification (basically the replacement of working-class by middle-class residents) became a noticeable phenomenon in many cities from about the early 1970s (Mills 1988; Hamnett 1991; Smith 1996; Smith and Williams 1986). From the earliest studies, it was shown that inner areas tended to be more attractive to less conformist households, or at least to that fraction of the middle class working in the arts and the media.

Thus Peter Williams (1976) found that in Islington, an area of inner London, employees in TV and journalism or in the arts more generally were the first-stage gentrifiers. Other researchers noted a dominance of single unrelated individuals living as a household – students or young workers, for example, single women or single mothers and gay men (Allen and McDowell 1989; Castells 1983; Knopp 1987, 1990). Damaris Rose and Paul Villeneuve (1988), working in Montreal, suggested that inner areas were particularly attractive to single mothers who found a range of support services there that made their lives possible. Bondi (1991), Lyons (1996) and McDowell (1997c) have also investigated the significance of single women in gentrification, but found only limited evidence so far in British cities, although Warde (1991) argued that dual-career, childless couples are an important part of the demand for gentrified inner area properties.

The key group of single gentrifiers, however, in cities such as New York (Chauncey 1995; Duberman et al. 1991), San Francisco (Castells 1983; Fitzgerald 1986), Los Angeles (Forest 1995) and Minneapolis (Knopp 1987, 1990; Lauria and Knopp 1985) in the US, and in London (Mort 1996) and Manchester in Britain (Hindle 1994) have been gay men rather than either straight women or lesbians. To some extent this is a reflection of the greater spending power of gay men compared with women, both because of their stronger labour market position and the greater likelihood of women being responsible for dependants, usually children or elderly relatives. Manuel Castells has argued however, that the formation of 'gay ghettos' is not a specific reflection of gayness but of a more general masculinity. He suggested that gay men in San Francisco chose to live in certain areas not only to make their gay identity visible to themselves and others, but rather that they were acting like all men in an assertion of their dominance through the desire to master space. Lesbians, Castells believed, have no desire to conquer space, being content with interior, and so invisible, networks and friendships. His argument has been roundly criticized, in my view correctly, by Adler and Brenner (1992). Such essentialism is now a discredited view of gender differences, as well as male blindness to the activities of lesbian gentrifiers in San Francisco (Casebourne 1997).

The assertion of identity through an association with territory is, however, an important part of gentrification by whatever group, be they gay or

Plate 4.1   Gay Pride flags in the Castro District, San Francisco

straight, middle-class professionals or more 'artistic' groups. As I suggested above, early gentrifiers distinguished themselves from suburban conformists though their residential choices, and for gay men gentrification has been a way of creating a whole range of neighbourhood services that facilitate their lifestyle. Thus in the Castro district of San Francisco, which was a key site of gay gentrification from the end of the 1960s onwards, cafés, bars, bookstores as well as estate agents, lawyers and other business services owned by gays grew up in close proximity to serve the local community (see plates 4.1 and 4.2). A fascinating fictional view of the Castro area in the 1980s may be found in the novels of Armistead Maupin 1980, 1984, 1986), whereas an alternative factual description to that of Castells, which emphasizes the impact of HIV and AIDS, is Frances Fitzgerald's *Cities on a Hill* (1986). The documentary film *The Life and Times of Harvey Milk* is a portrait of more complex aspects of gay residential concentration and associated political power. In the 1970s the Castro area elected an out gay congress man, Harvey Milk, who was the victim of extreme homophobia in local politics and of a successful assassination attempt.

While there are not such significant concentrations of gay men in British

Plate 4.2   The Women's Restaurant, on the edges of the Castro District,
San Francisco

cities, there are areas of London, Manchester and other large urban areas
that are associated with gay and lesbian life and politics. Frank Mort (1995,
1996) has written about the development of what he terms 'homosocial'
activities and spaces in London: I want to introduce his work on Soho in
central London, where he has excavated an archaeology of changing
masculinities and their reflection in the changing landscape and social
relations of the area since the 1960s. I shall postpone this, however, until
chapter 6 as it more easily fits into my designation of spaces of pleasure
than community *per se*.

Suburbia, ethnicity and identity: locating whiteness

As David Harvey and others have long argued, location in the city has a
major impact on the opportunities and life chances of the residents of
different areas, redistributing 'real income' and exacerbating inequalities
between social classes. Suburban location brings with it, in general, access
to clean air and more open space than in the city centre as well as a range
of educational opportunities in local schools, which tend to have a more

middle-class catchment area and are less ethnically mixed than schools in the inner city. The differences between schools in different parts of a city have recently become even more visible in Great Britain through the publication of rank order indicators of achievement as measured by examination results and test scores.

What has been less well explored by geographers, however, is the significance of urban location in the social construction of individual identity rather than material circumstances. This significance is illustrated in a moving article by Minnie Bruce Pratt, who has explored the links between her rejection of her white suburban lifestyle as a married woman, her coming out as a lesbian and her move to an inner area in Washington, D.C. 'I live in a part of Washington, D.C., that white suburbanites called "the jungle". When I walk the two and a half blocks to H St NE, to stop in at the bank, to leave my boots off at the shoe-repair-and-lock shop, I am most usually the only white person in sight' (M. B. Pratt 1992: 323).

Pratt explains that although she chose to live in this area and she is beginning to feel at home and accepted, as a white woman she is still an outsider. The janitor of her building is Mr Boone, 'a dark red-brown man from the Yemassee in South Carolina', and when he speaks to her 'he "yes ma'ams" me in a sing-song: I hear my voice replying in the horrid cheerful accents of a white lady: and I hate my white womanhood that drags between us the long bitter history of our region.' Unlike the neighbourhood where she grew up, where she took her position as an affluent white girl for granted,

> in this area when I walk out in the neighbourhood, each speaking-to another person has become fraught, for me, with the history of race and sex and class . . . It is an exhausting process, this moving from the experience of the 'unknowing majority' (as Maya Angelou called it) into consciousness. It would be a lie to say this process is comforting. (1992: 324)

Reflecting on her childhood, Pratt recognizes that

> I was shaped by my relation to those buildings and by the people in the buildings, by ideas of who should be working in the board of education, of who should be in the bank handling money, of who should have the guns and the keys to the jail, of who should be *in* the jail; and I was shaped by what I didn't see, or didn't notice on those streets.
>
> Not the way your town was laid out, you say? True, perhaps, but each one of us carries around those growing-up places, the institutions, a sort of back-drop, a stage-set. So often we act out the present against a back-drop of the past, within a frame of perception that is so familiar, so safe that it is terrifying to risk changing it even when we know our perceptions are distorted, limited, constricted by that old view.

So this is one gain for me as I change: I learn a way of looking at the
world that is more accurate, complex, multi-layered, multi-dimensional, more
truthful . . . I feel the need to look differently because I've learned that what
is presented to me as an accurate view of the world is frequently a lie. (1992:
325)

What Pratt describes so vividly and personally in this paper, with its
evocative title 'Identity: blood skin heart', is what Haraway (1991) refers to
as situated knowledge, when she argues that a view from a particular
position may be more truthful than what she termed 'the view from nowhere'. Pratt's taken-for-granted view of her home town in childhood, in
which she failed to recognize the class and race privileges of her position,
not only ignores the different view of the same town that may be held by
women of colour or gay men but also insists that its particular perspective
is the general truth. And, as Pratt argues, it is often painful to confront the
limits of our thinking, to recognize that what we think of as a universal
truth is a partial or particular position: 'The pain, when, for instance, I
realize how *habitually* I think of my culture, my ethics, my morality, as the
culmination of history, as the logical extension of what has gone before
. . . the kind of thinking that separates me from women in cultures different from mine' (1992: 327).

Growing up white

In an article that provides an astonishing complement to Pratt's, France
Winddance Twine (1996) discusses the impact that the failure to recognize
difference, to assume that a white suburban view of the world is *the* view,
had on her and other US-born women of African descent who were brought
up in white families as 'brown-skinned white girls' in suburban USA. She
shows how some girls of African descent, in the absence of a politicized
African-American residential community, acquire a white cultural identity
and not a black consciousness, before they leave home.

While Twine recognizes that in the last ten years or so there has been a
growing number of studies of whiteness (see, for example, Blee 1991;
Frankenberg 1993; hooks 1991c; Morrison 1992; Roediger 1991; Ware
1992) written both by women of colour and white women, she suggests
that this literature 'has not addressed the experiences of whites of African
descent'. The very assertion is so astonishing it tends to stop readers in
their tracks. But the texts about the social construction of whiteness have
assumed that white Americans are exclusively of European descent. Twine's
study expands the analysis of racialized gender identities in middle-class
suburban communities by examining how white identities are constructed

and enacted by women of African descent located in middle-class suburban communities. The central questions she asks are 'How do brown-skinned women of mixed African descent become socially constructed as white girls in the local context of middle-class suburban community?' and 'What social conditions are necessary for the acquisition of a white identity by African-descent girls?'.

In her work Twine brings together a social constructionist approach with the recognition of the importance of socioeconomic factors. Using qualitative methods she explored the experiences of sixteen women who became socially constructed as white prior to their puberty in their middle-class suburban communities, only to be forced to reconstruct themselves as black or biracial when they moved to become students at the University of California Berkeley where 'race awareness' is an important issue.

The women interviewed by Twine were all brought up in a 'family and social network which embraced a racially unmarked, middle-class identity' in which they had been

> the culturally unmarked peers of middle-class children. As children they had not been conscious of being culturally distinct from their peers. Not being distinguished from European-American peers in everyday interactions is critical to the maintenance of a white cultural identity. I am not referring to physical distinctions in colour, hair texture, or body type. Rather, these individuals experienced themselves as culturally neutral, and as not deviating from their peer group. (Twine 1996: 208)

In the acquisition of a white cultural identity, suburban residence played an important part. In 1980 US suburbia was an exclusive domain – blacks were only 6.1 per cent of all suburban residents compared with 23.4 per cent of city dwellers. At the time Twine's research subjects were growing up, the suburbs were also conservative, both socially and politically, a 'traditional' gender division of labour was common and conspicuous consumption was a prime activity which shaped identity and a sense of belonging. In addition the girls were often the sole or one of a tiny handful of non-European Americans at the school they attended, as well as living in adoptive families who were colour-blind or racially neutral, or with the white parent from a 'mixed' relationship. Thus spatial location, and especially residence in an exclusive area and attendance at a racially exclusive school, was crucial in the development of what at first seems a paradoxical assertion of racial neutrality.

Jessica, a twenty-one-year old woman in Twine's sample, who had lived with her single Anglo-American mother in the suburbs, explained that her mother never 'racialized' her and that she was not conscious of having a racial identity as a child: 'Well my mother is very idealistic. She was just. She would never use the word race. She would never say I was black or white. She would just say 'you're special' . . . She gave me a real sense of self but not a sense of racial self' (Twine 1996: 211).

For many of the women Twine interviewed it was not until they went to college and entered an environment where there were significant numbers of politicized people of colour that their own racial identity became an issue. Even though for some of the women patterns of anti-black sentiment and exclusion had become an issue when they reached puberty and started dating, it was not until they entered university that the women were forced to make hard decisions and relinquish their white identity. 'Before I came to Cal (University of California) I was white. I was all white culturally . . . I am perceived as black. I am treated as black so I don't have a problem with being black . . . But it's a difficult situation. It's really hard' (Tamala, African and European descent, adopted at birth and 'raised white').

At Berkeley the identity of these women was challenged and they were not allowed to be neutral. All but one of them experienced a shift in their identity during their first two years on the campus. Willingly or not, they were forced by the highly politicized atmosphere to 'recognize and claim a black racial identity as part of their campus socialization experience' (Twine 1996: 218).

This article remained in my mind for several months after I read it and I pondered whether in a less political environment the choices that faced these young women might be different. They were all between twenty-one and twenty-five when Twine interviewed them and I wondered what might have happened to them if they had moved straight into the workplace, if they had grown up in white working-class families in a different part of town. While it is impossible to know, my eye was drawn to an article in the *Guardian* in mid-1997. There an adopted woman speculated on her own experiences of being brought up 'colour blind' in Great Britain:

There were nine of us altogether. Four of us were adopted and mum and dad had five of their own: we were the original 'rainbow family'. By origin half the family spanned the globe. My eldest sister came from Lithuania, another from Newfoundland and my brother and I were Nigerian Irish mix and Nigerian Swiss respectively . . . At home we were all surrounded by indiscriminate, unyielding love. I didn't feel any different from my white brothers and sisters. Yet now I feel that the way I was loved – idyllic, colour-blind – however benign the intention, wasn't exactly representative of society's view of me. Society would define me by my colour, be it positively or negatively. I was 21 before I had my first dose of overt racism. It sounds like a bad B movie – "The Girl Who Woke Up After 21 Years and Realised She Was Black" – but that was the reality. I went to visit my brother Dominic who is also mixed race. He had always been a lot more 'rootsy' about his colour. He said to me a few years ago, while looking at a picture of our blonde, blue-eyed nieces and nephews: 'Sis, we've got to get some black into this family.' I thought he was being ridiculous at the time, but suddenly I knew what he meant. There were no visual points of reference for us. I had no visual connection with them.

The writer, Clare Gorham, then explained how she had struggled with feelings of resentment against her white adoptive parents before coming to an acceptance of her heritage and upbringing.

After a couple of years of beating breasts and lamenting my lost heritage, I began to realise that I was on an inane quest. I had my own heritage so why did I expect to find another? After a period I reached some semblance of long-awaited calm, and this was due mainly to the consistently deep love of my family and friends. We all have a tendency to put people into different societal boxes – race, financial status, class, religion and so on. Now I can really appreciate the fact that trans-racially adopted adults tend to defy those categories. I think that itself is a bonus. (Gorham 1997: 9)

Clare Gorham's resolution seems different from the young American women described first, who had come to, or been forced to, identify as 'black'. Although Gorham did not identify the town or city where she grew up, the examples are an interesting combination of the ways in which class, race, age, family circumstances and location intersect in the construction of subjectivity and identity, as well as a persuasive example of the fluidity of identity. For all these young women, leaving home was a significant factor in their reassessment of their identity, as of course it is for many young people. These two studies also clearly reveal the argument that 'race' or ethnicity is a social construct and a relational term without fixed referents. The idea that there are biological differences between people has been seriously challenged for a century or more and almost all social scientists now agree that a wide plethora of non-biological criteria are used to distinguish one group from another. Like gender differences, however, 'race' and ethnic differences have been naturalized and the historical social processes that construct people as 'different from' have been ignored in racist discourses.

While one consequence of the naturalization of difference has been the construction of 'whiteness' as the norm, as non 'ethnic' – which, as I argued above is now being challenged in careful empirical work – a second consequence is the facile assumption that all minority groups share identical cultural characteristics. Here, too, however, recent feminist work is exploring the fissures in 'ethnic communities' between men and women, first and second generations, the young and the old, documenting the huge diversity within communities of colour. While skin colour and ethnicity remain significant axes of discrimination and inequality, empirical work by feminists has challenged oversimple associations between the binary categories black–white/poor–affluent/empowered and powerless (DuCille 1996; Eisenstein 1994; Lamphere et al. 1997; Williams 1991). Recent work emphasizes the diversity within communities of colour and the successes and positive actions of their members in challenging racism (Mirza 1997).

For many young men, as well as young women, economic adversity leads to problems in establishing a confident sense of themselves as mature adults through labour market participation. In the following section, I turn to the 'choices' that young men are making in the 1990s. I shall return to questions about migration, culture, place and identity and ways to rethink these categories, in chapters 7 and 8.

Community, insecurity and working-class men on suburban estates

In her book *Goliath* (1993) Bea Campbell used an interest in the causes and consequences of urban riots in several British cities in 1991 to address a larger set of questions about changes in the social construction of masculinity that she perceived at the beginning of the 1990s. She was particularly interested in what made young and generally unemployed men, living in the main in municipal housing on outer estates in cities as different as Newcastle and Oxford, turn on people and property in their own localities, engaging not only in anti-social activities such as car theft and joyriding but also burglary and even arson in their own neighbourhoods. Campbell locates part of the explanation in the shift in national politics in the Thatcher years. The 1980s – that sexy/greedy decade identified by geographers Leyshon and Thrift (1996), albeit from a wildly different case study of the financial services sector – was a time which witnessed, in Campbell's words, 'the demise of the disciplined disorders that had characterised post-war politics in Britain. The national tone of what had always been a quarrelsome country was now reckless, butch and dangerous' (1993: 3).

The irony of a country, then headed by its first woman prime minister, Margaret Thatcher, becoming more 'butch' in its national culture is worth noting. One consequence of this shift was to deepen the coincidence of brutal and masculinist forms of behaviour in a wide range of locales. The 'hard men' in the inner city, with their love of speed exhibited in car chases, the 'hard men' in boardrooms up and down the country, where brutal takeovers and asset-stripping occurred and the 'lads' in the City of

London, with its celebration of 'fast' money and financial scandal (McDowell 1997a), all had certain characteristics in common. But for young working-class men without work and so excluded from the good life and its corre-lates – a car, a woman and adult responsibilities – by their lack of money, the only way to gain the accepted attributes of masculinity seemed to be through stealing and other forms of irresponsible behaviour. Here there are parallels with Kelly's study of Baltimore, although she focused mainly on young women rather than men in her study.

In the passage below Campbell describes a group of young men who for eighteen months, until the police intervened in the summer of 1991, both entertained and annoyed the residents of an estate in Oxford, the Blackbird Leys estate, by an illicit motor show, hotting or hotrodding stolen cars in the late evening and into the night.

> The night boys defied the definition of a passive underclass: these young men weren't *under* anyone. Economically they were spare, surplus, person-ally they were dependent on someone else for their upkeep, usually their mothers; socially they were fugitives, whose lawlessness kept them inside and yet outside their own community. They had no jobs, no incomes, no property, no cars, no responsibilities. But that is not to say that they weren't busy, with their 'own business'. And what they did have was a reputation.
>
> In many ways, they were the 'invisibles', their reputation derived none-theless from being seen, from performing. Their vanity powered their val-our. They planned, primed and timed a local drama that took place nightly in a small square. (Campbell 1993: 29–30)

The young men of Blackbird Leys lived in an area of Oxford that had relied on the car industry for jobs. 'The Leys was a major supplier of labour, both black and white, for the car industry, the industry associated for much of the twentieth century with a popular experience of modernity, mass production and mobility . . . It was also an industry associated with masculinity – cars were made mainly by men and for men' (Campbell 1993: 31–2). As the numbers of men employed in the Cowley works in Oxford declined from 30,000 to 5,000 between 1970 and 1990, the Leys estate was badly affected. As Campbell argued,

> Within a single generation a major tradition of employment, political align-ment, income and identity for working-class men, indeed a tradition that formed cultures of masculinity, was all but extinguished.
>
> The lads may have stopped making cars but that did not stop them stealing them. The collapse of manufacturing work for men was succeeded in Oxford by the rise in car theft.
>
> Car crime on the [Leys] estate . . . was about a relationship between young men and power, machinery, speed and transcendence'. (1993: 32–3)

113

So through theft, consumption and performance, these young men reconstructed a type of masculine identity that their fathers had created in the workplace but which economic restructuring, global shifts in the location of car production and high unemployment in 1990s Britain had denied them themselves.

In an interesting article published more recently, Fine et al. (1997) reported their results of a similar investigation of white working-class masculinity in two US cities, Buffalo in New York State and Jersey City in New Jersey. Here too the decline of heavy manufacturing severely reduced job opportunities for men, especially for young white men with few educational credentials. The authors undertook two independent qualitative studies of the locations – school, the neighbourhood and for some, the workplace – where working-class boys and men invent themselves as a group and relate to and distance themselves from other marginalized groups. Fine et al. studied their attempts both to create a sense of self-respect, and adapt to earlier hegemonic notions of working-class masculinity which had been constructed, in the main, in the workplaces which no longer existed.

The researchers found that

> in the late 1980s and early 1990s, the poor and working-class white boys and men whom we interviewed have narrated 'personal identities' as if they were wholly independent of corroding economic and social relations. Drenched in a kind of post-industrial, late twentieth-century individualism, the discourse of 'identity work' appears to be draped in Teflon. The more profoundly that economic and social conditions invade their personal well-being, the more the damage and disruption is denied. Hegemony works in funny ways, especially for white working-class men who wish to think they have a continued edge on 'others' – people of colour and white women. (Fine et al. 1997: 52–3)

For these men, the only way to resolve their anger about the lack of economic opportunities was to search for scapegoats. They refused either to see themselves 'inside history', suffering from a particular combination of social and economic relations, or, concomitantly, to organize along lines of class or economic location with other 'minorities', women and people of colour, who were also adversely affected by the same structural circumstances. 'These boys and men hold on, desperate and vigilant, to identities of white race and male gender as though these could gain them credit in increasingly class-segregated worlds' (Fine et al. 1997: 53). They have failed to recognize that the relatively privileged status of working-class men in US history throughout most of the twentieth century has come to an end. 'In the span of a few decades, foreign investment, corporate flight, downsizing, and automation have suddenly left members of the working-

class without a steady family wage, which compounded with the dissipa-
tion of labor unions, has left many white working-class men feeling angry
and emasculated' (1997: 54).

Although working-class men are not necessarily more racist or sexist
than middle-class men, in these circumstances Fine et al. found that their
frustration and anger took on 'virulent forms' in a displaced reaction to
global economic change. They constructed a discourse of blame against
those they felt were responsible for stealing their privileges. The degree of
hostility to 'Others' – blacks, gays and women – varied, however; some
men were more hostile than others. In a thought-provoking geographical
analogy, Fine et al. argue that, 'like cartographers working with different
tools on the same geopolitical space, all these men sculpt their identities as
if they were discernibly framed by, and contrasted through, race, gender
and sexuality' (1977: 59).

This type of work seems to me to offer a more sophisticated and nuanced
way of approaching questions of economic decline and restructuring than
analyses that fail to address questions of symbolic meaning and the social
construction of self, instead working with disembodied counts of the unemployed. It shows the power of analyses undertaken through a 'gender
lens' and is a powerful illustration of why gender matters in economic and
social geography.

New social movements, community power and community politics

In challenging and defending access to spatially unevenly distributed goods
and resources in local political actions, women have often played a key
role. In his early work on cities the sociologist Manuel Castells suggested
that struggles over urban goods and resources – what he termed collective
consumption goods – were the distinguishing feature of a specifically urban sociology (Castells 1978). In these struggles, or urban social movements, women play a key role, although Castells himself was rather neglectful
of this. He also failed to notice that the boundaries of collective provision
by the local or national state and the services provided by individual women
for their family members or for strangers in voluntary community work
were both permeable and changing as the ideological complexion of the
state changes and more or less money is transferred into local services (we
shall return to a more thorough feminist assessment of Castells's work in
chapter 7). Under the Thatcher governments in the 1980s in Great Britain, for example, as 'community care' replaced institutional provision for
the elderly and for people with mental illnesses, the burden of care fell

115

more heavily on the shoulders of individual women. And yet Castells did notice that cities only worked because women provided the time and means by which spatially separated services were connected: taking their children from school to the dentist, for example, or travelling to and from work via the childminder and the supermarket.

There is now a large feminist literature by geographers and others exploring the significance of women as participants in urban social movements and community politics, as well as gender questions and issues as the basis of struggles and organization in Western and non-Western societies. I shall return to questions about welfare provision and gender at the level of the nation-state in chapter 7, where I also address feminist theoretical perspectives on the state. Here I want to look at a study of women's local action in Brighton, England, and then at the work of women's committees established in a number of local authorities in the UK in the 1970s and 1980s.

In her book *Visible Histories* (1989) Suzanne Mackenzie examined the gamut of ways in which women living in the coastal resort of Brighton between the end of the Second World War and the end of the 1970s organized to improve their living and working conditions. Through a series of new organizational networks for fertility control, childbirth and childcare, and in the workplace, these women challenged the local state, patched up services, bridged gaps and filled emerging needs as women's lives changed over the postwar decades. Mackenzie documents the multiple ways in which women changed and improved their local environments in this single city.

One of the key issues raised by community politics, however, especially at the intra-urban level, is the NIMBY ('not in my backyard') question. If local residents organize to exclude unwanted activities from their own 'backyard', then by default another community or locality will suffer; conversely with desired goods and resources. In circumstances where money and other resources are limited, then their allocation to one area means that by default another area will go without. In order to ensure equity, or at least that the interests of the least powerful communities are not overlooked, strategic authorities at the level of the local state are necessary to oversee locality based disputes. Many policies – on childcare, safety and policing, for example – have differential impacts on men and women. Recognizing this, in the 1980s, in a number of areas in the UK, the local state established women's committees or equal opportunities committees to assess the extent to which local services might be altered or improved to achieve greater gender equity. Susan Halford (1992), has evaluated the impact of these initiatives.

Halford argues that the introduction of gender initiatives depends on a variety of factors, including resources, political commitment and leadership and the degree and nature of political mobilization in the local area; but, as she also notes, there are general features of local government bureaucracies that make any change difficult, as well as specific gendered structures and relations that hinder positive change in women's interests (1992: 160). In case studies of ten local authorities, Halford documented the ways in which empire building proved a dispiriting barrier to change. She found evidence of interdepartmental competition and organizational inertia in hierarchical structures. Further, local government departments often cross-cut gender issues, and so block gender initiatives. In addition the informal structures of power in organizations often operate to marginalize both individual women and women's issues in local workplace cultures which are not gender-neutral (and I shall return to a fuller exploration of workplace cultures in the next chapter) (Cockburn 1991; Kanter 1977, 1992; Marshall 1984; Pringle 1989; Watson 1992). Halford showed how the expertise and interests of male-dominated trade unions and professional and semi-professional groups such as district engineers, planners, surveyors and medical and related professions were often opposed to change. In many authorities these initiatives did not survive their early years.

New ways of living?

The case studies that I have included in this chapter illustrate some of the ways that the built environment and the uneven spatial distribution of opportunities, goods and resources through the city and between localities, neighbourhoods and villages have a significant impact not only on the life chances of urban residents but also on their sense of themselves as women and as men. It is clear that a complex set of interconnections between location, ethnicity and class position are related to gender divisions, creating particular understandings of what it means to be a woman or a man in different areas. For the young men in US ghettos and British municipal estates in both inner and outer city areas, the conventional routes to masculinity are closed by poverty and economic insecurity. And yet they continue to hold to mainstream definitions of masculinity that emphasize characteristics such as male solidarity in the face of danger and dominance over women – but also, ideally, the protection of 'their' women. If these aspects of masculinity elude men through legal activities, then often they are pursued through illegal channels. But, as Campbell argued, these men have a great deal in common with the very policemen and soldiers who are set up as their opposites and adversaries and who seek to control their illegal or anti-social behaviour.

117

These case studies also clearly illustrate the connections between urban and economic issues. The impact of location is partly a reflection of the distribution of economic activities throughout the urban area and the adverse impact of the decline of manufacturing and other job opportunities in particular areas of the city. I shall turn to examine more specific and detailed questions about the links between gender divisions and the workplace in the next chapter and in chapter 6 to the question of location, alternative spaces and gender identity. There the links between individual identity, place and fear and pleasure will be the focus rather than larger-scale issues of community and group identities.

Before concluding this chapter, I want to raise a few speculative questions about alternative forms of community and the possibility of differently gendered spaces. As the built environment is relatively permanent, it tends to reflect the gender divisions of an earlier age. As I argued in the introduction, the layout of cities, urban transport networks and timetables, as well as the internal layout of individual homes, are based on an assumption of permanent nine-to-five employment by a male breadwinner, with a wife who combines housework and childcare in the local neighbourhood. The reality of rising female employment and the transformation of working patterns that I shall describe in detail in the next chapter have yet to be reflected in new urban layouts and housing design. Indeed the most significant change that seems to have occurred so far is in the decline of the daily sit-down family meal (Bell and Valentine 1997; Gronow 1997) and its replacement by individual 'grazing', with the aid of the fridge and microwave. The development of more radical new ways of living seems remote.

There are, however, a number of historical precedents of regendered living and urban spaces. These include the utopian experiments of nineteenth-century socialists (Taylor 1983) and feminists, in the US in particular (Hayden 1976), as well as the example of an exciting new town constructed in the US during the war on quite different principles from the suburban conformity built into the British new town movement in the 1940s (McDowell 1983). A description of this town, Vanport City in Oregon, is the introduction to Dolores Hayden's magnificent book *Redesigning the American Dream* (1984), where she examines past and recent examples of communities that challenge 'traditional' gender assumptions. Vanport City was built for Wilhelm Kaiser to house the women who worked in his shipyard during the war, including that iconic figure Rosie the Riveter (see plate 3.1 in the previous chapter). Many of these women were married with children and their husbands were in the armed forces. Thus, for the duration, these working women were single mothers and Kaiser instructed his architect to build a town which would make their 'dual roles' as mothers and waged workers as easy as possible.

118

Each individual house was to be near a childcare centre. These centres were open twenty-four hours a day and provided hot food not only for the children but for their mothers to carry away at the end of their shifts, so they did not have to cook when they were tired. Each house was also designed with a large picture window facing the shipyards so that the children could see where their mothers had gone to work each morning. Unfortunately this splendid challenge to the patriarchal and familial principles that have dominated town planning and house-building throughout the twentieth century was demolished at the end of the war. The return to 'normality' meant that the men who returned were re-established in their 'proper' place, both in 'their' homes and in the workplace. As Hayden argues those old ideals – home, mom and apple pie – became dominant once again after the war ended.

There are other examples of communities and buildings where women and women's needs are central. These include a wide range of activities and buildings opened since the 1960s and the growth of the second wave women's movement. Here we might include the women's refuges and shelters, art centres and bookshops which were opened in many cities in the US, Canada and Britain (Wekerle et al. 1980). There are also other buildings which are open only for women at certain times: local authority swimming pools and sports centres are common examples in Britain, but parts of public transport systems, cafés, restaurants, bars and public gardens are also sometimes restricted to women. As I noted above, several local authorities in Britain established women's committees in the 1970s and 1980s to address questions about access and safety in public and in public buildings. There are also studies about the role of women planners and architects and their challenge to the masculinist assumptions common in their professions (Brion 1994; Greed 1991, 1994).

More recently projects have been started in Britain and the US to meet the needs of specific groups of women, defined perhaps by ethnicity, age or sexuality, rather than women *per se*. It is also important not to forget earlier examples of women-only communities and practices: schools, colleges and convents provided both refuge and an opportunity for women to gain confidence and credentials in this and previous centuries. Recent research on the culture of organizations has demonstrated how important it is for women to increase their representation at all levels in order to challenge discriminatory attitudes and behaviours as well as institutional practices and assumptions that construct women as atypical or abnormal (Cockburn 1991; Marshall 1984; McDowell 1997a; Wright 1995)

There is disagreement, however, about whether women-only provision and spaces empower women or trap them in a ghetto of special needs, reinforcing the argument that women are in need of protection from the rough and tumble of urban life in ways that parallel the assertions of the Victorian era that I outlined in the previous chapter. Perhaps a more interesting project might be to think through what a non-sexist or non-gender specific urban environment might look like. Here we enter the realm of speculation rather than current practice, although Dolores Hayden (1984) has designed combined workspaces and homes for single parents in Los Angeles, in the belief that home and work must be more closely connected. The design and location of 'work', home and neighbourhood communities interlock with assumptions about gender divisions which must be challenged to construct a non-sexist city.

Conclusions: rethinking community

A more radical challenge to the acceptability of community (defined as a territorially bounded space dominated by face-to-face exchanges) as a basis for urban organization has come from the feminist political theorist Iris Marion Young, whose work on the body we encountered in chapter 2. Young believes that feminists and other socially progressive theorists must abandon the concept of community altogether:

> The ideal of community privileges unity over difference, immediacy over mediation, sympathy over recognition of the limits of one's understanding of others from their point of view. Community is an understandable dream, expressing a desire for selves that are transparent to one another, relationships of mutual identification, social closeness and comfort. The dream is understandable, but politically problematic, I argue, because those motivated by it will tend to suppress their differences among themselves or implicitly to exclude from their political group persons with whom they do not identify. The vision of small, face-to-face, decentralized units this ideal promotes, moreover, is an unrealistic vision for transformative politics in mass urban society. (1990c: 300)

As Young recognizes, a city broken into separate spaces or communities, where people feel comfortable in their face-to-face interactions with people like themselves, too often tends to be based on a 'desire for social wholeness and identification that underlies racism and ethnic chauvinism on the one hand and political sectarianism on the other' (1990c: 302). Community-based organization, in other words, is almost always socially divisive. Young yearns for a city that does not suppress difference and oppress 'others' – all those differing from the dominant norm – but is instead open to 'unassimilated otherness' (p. 301).

120

She illustrates the type of change that would be necessary through the example of the women's movement, which, she argues, has moved from organizing based on the ideal of community or the common identity of women to this preferred state of unassimilated otherness. In the early days of the women's movement in the 1960s, Young argues, the 'strong pressure within women's groups for members to share the same understanding of the world . . . often led to homogeneity – primarily straight, or primarily lesbian, or primarily white, or primarily academic' (p. 312). The anger felt by many working-class or black women at their exclusion led to bitter factional disagreements in the 1970s, before the development in more recent years of a more tolerant perspective that celebrated the multiple ways of 'being a woman'. This leads to a movement based not on its members understanding one another as they understand themselves, but instead an acceptance of the differences and distance between them without it closing into exclusion.

I wonder, however, how this ideal might be translated into tolerance in cities, where spatial distances between people reinforce their differences. As Young notes, 'In a racist, sexist, homophobic society that has despised and devalued certain groups, it is necessary and desirable for members of these groups to adhere with one another and celebrate a common culture, heritage and experience' (1990c: 312). In contemporary cities, acceptance and celebration of 'others' seems a distant prospect.

Young suggests that the privileging of face-to-face communities as an ideal must be abandoned, although she does not deny the value of mutual friendship and cooperation in relatively localized city spaces. But in the complex urban societies of the present day a rich and diverse set of social relations and connections is possible, as the media that link people across time and space expand. In the non-places identified by Augé (1996), for example, our social characteristics – our gender, ethnicity, our age – become insignificant, and, as Harvey (1989) and Giddens (1991) noted, social networks increasingly straddle larger and larger distances. Does this mean, though, that we will become more tolerant, living as strangers with particular characteristics, backgrounds, needs and abilities, who do not, cannot and must not try to 'understand one another in a subjective and immediate sense, relating across time and distance' (Young 1990c: 317) but instead live in relations of mutual tolerance? I wonder, but suspect Young's vision is a utopian dream: but surely one worth pursuing. However, in the present, when so many people's lives remain localized in the sorts of areas and localities I have described above, it seems an impossibility. In smaller ways, however, it is important to struggle against the processes and practices that reinforce all sorts of social and spatial exclusions.

121

Further reading

One of the earliest collections on the relations between the built environment, localities and gender divisions, *Women and Space*, edited by Shirley Ardener in 1981, is still well worth reading and includes a number of comparative studies of different societies. Daphne Spain, in her book *Gendered Spaces* (1993), provides historical as well as geographical comparisons. Dolores Hayden's work is, in my view, exceptional. Her scholarly but supremely readable analyses of the different ways in which gender and spatial divisions are connected include *Seven American Utopias* (1976), *The Grand Domestic Revolution* (1981), *Redesigning the American Dream* (1984) and most recently *The Power of Place* (1995), in which gender, class and ethnic divisions and their representation in the landscape of twentieth-century Los Angeles are uncovered and illustrated. Sue Ruddick (1996) has examined the links between public space and the social construction of 'difference'. Gerda Wekerle with others (1980, 1995) has published widely on issues of gendered spaces, including planning safer cities, and Clara Greed (1994) has also assessed the prospects of gender-sensitive planning.

Although Mona Domosh concentrates on class relations, her book *Invented Cities* (1996a) about the landscape of New York and Boston in the nineteenth century is worth exploring. *Changing Places: Women's Lives in the City* (1996), edited by Chris Booth, Jane Darke and Susan Yeandle, is an extremely comprehensive introductory text with a good bibliography. Ruth Fincher and Jane Jacobs's (1998) recent edited collection includes papers by feminist urban geographers and others. The *International Journal of Urban and Regional Research* and *Gender, Place and Culture* publish numerous empirical explorations of gender divisions and relations in different circumstances and localities. While this chapter focuses solely on Western societies, there are many excellent papers and books about the gendered nature of space in colonial and post-colonial societies. Sara Mills (1996) has analysed colonial India in the late nineteenth century, for example; there are several papers on 'place' in Ashcroft et al. (1995) and in Momsen and Kinnaird (1993). Finally Iris Marion Young has developed her arguments about community in a number of places, including papers I have drawn on in Linda Nicholson's edited book *Feminism/Postmodernism* (1990) and in Judith Squires's collection *Principled Positions* (1992).

5

Work/Workplaces

Introduction

The literature about gender and waged work is enormous. This has been one of the key areas of feminist scholarship and perhaps the most significant focus of feminist geographers, at least until relatively recently. To some extent the issues that dominate this chapter are the reverse of those in chapter 3 – the Home. There the development of the ideal of feminized domesticity and its role in confining women to the home were explored. But the distinction between home and 'work', in the sense of waged labour, is made so routinely in industrial societies that it seems self-evident and we take it for granted that, for most people at least, going out to work entails leaving home. Ray Pahl forcefully reminded us, however, in his book *Divisions of Labour* (1984) that this has not always been the case, and nor is it the common pattern in many societies today. A great deal of work was, and still is in places, undertaken at home and goods are produced by the joint labours of household members in their own homes. As I argued in chapter 3, childcare and housework are certainly work, even if most women's labours here are not regarded as work and are not financially remunerated.

It was with the emergence of industrial production that home and work became spatially separated, but even in the most 'advanced' of advanced societies that separation is not complete today. As I also argued in the earlier chapter, a sizeable minority of women have always worked for wages, sometimes in their own home or in other women's. Indeed, I discussed both sweated and domestic labour in chapter 3, as that type of work conforms to the idealized notion that women's place is in the home. Going 'out' to work challenges this ideal, but even so millions of women did go out to work right through the nineteenth century. Many of them worked in types of employment where women constituted a feminized 'ghetto', working in the main only with other women or in jobs and occupations that were constructed as 'women's work' and consequently were much more poorly paid than 'men's work'. Since the middle of the twentieth century, women's participation in waged employment has expanded but their concentration in feminized occupations has remained a dominant feature of their employment pattern. Thus the key issue for feminist economists, sociologists and economic geographers has been to explain the reasons for women's initial exclusion and then their concentration or segregation within the labour market.

A remarkable series of theoretical and empirical studies, both aggregate analyses of national statistical series and detailed case studies of particular industries, sectors, occupations, localities and firms have been produced in the last twenty-five years or so. During this time, too, theoretical attention has moved from Marxist-inspired or socialist feminist analyses of divisions of labour to questions about workplace cultures, the embodiment of labour power and sexuality at work. As many extremely good surveys of these shifts are now available (Auster 1996; Bradley 1989; Crompton and Sanderson 1990; Dex 1985; Fuentes and Ehrenreich 1983; Nash and Kelly 1983; Stichter and Parpart 1988; Walby 1986), I shall summarize them relatively briefly and focus in greater detail in this chapter on some of the empirical work done in the different theoretical traditions.

In the 1990s, there has been a further shift in emphasis, as much empirical as theoretical. Partly as a reflection of the recognition that men and masculinity needed to explicitly enter feminist labour market studies as much as other areas, but also as a response to the material changes that have been the consequence of the deep economic restructuring that has occurred in industrial societies since around the early 1970s, and which culminated in a transition to service-based economies, a new emphasis on the social construction of masculinity in the workplace has become more evident. As manufacturing jobs for unqualified young men have almost disappeared in particular regions of the industrial West, the opportunity for these men to develop that characteristic working-class masculinity – built around shared risks and hardship at work and communal solidarity – that marked, for example, localities dominated by coal mining, shipbuilding and steel or chemicals production has vanished with them (Campbell 1984; Beynon et al. 1988; Fine et al. 1997; McDowell and Massey 1984). I discussed some of the implications of unemployment for young men in Britain and the US in the last chapter. Later on in this chapter, therefore, in the final part, I shall turn to a consideration of how new forms of work that seem in many senses to embody the social characteristics of femininity are interpreted by men in ways that conform to hegemonic notions of masculinity.

124

Explaining gender divisions of labour

In recent decades women's participation in waged labour has risen in virtually every country in the world as capitalist industrialization has proletarianized women. There are still, however, considerable geographical variations in the proportion of women who are in the labour force, as comparative statistics collected by the International Labour Organization reveal. Although the bases of comparison are not always entirely compatible and the years of collection vary somewhat, in the early to mid 1990s, women's labour market participation in Western countries varied from a high of 78% for women of working age in Denmark to only 43% in Spain and 44% in Italy and Greece. Participation rates in the 'rest' of the world are even more varied. Extremely low rates are still common in parts of Africa: in Algeria, for example, less than 5% of women were in waged employment in the early 1990s, in Egypt 14% and in Senegal and Morocco 17%. In other 'developing' societies at that time, between 50 and 65% of women were employed in such countries as India and Bangladesh, Singapore and Barbados, while only 40% of Chinese women were employed; in most of Latin America, typically less than a third of women of working age were in officially recorded employment.

A wide range of factors influences these rates and the variations among them. As well as clear differences between 'Western' industrialized nations and others, religious attitudes, for example, affect participation rates. Thus in the West, Catholic countries traditionally have had low levels of female participation. The rate for Italian women, for example, is almost the lowest in Western Europe (although the rate of growth in Italy between 1970 and 1990 was, in fact, among the highest in the West). Elsewhere, it is in Islamic nations that women's participation is lower, as the figure for Algeria illustrates (information for Pakistan and Afghanistan is too unreliable to use for comparisons). Similarly the extent and pace of industrial development is significant. In the Asian 'tigers', for example, now suffering from economic crisis but where rapid industrial growth occurred in the 1980s, large numbers of women were drawn into employment in the electronics and clothing industries.

Before examining the reasons for women's employment patterns, it is important to briefly assess the statistical basis of comparisons. Measuring and defining women's work raise methodological and theoretical problems. To take the former first, as feminists have long argued, the definition of work as waged labour in a formally structured employment relation is based on a masculine ideal of work. Many women 'work' for love and many others are employed in all sorts of arrangements where their financial

125

rewards may be temporary or periodic, paid in kind or unrecorded (Glucksmann 1995). This is particularly the case in less industrialized economies, although common too in industrial societies. Women work, for example, as unpaid helpers on family farms or in family businesses, as periodic and often peripatetic workers in agriculture, or part-time for cash payments in, for example, pubs, clubs and restaurants, or cleaning offices or other women's homes. A great deal of this work is not recorded in national statistical accounts (Waring 1989).

The basis for cross-national comparisons is also often uncertain, as different countries use different measures, recorded over different time periods, and the figures may be more or less reliable. Thus it is clear that what we count as 'work' is both socially and statistically defined and is subject to a variety of meanings in different contexts so comparisons between countries are difficult. The data collected by the International Labour Organization are the best that are available at present.

Despite the significant geographical variations in participation rates (at least as in official records), the pattern of women's waged employment is universally distinguished by three key features. Women are concentrated into certain sectors and occupations (this is known as *horizontal segregation*); they tend to be in positions at the bottom end of the occupational hierarchy (this is known as *vertical segregation*), and women as a group earn less than men as a group. This latter feature is not merely a reflection of the fact that women do different jobs than men; even when men and women do the same types of work, indeed even if they do jobs with similar levels of responsibility, women tend to earn less than men. In Great Britain in the mid-1990s, for example, women working full-time earned on average 73p for every £1 earned by a man in a full-time work. The disparities are greater if women employed on a part-time or casual basis are included in the comparisons.

The segregation of men and women into different occupations is related to societal expectations about gender. Women are found in jobs in which the social expectations that they are nurturing, caring and supportive of others tend to be confirmed. In the United States for example, women account for over 90 per cent of dental hygienists, secretaries, childcare workers, registered nurses and pre-kindergarten and kindergarten teachers (Auster 1996). Similarly for men, beliefs that strength or analytical abilities come with masculine genes result in men's domination of both manual jobs depending on strength and occupations requiring analytical skills. Thus in the US men account for 90 per cent of truck drivers, car mechanics and firefighters as well as of airline pilots and navigators, and over 80 per cent of doctors, dentists and architects (Auster 1996). In Britain and other countries in Western Europe the patterns of gender segregation are similar.

In countries where women dominate occupations which are defined as 'male' in the 'West' – in the countries of the former Soviet Union, for example, the majority of doctors are women – these occupations themselves are regarded as less prestigious than other, male-dominated occupations and so are less well rewarded financially. These variations suggest that it is not the characteristics of jobs themselves that demand attributes or skills that are associated with supposedly masculine or feminine traits, but rather it seems that *who does a job* depends on how it is socially constructed, valued and concomitantly rewarded. Feminist economists, sociologists and geographers, however, have had a long struggle in establishing this relationship and in the process have had to provide counter-arguments to traditional explanations for this widespread pattern of gender segregation.

There is a wide range of theories to explain occupational segregation that vary in the emphases placed on individual choice and large-scale structural factors, although in most theoretical frameworks the outcomes are assumed to be a compromise between individual abilities, aptitudes and interests, the possession of credentials, including class-related attributes as well as educational contacts (what the French sociologist Pierre Bourdieu, whose work we met in chapter 2, termed cultural capital (Bourdieu 1984)), and the rules and regulations that determine access to particular occupations and positions. As many of the theories of occupational choice were developed before feminists insisted that aggregate social and economic processes affected men and women in different ways, gender differences were either ignored or explained in naturalistic ways. In other words women's 'natural' talents rather than discrimination on the basis of gender were taken as the reason for their relegation to female-dominated job ghettos. Let's look at some of the main types of explanation for occupational segregation and the alternatives to these developed by feminist social scientists over the last twenty-five years.

Orthodox economic explanations

Supply and demand theory

One of the most straightforward economic explanations for women's rising labour market participation lies in the coincidence of changes in both the supply of and demand for labour. A range of changes that mean that women are both more appropriately qualified for waged work and more available, combined with a growing demand for labour, are outlined. These include women's improving educational credentials, the widespread availability of birth control, at least in more 'developed' countries, and the associated decline in average numbers of children born to individual women.

In addition, in some countries the wider availability of a range of consumer durables and services that in theory reduce the burden of housework and childcare should 'free' women for waged work. The evidence about the impact of 'labour saving' devices is complicated, however. In many cases their introduction has led to women aiming for higher standards of cleanliness, for example, rather than reducing the hours spent in domestic work (Cowan 1983; Oakley 1974). In several countries, campaigns around 'women's issues' (childcare provisions, abortion and sexual harassment campaigns, for example) and legislative changes which have improved women's position and led towards greater equality in women's and men's opportunities have also facilitated women's entry into waged work.

On the demand side, economists have pointed to the growing demand for workers in periods of economic growth and as capitalist forms of organization have spread into economically buoyant areas of the world. In simple demand models it is assumed that capital is indifferent to the sex of workers, although in other models it is assumed that women's entry is related to periods of boom when labour shortages are intense. Women, it is argued, are drawn into the economy during upturns and are expelled again in periods of economic downturn. The empirical evidence for this argument is limited, however. Both longitudinal and cross-national figures indicate a steady increase in women's participation in the majority of countries since the postwar period, even in periods of general recession (Rubery 1988). The exceptions are some of the former socialist societies where women's participation was extremely high in the communist era and has declined since 1989, both as a consequence of economic difficulties (rising unemployment has also hit men) but also through women deciding to withdraw from the labour market in circumstances where domestic labour remains time-consuming and arduous.

Human capital theory

A variant of basic supply and demand theories which is more explicit about the significance of gender divisions has been developed by a number of neoclassical economists. Known as human capital theory and represented by the work of Becker (1975), the assumptions that lie behind supply and demand theory about women's responsibilities for domestic work and childcare, for example, are made explicit. In this theory it is assumed that the correct unit of analysis is not the individual but the family or household, which has a finite amount of work and particular tasks to achieve. A rational division of labour is constructed based on the amount of human capital each member embodies and on the relative rates of return that might be achieved through its sale in the labour market. Men, it is argued, are, in general, better educated than women and have invested more time and energy gaining skills or credentials. Thus it is sensible for them to enter the labour market as they receive commensurately higher rewards than their female partners, who more appropriately undertake the essential unwaged labour necessary to run a home and bring up children. Further if women do enter the labour market, this model predicts they will take up part-time employment and/or work close to home, as the returns for each hour worked or mile travelled are lower than for men.

That these gender-specific patterns exist is not in doubt. A number of feminist geographers, for example, have addressed the specifically spatial question, investigating the impact of distance and location on job search and employment patterns. Empirical associations between gender and travel-to-work distances have been established. In general women travel shorter distances as a consequence of their childcare responsibilities and their more limited access to private cars, although these relationships are affected by social class, credentials and salary levels, and by ethnicity. Women who are better qualified, for example, achieve higher earnings and are more likely to travel further to work; it also seems that women from ethnic minority groups may travel longer distances than other women. But even for well-educated and well-paid women the association between distance and pay rates is less marked than for men (Hanson and Johnston 1985; Johnston-Anumonwo 1992; Villeneuve and Rose 1988). Hanson and Pratt's (1995) work has been particularly influential in drawing attention to spatial issues, extending the understanding of the role of residential location and gender differences in job search behaviour in the maintenance of occupational sex segregation. They developed the idea of spatial containment, which is related to women's domestic responsibilities, to explain gender differences in labour market behaviour.

While the human capital model may have fitted empirical patterns of women's employment in advanced industrial nations in the 1970s, it increasingly diverges from reality in the 1990s, when women are better educated than ever before (in Britain, for example, girls outperform boys in school-leaving examinations, and in 1996 for the first time more young women than young men graduated from British universities). More and more women are also working full-time and growing numbers of men are having to accept part-time temporary or casualized employment in the new 'flexible' labour markets of the West: patterns that were previously thought appropriate only for women. Neo-classical economic models also tended to take gender divisions for granted. Thus the models developed in the 1970s and early 1980s failed to ask why it was that girls left school earlier or did not achieve the same level of qualifications as their brothers. Thus a particular sexual division of labour is assumed rather than explained in these models.

For an explanation, feminist economists turned to a different approach that I shall outline below. More recently, however, human capital theorists have begun to modify their assumptions to consider contemporary realities of (some) women's lives. A *Guardian* report (19 May 1997, p. 18) based on an unpublished paper by an economist suggested that a more nuanced view of domestic labour should be introduced to explain why women who could (and do) earn high salaries still do (some of) their own housework and childcare. It was argued that domestic labour should be valued at the hourly rate a woman would have earned by undertaking an additional hour's work in the labour market. In the *Guardian* article this approach was illustrated through the example of Cherie Blair, the British Prime Minister's wife and also a lawyer: 'If Cherie Blair does some cleaning, you can either say that it is worth what a char lady would have cost, say £3 an hour, or you can look at what she would have earned if she had spent that time in the High Court instead, say £200 an hour.' It is assumed that we are all rational beings who make trade-offs, and so to Mrs Blair 'the cleaning must be worth more than £200, or she wouldn't be doing it'. Academic economists clearly know little about the guilt that working women face and the reasons why they might choose to do their own cleaning!

The model is then developed to include the choices made by men and women within a household and here the old assumptions of human capital theorists are re-established. It is argued that the value of a man's labour is higher because he earns more (this is still a correct assumption, even for women in professional and managerial occupations, as figure 5.1 shows), so the value of his spending half an hour at the kitchen sink is greater than if his wife does it. Or to put this argument the other way round, the earnings foregone are greater. Under the assumption of this revised human capital model the overall value of domestic labour in the British economy is then imputed, with the argument that 'mothers contribute 70 per cent of domestic labour, but only 50–60 per cent of the *value* of domestic labour.' In this model, a typical mother contributes just 36 per cent of the value of a family's labour, although a more highly skilled woman's contribution may rise to 46 per cent. It is also assumed that the value of a woman's domestic labour diminishes over time as her 'human capital' declines and her employability diminishes.

It should be clear that this model merely replicates the sexism of the current labour market, rather than explaining its gendered nature. It reinforces current assumptions, women's social construction as inferior labour power and their categorization as 'less skilled' workers.

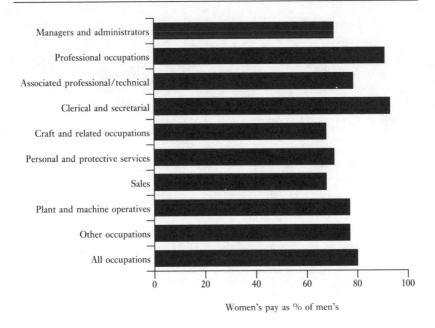

Figure 5.1   Women's pay as a percentage of men's pay (full-time employment), Great Britain, 1996 (data from Labour Force Survey, 1997)

Dual and segregated labour markets

If we turn to the work of labour economists, rather than neo-classical theorists, we find there a challenge to orthodox assumptions that the allocation of labour is based on rational decision-making by individuals or by household units. Labour economists have argued instead that the institutional structure of the labour market is based on discriminatory practices. Two related approaches are important in explaining gender divisions: dual or segmented labour market theory and labour process theory. Dual labour market theorists (see, for example, an early paper by Barron and Norris 1976), as the name indicates, argue that there are two labour markets, a primary one and a secondary one, differentiated by the terms and conditions of employment. The former offers high wages, good working conditions, security of employment and opportunities for promotion, whereas jobs in the secondary sector tend to be poorly paid and offer few opportunities for advancement. The majority of women are assumed to work in the secondary sector, although the explanatory mechanisms are left untheorized.

This dual model has been further developed to take account of greater degrees of segmentation that are evident in the labour market, through the exploitation by employers of racial and ethnic differences among workers, for example, and of differences based on age as well as gender to control the workforce (Craig et al. 1982; Rubery 1988). These models thus create space for treating gender as a central element structuring labour markets, as well as a reflection of women's domestic and family responsibilities.

Marxist theories: the reserve army of labour

Although labour economists were writing from a left perspective, they did not adopt an explicitly Marxist framework, and as I noted above they tended to leave untheorized the ways in which women were constructed as inferior labour power. Some of the earliest work by explicitly feminist sociologists, economists and geographers, however, was within a broadly socialist or marxist framework of analysis. Utilizing Marx's concept of the reserve army of labour – that group of workers who are underemployed or unemployed as capitalist production expands and changes (the people, for example, made redundant by technological change in the agricultural and manufacturing sectors) – feminists examined the role of women in general and married women in particular.

British sociologist Veronica Beechey (1977, 1987) was an early and key exponent of this approach. Her aim was to explain the noticeable growth of employment among married women in Britain in the 1960s and 1970s. She suggested that in this period married women were constructed as a uniquely disposable labour force for capital. They had low levels of union membership, and they were ineligible for many work-related benefits, for redundancy payments, and also for state unemployment benefits. Their ineligibility lay in the assumption in the tax and welfare systems that married women should be economically dependent on their husbands as their first responsibility is to create a home and care for these men and their children. Thus women were constructed as a flexible, disposable and low-paid workforce because domestic work was seen as their first responsibility.

Unlike the human capital theorists, Beechey did not see this gendered division as inevitable, but instead argued that the ways in which state legislation and employers' attitudes construct women as a dependent group are the reason both for their continued responsibility for domestic work and childcare and for their segregation into a limited number of 'appropriate' jobs and occupations. Feminists in the United States (see Power 1983, for example) have extended these arguments and also demonstrated how women's domestic work was tied increasingly into capitalist production

132

over time, not only 'freeing' women to work but also making it necessary so that they were able to purchase goods they previously made at home. Thus, as I noted in chapter 3, skills such as soap and jam making, home sewing, brewing and baking declined during the twentieth century as cheap factory produced goods replaced domestic production.

During the 1970s and 1980s feminist geographers interested in the labour market drew on versions of these approaches, working within the field now known as the division of labour approach (Frobel et al. 1980; Massey 1984). In both advanced and newly industrializing countries, it was argued, women were a reserve of cheap labour, attractive to newly mobile capital in search of higher rates of profit. While this 'division of labour' approach implicitly drew on feminist analyses of how women's domestic responsibilities were part of the explanation for their construction as a reserve army, theoretically women were seen to enter the labour market with their gender attributes firmly in place. Indeed versions of this approach, especially in its application to newly industrializing countries, relied on some of the most stereotypical notions of femininity in their explanations – women were widely portrayed as young, submissive and dextrous, for example, and as exotic and 'oriental' (Said 1978).

Feminist economists Diane Elson and Ruth Pearson, (1981) challenged these views and the notion of women passively waiting as a reserve of 'green' labour, ready to move into factories and offices as demand necessitated. Instead they argued that in both industrial and industrializing nations, actions by the state and capital were necessary to construct and train women as 'labour' and to extricate them from patriarchal familial relations. The active agency of women was also stressed, and the ways in which they resisted some of the most exploitative actions of their employers were investigated. In their case studies of women's work in electronics assembly in a range of locations, from Scotland to Korea, for example, Women Working Worldwide (1991) illustrated different strategies of resistance. A lively controversy has also developed in the feminist development literature about the extent to which women's entry into the labour market has increased or reduced their inferior position and their domination and oppression by capital and by men. A number of scholars (see, for example, Lim 1983) have suggested that the tendency for Western feminists to emphasize the exploitative nature of the capitalist social relations underemphasises overall improvements in living standards and the increase in independence and self-worth that may be achieved by women who enter the labour market. Labour force participation may also enable women to escape oppressive family circumstances.

As the growing number of excellent empirical studies of different sectors in different parts of the world reveal, however, the actual effects for

133

different groups of women are often complex and varied and depend on both their past and present circumstances, the type of work they do and the industry which they enter. There is a fascinating history and geography to the changing patterns.

Sexing work and workplace cultures

Although all these theoretical approaches have proved influential ways of describing the sexual division of labour in postwar advanced economies and in the newly industrializing nations, none of them is really able fully to explain why women continued to be recruited to a narrow range of occupations. As the decades advanced, these explanations also came to seem increasingly inadequate in their relevance to so-called post-Fordist patterns of work in the 'West'. Their assumption that women were secondary or temporary workers, whereas men had a primary and full-time attachment to the labour market, was challenged by the decline of manufacturing, by the growth of services, by rising female employment and by the introduction of flexible working patterns for both sexes. As Shirley Dex (1985) argued in her useful survey of explanations of women's labour market participation:

> Women are not a marginal workforce and should be viewed as permanently attached to the labour force. . . . The issues of whether women are a reserve army of labour or a disposable workforce buffeted by economic fluctuations have both been found to be asking the wrong questions about women's employment. The questions have been informed by too much male-centred theorising. More specific gender-related questions need to be formulated about women's and men's work as a further step towards the reconceptualisation of the socio-economic changes that are occurring. (1985: 203–4)

The emphasis needed to shift to the characteristics of work rather than the workers, to explore the ways in which gender-specific traits and characteristics are attributed to men and women through the work they do. Gendered identities are created and recreated at work, rather than individuals entering the labour market with their unchanging gender identity fixed firmly in place. A growing number of case studies of women's work began to shed light on a wide and varied range of social practices on the 'shopfloor' that construct women as 'embodied' – different from the disembodied masculine taken as the norm – and so act as an obstacle to women's advancement because of their perceived inferiority (Bradley 1989; Cockburn 1983, 1991; Game and Pringle 1984; Milkman 1987; Pringle 1989; Westwood 1984).

134

Increasingly feminist analysts recognized that the gender identities of both jobs and workers are negotiable and contestable at work. As Joan Scott recognized,

> if we write the history of women's work by gathering data that describe the activities, needs, interests, and culture of 'women workers', we leave in place the naturalized contrast and reify a fixed categorical difference between women and men. We start the story, in other words, too late, by uncritically accepting a gendered category (the 'woman worker') that itself needs investigation because its meaning is relative to its history. (1988: 47)

The same observation is applicable to occupations, and thus the processes of occupational sex typing – or, better, stereotyping – began to be unpacked.

Jobs are not gender-neutral – rather they are created as appropriate for either men, or women, and the sets of social practices that constitute and maintain them, are constructed so as to embody socially sanctioned but *variable* characteristics of masculinity and femininity. This association seems self-evident in the analysis of classically 'masculine' occupations; consider, for example, the heroic struggle and camaraderie involved in heavy male manual labour (McDowell and Massey 1984). The same belief now holds with respect to self-evidently female occupations such as secretarial work (and see Pringle 1989), but it is salutary to remember that these latter have changed their gender associations over the century (Bradley 1989). Less obviously 'sexed' jobs and new occupations are struggled over and negotiated to establish their gender coding (Crompton and Sanderson 1990). Attention has turned, therefore, to the ways in which workplace cultures and management and workers' attitudes maintain or challenge patterns of gender attribution and segregation. New questions about struggles and power relations between men and women, about daily practices and about the production and maintenance of acceptable versions of femininity and masculinity in the workplace have entered feminist analyses of waged work and individual workers have become active agents colluding in or challenging their gender attributions.

The focus of new research has also shifted to include management and organizational structures as well as individual workers. Formal organizational structures and informal workplace practices are not gender neutral as in the traditional view of the bureaucratic organization but are in fact saturated with gendered meanings and practices that construct both gendered subjectivities at work and different categories of work as congruent with particular gender identities. Interesting work is being undertaken by sociologists (Leidner 1993; Halford et al. 1997), organizational theorists (Casey 1995; Hearn and Parkin 1987; Knights and Willmott 1986) and increasingly by anthropologists interested in the multiple constructions of femininity and masculinity in different types of jobs and at different workplace sites (Wright 1995). The ways in which 'resexing' jobs is a significant part or consequence of economic restructuring, often leading to loss of status, power or financial rewards are also beginning to be investigated, linking the specificities of doing gender on the job to wider economic processes (Halford and Savage 1995; Halford et al. 1997; Morgan and Knights 1991; Kerfoot and Knights 1994).

There has been a shift in recent studies from what might be termed the 'gender-in-organization model' in which organizations are seen as settings in which gendered actors behave – as gender-neutral places which affect men and women differently because of their own different attributes – to theorizing organizations themselves as embedded with gendered meanings and structured by the social relations of sexuality. In these studies, sexuality is defined as a socially constructed set of processes that includes patterns of desire, fantasy, pleasure and self-image. Hence it is not restricted solely, or indeed mainly, to sexual relations and the associated policy implications around the issue of sexual harassment. Rather the focus is on power and domination and the way in which assumptions about gender-appropriate behaviour and sexuality as broadly defined influence management practices, the organizational logic of job evaluations, promotion procedures and job specifications (Acker 1990; Cockburn 1991), and the everyday social relations between workers. The growing recognition of the ways in which male sexuality structures organizational practices also counters commonly held views that sexuality at work is a defining characteristic of *women* workers. The realization that male embodiment and masculine sexuality must also be rendered visible and interrogated resulted in a significant shift in feminist analyses of the gendering of occupations. Men began to enter the feminist analyses of work, and more slowly organizational sociology, where the significance of gender previously had been ignored.

Organizations reflect masculine values and men's power, permeating all aspects of the workplace in often taken-for-granted ways. Male power is implicitly reinforced in everyday interactions and in many of the microscale interactions in organizations: in talk and workplace jokes, for example, 'men see humour, teasing, camaraderie and strength, for example, women often perceive crude, specifically masculine aggression, competition, harassment, intimidation and misogyny' (Collinson and Hearn 1994: 3). There are numerous other ways in which particular workplace cultures in a range of occupations, in both the service and manufacturing sectors, appeal to 'highly masculine values of individualism, aggression, competition, sport and drinking' (Collinson and Hearn 1994: 4).

The expansion of work about masculinity and organizations, about male power, masculine discourse and gendered social practices is part of a wider move in feminist-influenced scholarship to understand the complexity of gendered subjectivities and the ways in which they are constructed in and vary between different sites – the home, the street and the workplace, for example. It coincided with attempts by feminists, particularly feminists of colour, to reveal the specific assumptions about 'woman' that lie behind the early feminist scholarship. Criticized for its implicit focus on a version of white, anglo-centric and middle-class femininity, feminist scholarship is increasingly working on the ways in which race, class and gender are mutually constituted. In chapter 3, the racialization of waged domestic work was examined, for example. However, it is an accurate criticism that the situation of Third World women was, in the main, equated with the circumstances of women in the preindustrial period in the West and insufficient attention has been paid by geographers and others to the specificities of gender relations in employment practices shaped by, for example, imperialism.

There has been a rise of queer scholarship. Lesbian feminists such as Butler (1990a, 1993), whose work I introduced in chapter 2, Fuss (1990) and Wittig (1992) have shown how the 'regulatory fiction' of heterosexuality (Rubin 1975; Rich 1980) reinforces a naturalized binary distinction between men and women. Similarly, in a remarkable growth of male gay scholarship from the mid-1980s, the construction and dominance of a hegemonic heterosexual masculinity which excludes other forms of masculinity has been revealed (Craig 1992; Herdt 1992; Kimmel 1988; Metcalf and Humphries 1985; Weeks 1986). In recent work on gender, therefore, in general as well as in the sociology of organizations school, the notion of multiple masculinities has been developed to refer to the variety of forms of masculinity across space and time. There has been a rapid expansion of an exciting literature demonstrating the extent of historical and geographical variations (J. W. Gibson 1994; Gilmore 1990; Herzfeld 1985; Kaufman 1993; Klein 1993; Mangan and Walvin 1992; Messner 1992; Nye 1993; Roper and Tosh 1991; Segal 1990).

Connell (1995) argues that new scholarship from history and anthropology has led to important research on the ways in which masculinities are produced as cultural forms. To understand the diversity of forms and the transformations that occur it is important to analyse masculinity in specific contexts, in different organizations and in different places. A geography of masculinity and femininity is essential and here a great deal more comparative work is needed. There is scope, for example, for studies that examine the different workplace practices in particular branches of 'global' organizations. There is also a virtual absence of comparisons of men and women doing the same jobs, whether in the same or different locations, although this absence partly reflects the fact that so few women do the same jobs as men. With women's growing access to professional occupations, this should change, although the pace of change is too slow, in terms both of access and changing research foci.

I want now to turn to a small number of some of the fascinating case studies of gender at work in order to illustrate the more general arguments in this chapter so far.

Case studies of gendered work

1 Secretaries talk: a female ghetto

As I suggested above, until feminist scholarship began to have an impact in the academy – from about the mid-1970s onwards – case studies of the labour process and working lives were dominated by men's experiences. Indeed analysts of the workplace seemed to be fascinated by the heroic struggles of men in manual occupations, in much the same way as in early work on the city analysts were fascinated by the social life of inner areas. Women's working lives remained relatively invisible, both because women's work was not seen as interesting and also because the dominant focus on case studies of manufacturing jobs meant that the service sector, where the majority of women were employed, was neglected. In the small number of early studies of women's work, the main focus tended to be on the way in which women combined their 'dual roles' as mothers and as employees. The actual experiences of women working on the factory floor, in schools, hospitals and offices were not seen as an area for serious consideration. When this absence began to be remedied from the early 1980s, a number of fascinating case studies of single workplaces were undertaken: of a tobacco factory in Bristol (West 1982), a car components assembly line (Cavendish 1983), a hosiery factory in Leicester (Westwood 1984), and – more rarely studied – office employment (Webster 1986), where the impact of new technology on skills was assessed.

These studies in the 1980s belonged in the main to what might be described as a political economy or socialist feminist approach, and tended to ignore contemporaneous changes in feminist theorizing in other areas. As Rosemary Pringle suggested in 1989, 'There is a vast gulf between feminist debates on psychoanalysis, discourse theory, cultural production and semiotics, and the frameworks of political economy and industrial sociology within which most studies of work are situated' (1989: ix). Pringle's own study, *Secretaries Talk*, was an attempt to break down this divide and locate workplace studies 'in the context of debates concerning culture,

138

sexuality and subjectivity' (1989: x). It has since become a classic study of women's work and has inspired others to address questions about the social construction of gender *in* the workplace.

As I have already argued, women are employed in a range of occupations in which the characteristics associated with femininity and those associated with the jobs women do are congruent. Secretarial work is now seen as essentially feminine and is overwhelmingly carried out by women. Indeed men who work as secretaries are represented as demasculinized and often ridiculed. This is not only because the notion of a secretary is itself gendered but also because it is defined in relation to the category 'boss', another gendered category but in this case a masculine one. Thus, as Pringle pointed out, just as women are defined by 'lack', lacking what it takes to be a man, so secretaries lack what it takes to be a boss. If these naturalized and taken-for-granted associations trouble male secretaries, they also raise difficult issues for women who become 'the boss'. As all the associations of power in the workplace are masculine, can a women take this power and remain a woman?

Joan Acker (1990) has argued that to succeed at the highest levels in the public world of work, women do indeed have to become 'honorary men', disguising their femininity and adopting masculinist standards of style and behaviour. Based on my own work in merchant banks (McDowell 1997a), however, I suggest that this is an impossible strategy. Despite recent arguments about the plasticity and fluidity of identity, material differences still have an impact and a masculine performance by a man is still more highly valorized than that by a woman. As one of my own interviewees remarked, 'a woman can never be a man as well as a man can.' Women in the workforce have to find strategies of resistance that enable them to challenge their designation as 'other' and find acceptable ways of being women which do not automatically define them as powerless or 'lacking'.

In her book, Rosemary Pringle drew on interviews with senior secretaries to show how a secretary is constructed in a 'way that plays down the importance of what she *does*, in favour of a discussion of what she *is*' (1989: 2, original emphasis). Thus the nature of the work, the secretarial labour process, is trivialized and the characteristics of femininity are emphasized. So dominant is this process that secretarial work is seen as self-evidently 'natural' for women and all women are assumed to be capable of it. As one secretary whom Pringle interviewed bitterly remarked, 'typing is seen as something every woman can do – like washing up!' (p. 3). The association between 'woman' and 'secretary' is cemented in other ways as well. Secretaries are also 'represented in familial or sexual terms: as wives, mothers, spinsters, mistresses and femmes fatales' (p. 3). This further reinforces the trivialization of their labour. As Pringle found in her fieldwork, 'it was impossible to talk to secretaries about what they do without the talk running fairly quickly onto questions about coffee-making, personal services, clothes, femininity and sexuality: these themes are central to their self-definition and their working relations' (p. 4). As she noted, the relationship between secretaries and bosses is often based on images of sexuality and fantasy. It is an intimate and often emotional relationship, as well as one constructed through unequal power relations.

But power does not only operate one way: as male power over female employees. While bosses clearly have power over their secretaries, secretaries may also make or break their bosses. As Pringle demonstrated, the relationship is frequently one of mutual power and vulnerability. The relationship between Sarah Keays and Cecil Parkinson in Britain is an instructive one. Keays was the secretary and mistress of Parkinson, a conservative minister in Thatcher's first government. He was forced to resign when Keays made public their relationship, the fact that she had had a child and Parkinson's failure to redeem his promise to divorce his wife and marry her. It is important to remember, however, that the structures of power and the pretence that politicians observe, or should observe, exceptional standards of behaviour meant that Parkinson also suffered, although to a less significant extent, at least economically, than his abandoned mistress and daughter.

Pringle's study was an early, and magnificent, demonstration of how to link discursive and structural analyses when investigating the labour market position of women and it provided a welcome shot in the arm for feminist research on work. Through a mix of methods and sources she showed how representations of secretaries in a wide range of media – adverts, films, management textbooks – as well as in everyday social relations in the office combine with structures of inequality – in pay and conditions and in career prospects, for example – to reproduce gendered inequalities in the workplace.

I want to turn now to another splendid piece of empirical research which reveals how certain men are able to redesignate tasks that seem essentially feminine – typing is the example again – and hold on to their power in the labour market.

2 Typing for men? Restructuring the printing industry

For many men, the social construction of masculinity in the labour market is bound up with physicality, with a bodily performance. To be masculine in the workplace means being endowed with strength and endurance which are key elements of the work undertaken. Thus for working-class men, heavy manual work involves physical effort and often shared dangers, through which a group solidarity and a spirit of masculine camaraderie is created, as I described in chapter 4. This masculinity is one of the ways in which working-class men create their own sense of worth. As Connell suggests, 'Emphasizing the masculinity of industrial labour has been both a means of survival, in exploitative class relations, and a means of asserting superiority over women' (1995: 55).

The decline, deskilling and casualization of many industrial jobs has threatened working-class masculinity. In addition, restructuring through technological innovation has challenged the gender attribution of certain occupations, and altered traditional associations between masculinity and machinery.

Cynthia Cockburn (1983, 1986), in a fascinating series of case studies, has examined the introduction of new technology into a range of occupations, including the clothing industry and hospital radiology departments. She has shown how women are being trained to operate new machinery, thus deskilling and often replacing men. In the tailoring trade, for example, Cockburn found that computer-assisted design and cutting replaced traditional male skills based on manual processes. In some occupations and industries, however, men have been able to retain their traditional dominance by endowing the new technology and new machines with masculine attributes. As Connell has noted:

> The new information technology requires much sedentary keyboard work, which was initially classified as women's work (key-punch operators). The marketing of personal computers, however, has redefined some of this work as an arena of competition and power – masculine, technical but not working class. These revised meanings are promoted in the text and graphics of computer magazines, in manufacturers' ad-text and graphics that emphasizes 'power' (Apple Computers named its laptop the 'PowerBook') and in the booming industry of violent computer games. (1995: 55–56)

In her exemplary study of the impact of new technology on gender relations in the printing industry, Cockburn (1983) illustrated how skilled working-class men did manage to revise the meaning of keyboard work, constructing it as masculine and so maintaining their hold on the key occupations, their power and high salaries. Cockburn's study of technical change in the printing industry as it faced up to the end of 'hot metal' compositing, is, in her own words, about 'the making and remaking of men' (p. 3). Until the end of the 1960s the work done by compositors in the printing industry was similar to that of their fathers and grandfathers. Indeed, the industry was one in which boys followed their father or other

141

male relatives into the trade and printing was distinguished by its 'patriar-chal craft culture, with a strong trade union identification' (p. 3).

The men interviewed by Cockburn who had entered the trade in the 1960s 'stepped into a set of class and gender relations that were relatively unchanged' (p. 43). But in the 1970s, newspaper owners hoped, through the introduction of computerized photo compositing, to restructure the industry, breaking the strength of the trades unions in order to allow them to cut jobs. For some papers and presses, restructuring was associated with a geographical move from the centre of London to the Isle of Dogs in the newly redeveloped Docklands. In this area, the struggle between, for ex-ample, the unions and the Murdoch-owned papers was extremely bitter. Cockburn's interviews with fifty London newspaper compositors took place before the most violent clashes.

Although the newspaper owners hoped, when the new technology was introduced, to use external typesetting companies, many of them employ-ing women, the unions insisted that the male formerly hot-metal composi-tors were retrained. This raised interesting questions about the gendering of skills. Cockburn recorded her surprise at seeing these men at work. 'To our eyes, used to seeing women and girls sitting at typewriters, the men in their shirt sleeves, often quite heavily built men used to more strenuous manual work, do indeed seem out of scale with the new equipment' (p. 96). In the 1990s, of course, we are now more familiar with the sight of men at keyboards, as the national press regularly portrays City dealers at their screens.

Although many of the newspapermen who managed to hold on to their compositing jobs were retrained by young women, they insisted that their own skills were superior. ' "They [the women] weren't ever operators, they didn't understand things," the men said. "They were *typists*" ' (p. 97 original emphasis). Thus the former hot-metal compositors managed to re-endow their work with masculine skills, albeit this time those of brain not brawn. The job required men who were able to understand what they were entering, compared to the women with their touch-typing skills which reduced them, in the opinion of Cockburn's interviewees', to 'an optical character recognition machine' (p. 97) rather than skilled and experienced workers.

3   Selling insurance: constructing masculinity on the streets

Robin Leidner, an American sociologist, has also undertaken case studies of gender stereotyping in the workplace. She has examined the fast food industry and insurance selling (Leidner 1991); I shall focus here on her study of the latter job. Occupations that involve selling of some kind, whether telephone saleswork, selling insurance, or the door-to-door selling of all sorts of goods, may seem at first glance to embody a number of the socially constructed attributes of femininity. In these jobs, the employee's task is to persuade people, often against their will, that they wish to purchase a good or a service. Charm, tact, persistence and persuasion are required, all of which seem to be characteristics more readily associated with women than with men. On the other hand, however, many of these jobs are performed in the public spaces that are linked with masculinity – in the streets for example – or may involve travel between towns and cities. These travelling jobs are often done by sales'men', and it is noticeable that in their representation in plays and films these men, perhaps because of those very attributes of charm and persuasion just mentioned, are often portrayed as slightly shady or dubious characters, somewhat effeminate and definitely untrustworthy.

To investigate how these contradictory attributes are resolved into a coherent performance that is congruent with masculine or feminine gender identities, Leidner interviewed a sample of men and a smaller number of women who sold insurance for a national company through 'cold calling' (that is, arriving unannounced) at homes in rural areas and small towns in the US. Almost all the male employees were young, the majority in their twenties, and they were predominantly white. The men were adamant that a woman would find it difficult to succeed in their job, even though, as Leidner noted, 'the job presented interactive imperatives that are generally identified with femininity. The skills required for establishing and maintaining rapport – drawing people out, bolstering their egos, displaying interest in their interests and carefully monitoring one's own behaviour so as not to offend – are usually considered womanly arts' (1991: 171). This meant that 'since some aspects of the agents' jobs required skills that are not generally considered manly, the agents' understanding of the job as demanding masculine attributes meant that these skills had to be reinterpreted or de-emphasized' (p. 171).

Leidner found that the men whom she interviewed 'assigned a heroic character to the job, framing interactions with customers as contests of will. To succeed, they emphasized, required determination, aggressiveness, persistence, and stoicism . . . through this need for toughness . . . the work was constructed as manly' (p.172). The male agents believed women were too sensitive or not aggressive enough to succeed. Thus Josh, one of Leidner's interviewees, claimed, 'Most girls don't have what it takes. They don't have that killer instinct' (p. 173). The women found it a constant struggle to deal with the sexist attitudes of their male colleagues, as well as to cope with a life 'on the road', and many of them left of their own accord.

In my own work in merchant banks I also found that male dealers and traders made similar gendered claims about the attributes needed for success (McDowell 1997a), making it more difficult for women to be successful. In an interesting study of a range of occupations in British retail banks, however, Knights and Willmott (1986) found that men were unsuccessful in protecting their dominance of certain job categories. In their case study, they documented, as Leidner did, the numerous ways in which the male cold callers selling insurance constructed themselves as aggressive agents overcoming resistance. These British men, though, lost their jobs in an internal restructuring in which management took advantage of idealized feminine characteristics of nurturance, helpfulness and service to customers as an alternative way to selling insurance. Women employees in the British bank were upgraded from bank tellers to insurance sellers and advice givers. The work was reorganized by bringing it inside to take place in open plan areas within the banks' premises. The cold-calling external sales teams who had worked the streets were abolished. The geographical shift was part of the regendering of this occupation, which brought financial advantages with it. The bank was able to reduce its salary bill as the newly promoted women were paid less than the men whom they replaced, providing an excellent illustration of the argument that when women replace men in the same occupations, then the jobs are automatically classified as less prestigious and so less well paid.

4   Working in gendered places

In the final case study I want to reverse the focus, as it were, and instead of discussing the ways in which organizational cultures and practices are part of the social constitution of gendered subjectivities in the workplace, I want to show how workspaces are constructed as gendered places. As many geographers have demonstrated, places themselves embody gendered attributes – the masculinized space of the pub for example that we considered briefly in chapter 2, in which lesbians may feel out of place. In this case study I want to draw on my own work with Gill Court in merchant banks in the City of London and on Doreen Massey's work with Nick Henry in high-tech workplaces in the science parks of Cambridge, England. These two studies were initiated as part of a project on the changing geographies of south-east England (and see Allen et al. 1998).

The City of London – and merchant banks, as Pryke (1991) among others has noted – has long been a space dominated by men. Indeed

Virginia Woolf in her passionate anti-war polemic *Three Guineas* (originally published in 1938) commented on the male dominance of central London.

> Within quite a small space are crowded together St Paul's, the Bank of England, Mansion House, the massive if funereal battlements of the Law Courts; and on the other side, Westminster Abbey and the Houses of Parliament. There . . . our fathers and brothers have spent their lives. All these hundreds of years they have been mounting those steps, passing in and out of those doors, ascending those pulpits, preaching, money making, administering justice. (Woolf 1977: 22)

As I argued in my book *Capital Culture* (McDowell 1997a), both the external and internal design and layout of the City symbolize male power and authority and men's legitimate occupation of these spaces. The streets and squares, the spaces between them, the facades of buildings and the internal layout of dealing rooms and trading floors reflect and reinforce the idealization of a city worker as masculine. In these spaces, feminine bodies are 'out of place'. I showed that whether in the coldly rational and intellectual arena of the corporate bankers – in offices and boardrooms – or in the carnivalesque atmosphere of the trading floors, the female body is 'othered'.

In her study of high-tech firms in Cambridge, Massey (1997) drew a parallel between male-dominated monasteries and the laboratories and research rooms in which 'boffins' spend their daily working lives. Like the elite spaces of the 'ivory tower' university, both monasteries and high-tech spaces are spaces of the mind, of knowledge and reason and the disinterested pursuit of truth and science. The obsession with an abstract, instrumental form of rationality codes the scientific laboratory as masculine, in which their 'dedication' to the pursuit of truth leads the almost universally male employees of science-based high-tech firms to work long hours and neglect their family and social lives. As Massey concludes from her historical comparisons between organized religion, the pre-twentieth-century universities and contemporary high-tech workplaces: 'Spatialities, identities, genders and social orders – such has been the long history of . . . their co-constitution. It is a history even now embedded in the laboratories, the excluding masculinities, the elitist and specialized time-spaces of today's new industry of high-technology R&D' (1997: 33).

And as we see again and again, this co-constitution, in different forms and with different histories and geographies, is a dominant feature of the landscapes of the industrial Western societies considered in this book. But as we also see, feminist research, scholarship, argument and action reveal and challenge this dominance.

145

Conclusions

In terms of theoretical emphasis, it is possible to trace a shift in feminist analyses of the labour market and working lives from a predominantly political economy approach dealing with large-scale societal structures – the nature of capitalism and patriarchy for example – to recent studies influenced by poststructuralist ideas. Questions about the discursive construction of identities, about workplace culture, symbols and representations of work and workers, and about sexuality and power in the production and reproduction of workplace inequalities increasingly are the focus of feminist analyses. Organizations are commonly theorized as embedded institutions, affected by and influencing a set of structures and meanings that operate at different spatial scales, all of which affect their social practices. This is not to deny the continuing importance of structural factors and the imperative in capitalist institutions and economies of the relentless search for profit that affects how and why gendered divisions are created and maintained. I want to suggest that there is scope for fruitful analyses of the labour market that combine different theoretical approaches and methods, setting the analysis of individual behaviour, for example, within a framework of the institutional regulation of the individual firm and the economy as a whole.

It is also important, as I have argued in earlier chapters, to examine the interrelationships between gender, class and other social divisions and their changing forms over time, both in the workplace and outside it. Capital creates and exploits differences between workers, as the labour process theorists argue and gender is but one, albeit an extremely significant one, of these differences. It may be that as the economies of countries change, other divisions become as significant as gender divisions of labour. Indeed it might be argued that in advanced industrial societies, as working-class men lose their livelihoods and middle-class women enter the professions in growing numbers, class divisions are recutting the old gender divisions of an earlier era. This is an argument that I have made elsewhere in outline form (McDowell 1991a) but which needs a great deal more investigation in comparative analyses of firms, regions and nations. At present, however, on the global scale it seems as if more and more people in the world are being drawn into the social relations of what we might term a patriarchal form of capitalism. In this form, women workers are constructed as inferior bearers of labour power compared with their male compatriates. As this brings lower wages, challenges to these circumstances will remain as crucial a part of a feminist politics in the next century as they have been in the second half of the twentieth century.

146

Further reading

The literature about gender and waged work has expanded enormously in recent years and there is a wide range of fascinating books, journals and articles that are easily accessible. In geography, the main journals to keep an eye on include *Economic Geography, Geoforum, Regional Studies* and *Environment and Planning A* and *Environment and Planning D: Society and Space* although case-study material and detailed analyses of particular organizations from a feminist perspective are not yet common in our discipline, except perhaps in *Gender, Place and Culture*, which has included articles about sex work, farm work and community work in recent issues. *Situated Lives*, edited by Louise Lamphere and others (1997) examines the differences in the lives of US workers, including black and Chicana women.

Feminist scholars have long had an interest in gender and economic change and there is a large literature about the proletarianization of Third World women. Useful introductions and case studies of industries and places include the books by Haleh Afshar (1991), Richard Anker and Catherine Hein (1986), Lynn Brydon and Sylvia Chant (1989), Annette Fuentes and Barbara Ehrenreich (1983), Janet Momsen (1991), Janet Momsen and Janet Townsend (1987) and Katherine Ward (1990). There is also an excellent summary of gender and development issues in a chapter by Pearson (1992). Among geographers, Sylvia Chant (1991) has worked in Mexico, and with Cathy McIllwaine (1995) in the Philippines, and Anne Faulkner and Vicky Lawson (1991) have worked in Ecuador.

For case studies from other disciplines turn to *Work, Employment and Society, Gender, Work and Organizations* and *Gender and Society*. For historical studies *Gender and History* and the *History Workshop Journal* are good sources. For studies of gender divisions of labour in other societies look at *Development and Change* and *Journal of Peasant Studies*, for example. There are some reviews of gender and development and gender issues in the Third World by geographers (for example, Brydon and Chant 1989; Momsen 1991; Momsen and Townsend 1987), but these are dated now. There is a good summary review of gender and development issues in the chapter by Pearson (1992). Other recent books worth a look include C. Auster, *The Sociology of Work* (1996), S. Halford, M. Savage, and A. Witz, *Gender, Careers and Organizations* (1997), L. McDowell, *Capital Culture: Gender at Work in the City* (1997a); R. Pringle, *Sex and Medicine* (1998) and S. Walby, *Gender Transformations* (1997). J. K. Gibson-Graham's (1996) book is a thought-provoking feminist critique of capitalism and political economy approaches.

6

In Public: the Street and Spaces of Pleasure

Introduction

In this chapter we move from the internal spaces of the home and the workplace back outside, to the public or open spaces of the street and the park, and the public or quasi-public spaces of leisure: bar, cafés, swimming pools and pool or snooker clubs, the department store and the public house. Here many of the themes that we have already examined in previous chapters reoccur: about the ideal and beautiful female body, for example, from chapter 2, and about the social constitution and gendered nature of different spaces and activities. However, I suggest that it is important to distinguish public and quasi-public spaces of leisure because they are a different *kind* of space than either the home or the workplace, and in them the constitution and maintenance of gender relations take particular forms. Thus, according to Neil Smith's (1993) definition which I introduced earlier, these spaces are spaces at a different scale from the ones we have considered already. This is not to deny that spaces or scales are social constructions, with complex and messy overlaps between them. The public spaces of leisure that we shall consider here, for example, are also workplaces for the many waged employees who maintain the services provided within them, but in this chapter the focus will be solidly on the gendered social relations of consumption.

When we turn to public spaces we clearly see the effect of the associations of the public/private divide with gender divisions. Because of the strong associations between women and the home, those interior spaces of domesticity, feminist investigations of public spaces have often focused on the problems and dangers that women experience 'outside' compared with an assumption that men may take for granted their freedom in and dominance of these spaces. Thus there is a significant literature about the ways in which women experience fear and anxiety, as well as physical danger, harassment and attack in streets and open spaces. I want to discuss this work but I also want to show that, paradoxically, the public spaces of the city have been significant locations in women's escape from male dominance and from the bourgeois norms of modern society. Indeed, I want to start with this latter area and return to the connections between gender divisions and the establishment and growing dominance of the norms of bourgeois respectability during the modern era. First, however, it is important to remember, as I have emphasized elsewhere, that here too the division between the public and private, just like the distinction between geographical scales, is a socially constructed and gendered division that feminist scholarship has challenged and attempted to overturn.

As you may remember, I suggested earlier that industrial societies, in the mid to late nineteenth century, witnessed the establishment of an ideology that constructed women (or rather so-called decent women) as angels of the hearth. This ideology has dominated Western thought, housing provision and urban planning since that period. Its significance for definitions of 'the home' was outlined in chapter 3, and some of the implications for urban land-use divisions in chapter 4. Here I want to look at the converse as it were: at how women who did not conform or keep to their place were constructed as wicked or fallen, subjected to abuse or vulnerable to physical danger, forcing them to reconsider their decision to participate in the public sphere. But I also want to show how semi-public spaces, such as the large department stores that began to be built in nineteenth century cities, created a place where women might escape from the confines of domesticity and male presence/control, even if only for short and temporary periods. Thus the public and semi-public arenas of industrial towns and cities were paradoxical spaces for women, where danger but also relative freedom awaited them.

I then want to move on to twentieth-century spaces and contemporary issues about gender and the public arena, through a discussion of women's relationship to open spaces, as seen variously through the eyes of women artists and writers. I also want to look at men's relationship to open spaces, to streets and to parks, especially the relationship of those men who cannot or choose not to conform to hegemonic notions of masculinity. Finally I want to assess the effects of the images of familialism and heterosexuality that pervade a wide range of spaces of pleasure. Here I shall focus in particular on beach holidays and other holiday places, and on urban spectacles presented in spaces of pleasure and desire.

Citizenship and public space

In this chapter the predominant emphasis is on the case-study material, as the theoretical basis of the divisions between public and private space and their implications for gender have been thoroughly discussed already. But here I want to blur that sharp association between gender and space and suggest that there is a messier and more complicated set of relationships to be uncovered since so many activities transgress the clear associations between femininity and privacy on the one hand, and masculinity and public spaces on the other. Men and women are variously divided and united by social characteristics – their race, age and sexuality, for example – and so do not always line up clearly on one side or other of a gender divide.

Here, in this chapter, I also want to introduce debates about the definition of citizenship and human rights, because conflicts over the use of public spaces often revolve round differential claims about the right of occupation. Liberal theorists argue that each and every individual as a member of the polity has an equal right to be in the public arena, but as feminists and others have pointed out, this right is often denied in practice. There is, in the operation of state-defined rules and in common practices, an assumption of moral worth in which *de facto* as opposed to *de jure* rights of citizenship are defined as open to those who are deserving or who are capable of acting responsibly. The less deserving and less responsible are defined as unworthy of or unfitted for the privileges of full citizenship. Thus in practice, as critics from both the left and the right have recognized (Sandel 1996; Sklar 1991; Young 1990b), citizenship is not an inclusive but an exclusive concept.

A range of individuals and particular social groups are excluded from the widest spectrum of access to public spaces and arenas, on the grounds either of their transgressive behaviour and their refusal to recognize the common rights of all or, alternatively, on the grounds of their need for protection from the hurly-burly of the public arena. It is on this latter set of grounds that women have been, and continue to be, excluded from equal access to the public arena. Thus women's construction as dependent on men, both economically and morally, or as lesser beings – as fragile or in need of protection – reduces their rights to freedom (Pateman 1988, 1989). A clear illustration here lies in the judgments made in cases of rape and harassment, when judges often argue that women should remain indoors for their own protection. Calls for curfews for women and girls when men who are suspected to be dangerous are 'loose' are common. Feminist campaigns to 'reclaim the streets' or 'reclaim the night', along with counterclaims for curfews for men, challenge the assumed greater freedom for men to occupy open and public space.

Interestingly, in these cases of rape or murder, women also appear as trangressors who through their actions should also be excluded from the public sphere. Thus the British judiciary often indicates in such cases that a woman who has been out too late or in the wrong place deserves what happened; the element of fault, it is implied, is on her part rather than on

150

the part of the man who attacked her (see J. Smith 1989). A number of feminist geographers have looked at questions of women's safety on the streets (Valentine 1990; Pain 1991), although it is also salutary to remember that abuse and physical harm are more likely to be perpetrated by someone known to the victim, often within the 'haven' of the home, than by a stranger in a public arena.

A range of other groups are also discriminated against in terms of access to particular spaces. Young people, people of colour and 'countercultural' groups often find that they are harassed and moved along (McKay 1995; Valentine 1996) as urban public spaces become increasingly less accessible and privatized through, for example, the use of private security firms to patrol the spaces between corporate buildings (see M. Davis's vivid description of this in Los Angeles (1989) and Zukin's work on New York (1995)). For the growing number of homeless people living on the streets, in doorways, subways and other tunnels (Morton 1995), increasing surveillance of urban spaces causes great problems.

Feminist political theorist Nancy Fraser has argued that if we are to take these exclusions seriously, then we have to rethink our notion of public space as sets of multiple and differentiated public arenas to which some groups have access but from which others are excluded. Like the postcolonial theorists who argue that there are subaltern subjects who are able to challenge the power and discourses of colonialism, Fraser suggests the notion of 'subaltern counterpublics', which are public spaces where marginalized groups might articulate their needs, so constructing them in opposition to the dominant or legitimate uses of these spaces (Fraser 1990).

Some subaltern counterpublics perhaps exist already. We might include spaces of protest, such as New Age encampments perhaps, or the tunnels and trees of road protesters, although the work of the geographer Don Mitchell (1995) on the history of the People's Park in Berkeley, which was claimed by countercultural groups in the late 1960s, shows how hard it is to preserve spaces like these in the face of the state and private property interests. Protest movements trying to maintain subaltern spaces in Britain have had the same experience, as participants are torn out of trees and tunnels or evicted from squatted houses by police and specialist security firms.

But public spaces are important in that they are where the diversity that constitutes 'the public' is most apparent and where idealized notions of 'the public interest' are challenged. As David Harvey (1992) showed in his analysis of the use of Tompkins Square, a park in Manhattan, the multiple users of this space – young women and children, Hell's Angels and bikers, the deinstitutionalized, people who abuse a variety of substances, the homeless and business people – found mutual and tolerant coexistence impossible. Harvey drew on a range of sources for his paper and made vivid use of press coverage. He starts, for example, with extracts from an article in the *International Herald Tribune* (1 August 1989) by John Kifner. At the time Kifner wrote his report, as well as three hundred homeless people living in the park there were also:

> Skateboarders, basketball players, mothers with small children, radicals looking like 1960s retreads, spikey-haired punk rockers in black, skinheads in heavy working boots looking to beat up the radicals and punks, dreadlocked Rasta-farians, heavy metal bands, chess players, dog walkers – all occupy their spaces in the park, along with professionals carrying their dry-cleaned suits to the renovated 'gentrified' buildings that are changing the character of the neighbourhood. (Quoted in Harvey 1992: 588)

Two years later an article in the *New York Times* pointed out the dilemma that faced the city's planners in attempting to resolve the conflicts arising from these multiple users:

> There are neighborhood associations clamouring for the city to close the park and others just as insistent that it remain a refuge for the city's down-trodden. The local Assemblyman yesterday called for a curfew that would effectively evict more than a hundred homeless people camped out in the park. Councilwoman Miriam Friedlander instead recommended that Social Services, like healthcare and drug treatment, be brought directly to the people living in the tent city. 'We do not find the park is being used appro-priately,' said Deputy Mayor Barbara J. Fife, 'but we do recognize that there are various interests.' There is, they go on to say, only one thing that is a consensus, first that there isn't a consensus over what should be done, except that any new plan is likely to provoke more disturbances, more violence. (Quoted in Harvey 1992: 590)

Clearly issues about the multiple occupancy of urban spaces raise difficult questions about how to adjudicate between conflicting notions of appropri-ate access and use. As I shall show below, twentieth-century concerns about differential access to particular spaces and places in the city have historical precedents.

Modernity and urban public spaces: the city flâneur and the flâneuse

At the end of the millennium when issues about difference and diversity are central in geographic research agendas, there is a noticeable retrospec-tive flavour to many analyses in their return to how these issues developed a century previously. Although the turmoil of a postmodern world seems challenging to many, the huge social and economic upheavals that wrenched people from the land and from their homelands in the vast expansion of industrial urbanization in Western Europe and the US in the nineteenth and early twentieth centuries not only reshaped the relations between space, gender and identity but also transformed cultural representations. One of the reactions to the huge and unprecedented growth of cities in the nineteenth century was a set of new movements in the arts, in painting, poetry and literature, and the development of new cultural forms such as photography and the cinema in which reactions to the vast social changes were explored. Thus Raymond Williams has argued that

> the facts of the development of the city into the metropolis are basic. We can
> see how certain themes in art and thought developed as specific responses to
> the new and expanding kinds of nineteenth-century city and then, as the
> central point of analysis, see how these went through a variety of actual
> artistic transformations . . . in certain metropolitan conditions of the early
> twentieth century. (Williams 1989: 39)

During this period, between about 1850 and 1920, modernism as an artistic movement became established, challenging previous ideals of artistic representation and culminating in movements such as Dadaism, surrealism, cubism and so on. It was also a key period of political unrest and social ferment in Western Europe and the US, of which the suffrage movement was an important part. So changes in women's status and their everyday lives were also a key part of urbanization and modernity.

The artistic and cultural movements of modernity, as well as the social upheavals, have attracted a great deal of research attention recently from a range of disciplinary perspectives, including geography. In the so-called 'cultural turn' in our discipline, for example, there has been a new interest in literature and art as source materials (see, for example, the work by Cosgrove and Daniels (1988) on painting and architecture) and in the built environment of the period (see, for example, Mona Domosh's book about New York and Boston (1996a) that I mentioned in chapter 4) in understanding modernity. It has been argued, however, that in this work in general, the experiences of women have received insufficient attention. The key reason for this, Janet Wolff (1985) has suggested, is an overwhelming focus on the public arena of life, that is the sphere dominated by men, since industrial urbanization was accompanied by a growing spatial separation of men's and women's lives. In the great new cities of the nineteenth century, a new male figure appeared, that of the flâneur or voyeur who took pleasure in his role as an urban onlooker. I want to examine some of the arguments about the

153

place of these male urban observers and, in particular, assess the possibility that they might have had a female counterpart.

The writings of French poet and commentator, Charles Baudelaire, were crucial in the recognition of the significance of urban change. Indeed, modernism as an urban artistic movement drew some of its earliest inspiration from his work. In an essay 'The painter of modern life', written between 1859 and 1860, Baudelaire (1963) outlined a set of arguments about the fleeting and transitory nature of urban experience. He suggested that the artificiality of urban life was based on a confusion between images and reality in cities where dreams and spectacles were the basis of consumption. The quintessential figure of the modern metropolis, according to Baudelaire, was that of the flâneur: the strolling observer, who gazed at but did not participate in the spectacular developments in the city. The flâneur was an anonymous figure in the urban crowd, invisible but all-seeing, a spectator who was, according to Frisby, 'a prince who everywhere rejoices in his incognito' (1985: 19).

These ideas about the fleeting and anonymous nature of social interactions in the metropolis became an important element in the sociology of urbanism developed later in the century, predominantly in Germany, by Simmel, Tönnies and others, whose work so influenced the Chicago School of urban sociology in the US in the first two decades of the new century, and later the development of urban geography. (Interestingly Simmel was one of the first academics to permit women to attend his seminars at the University of Berlin before they were formally admitted as students.)

For Baudelaire, and succeeding theorists, the flaneur inevitably was a man, as it was only men at that time who had the freedom to 'hang out' and spectate. Women in the mid-nineteenth century, or rather respectable middle-class women, were not accepted participants in the urban spectacle, but instead were those angels of the hearth confined to the sylvan peace of suburbia. Their less respectable sisters, however, joined the flâneur, or the urban dandy, as urban outsiders. As well as the flâneur, these outsiders or observers included, according to Baudelaire, poets, rag-pickers, lesbians, old women and widows (this group presumably assumed to be free from the unwanted heterosexual gaze) and prostitutes or whores, all of whom lived on their wits in the developing metropolises. The latter group of women, commonly and accurately termed 'streetwalkers', were regarded as fallen women in the hypocritical sexual double standard of the Victorian era. The very act of their appearance on the streets left the status of women open to interpretation and, often, to unwanted sexual attentions. In late Victorian Cambridge, for example, the early women students were required to wear gloves and hats when they ventured out into public in an attempt to distinguish them from the many women of 'easy virtue' in the city.

In her interesting paper, Janet Wolff pursued her claim that the sociology (and we might add the geography) of modernity neglects the specificities of most women's experiences of urban living. In her view 'the flâneur can only be male' (1985: 37). She suggests that the heroes of modernity, and modern urbanization – the flâneurs, the migrant and the stranger, who 'share the prospect and possibility of lone travel, of voluntary uprooting and of anonymous arrival at a new place' (p. 40) – are all men. It is perhaps her emphasis on the voluntary nature of travel that is significant here, as during the nineteenth and twentieth centuries as I describe in the next chapter, millions of women also became migrants, but more often through necessity than choice. But in Wolff's view the insistence in a wide range of writing on the transitory and fugitive nature of encounters as typical of life in the modern metropolis did not match the experience of most women.

In her book *The Sphinx in the City* and in a specific response to Wolff, Elizabeth Wilson (1991, 1992) disagreed with Wolff's contention that a female flâneur – a flâneuse – was an impossibility. She suggested that women actually had a great deal more freedom in nineteenth- and twentieth-century cities than Wolff allows, as the city was an arena where the strict and hierarchical ties of small towns and villages were relaxed and dissolved. Consequently, women too were able to experience something of the rootlessness and displacement at the heart of the urban experience.

In her edited collection of women's twentieth-century fiction about the city, Liz Heron (1993) also argues that the city is an important locus in the challenge to gender divisions. The city is, Heron suggests, a crucible for destabilizing the dichotomies that traditionally divide women's and men's lives. Thus, she suggests,

> the classic narrative of the city as a new beginning, a stage embarked upon in early adult life, has specific features for women in that the very notion of female self-invention defies the nature–culture divide; women being traditionally the stable, fixed point in a universe whose spaces wait to be explored by men, so that woman endures while man transcends. (Heron 1993: 3)

Instead, in the city the active independent woman came into her own. In the fiction that Heron included in her collection, associations between migration to the city and urban living and women's sexual and economic freedom are a central theme.

As Wilson noted, as the nineteenth century ended, women became increasingly visible in cities, passing through the streets on their way to the new employment opportunities afforded by the rise of clerical occupations and to go shopping in the growing number of department stores, where solitary women were able to linger, gazing at the goods in a manner remi-

155

niscent of the flâneur. This is not to deny, however, that women were still subjected to and constrained by the intrusive male gaze and, on occasion, actual verbal or physical harassment. However, as Heron notes, 'this can be less of a feature of city life than of a narrower social environment like that of the provincial town' (1993: 7). The very anonymity of the urban crowd may protect women, while at the same time that edge of danger is a lure to explore the city landscape.

Interestingly, Wilson has extended the argument about the significance of gender by suggesting that, far from being a representative of solid hegemonic masculinity, the figure of the flâneur was actually a transgressive one, a sexually insecure figure, and a passive spectator rather than, as is more commonly associated with masculinity, a participant. Indeed with his interest in clothes and shopping, the flâneur represented an unstable and unsettling version of a feminized masculinity. Heron also argued that the socially marginal female figures that dominate a large number of women's writings about the city are androgenous figures: independent and hard-pressed working-class women, artists' models or writers, if not deviants and misfits, outside the conventional bounds that define femininity. These female protagonists are women without family, often without men, and certainly escapees from the stultifying bonds of domesticity.

The work of scholars such as Elizabeth Wilson and writers such as Liz Heron, and now many others who are exploring the neglected aspects of women's experiences in the transformations associated with modernity, is crucial in countering previous dominantly male-centred accounts of these changes. Indeed the central burden of Wolff's original argument about the impossibility of a female flâneur was the theoretical impact this denial had on the development of the social sciences. Wolff documented the long disciplinary neglect of the private sphere and analysis of the reasons for women's exclusion from and/or limited participation in the public worlds of work and politics in the social sciences in general. This neglect, as I have noted already, was also a central feature of the history of geographical thought.

Transgressive spaces for men

The association of city spaces with the possibility of transgressing hegemonic versions of sexuality has not only been documented by feminist scholars as important for women. For men too the city is an arena permitting greater sexual freedoms, and the associations have been explored by several urban and gender theorists in different ways. Mapping the spatial significance of particular parts of a city for both hetero- and homosexual behaviour is a feature of some of this work. In, for example, her fascinating examination of paradoxical responses to nineteenth-century cities entitled *City of Dreadful Delight* (1992) Judith Walkowitz has looked at the ways in which bourgeois and ruling-class young men in Victorian England were drawn to particular urban spaces in their attempts to escape from what they saw as the stifling codes of conventional Victorian morality. For example, young men who lived in upper-class residential districts in the West End of London used the East End as their playground. Here they engaged in gambling and forbidden sports such as cockfighting and bearbaiting, as well as in varieties of heterosexual and homosexual experience outside the bounds of their 'normal' social and sexual relations with women of their own class background.

Other researchers have concentrated on uncovering the histories of public displays of homosexual behaviour and their urban associations. Thus in the expanding scholarship about gay men by queer theorists and others, an important emphasis is placed on the significance of particular places and spaces in the city which are identified with non-heterosexual identity. Indeed in some of the earliest work about gay gentrification, it was even claimed that gay men were not gay unless they had a visible territorial identity that marked them out as different

Gay New York by the historian George Chauncey (1995) is a recent and interesting book that charts the significance of different spaces in the city for gay men between 1890 and 1940. Chauncey argues that gay men in the period before the Second World War were involved in a public world of gay social relationships that took place in certain parts of the city, especially in working-class areas. He shows how, in the Bowery for example, middle-class men were able to act out a gendered performance that both threatened and reinvented hegemonic notions of straight and gay masculinity. Chauncey used a wide array of sources, from newspapers to diaries, to reveal a network of clubs, bars, rooming houses, restaurants, YMCAs, areas in Central Park and public baths in New York City that were part of the landscape of gay sexuality. Over the period he studied, however, the visibility of gay cultures disappeared as gay men were forced back into the closet, especially through the strict enforcement of a public discourse about 'vice'.

His book is a welcome attempt to connect the social construction of alternative sexual identities to the symbolism and meaning of the urban landscape and also an important corrective to the idea that a visible gay male identity in New York City had to await the Stonewall riot of 1967 when the police raided a gay bar. Chauncey is currently working on a second volume to bring his analysis up to the present. Indeed it may be published before this book: if you are interested in contemporary New York, keep an eye out for it.

In a somewhat similar project in London, Frank Mort (1995) has constructed a series of what he termed 'archaeologies of city life'. Focusing on the Soho district in central London in the 1980s, he has shown how a regime of gendered commerce drew on a range of cultural constructions of urban space as an arena of consumption to create Soho as an area associated with a series of particular versions of masculine identity. Mort argues that a distinctive breed of media professionals and cultural entrepreneurs was responsible for the promotion of London as a renewed site of conspicuous wealth during the 1980s, creating a plurality of identities for men. Homosexual men were particularly important actors as their social and sexual identities were shaped by the new consumer regime. These new consumer-based forms of masculine identity were mapped on to the urban landscape, creating particular zones in the city which became closely associated with the new configurations of gendered culture and business. Mort identified Soho as an area that had long been associated with gendered regimes, although, at least visually, it was dominantly a seedy form of heterosexuality in previous decades. In the postwar period, however, and especially in the 1980s, Soho became a crucial quarter for the development of a particular type of homosexual identity.

Using a similar set of sources to Chauncey, Mort uncovered the uneven archaeology of Soho as a space with a history of sexual dissidence and cultural hybridity. In the early twentieth century, it was an area of bohemian habits and behaviour where an early mixture of immigrants, artists, theatre people, prostitutes, and jazz musicians rubbed shoulders. This bohemian and avant-garde culture, according to Mort, 'privileged a range of masculine types, [and] revolved around the personalities of the bohemian, the flaneur, and the man about town' (1995: 577). From the late 1960s onwards an organized sex trade dominated the area, but in its 1980s renaissance its older bohemian character was resurrected. The new consumer culture that developed in that decade drew on 'the gendered representations of city life which had been laid down at different historical moments'. Distinctive heterosocial and homosocial spaces were constructed, with differential access for particular versions of masculine identity.

But it was a particular version of homosexual masculinity that came to dominate the area. According to Mort there was a

> growing commercialization of homosexuality. Bars and clubs, cafés and shops held out the promise of a homosexual life, shaped by the world of goods. In these commercial spaces the carnival promised a 'mixed' utopia – a co-mingling of lesbians, gay men, and their friends. But it was one constituency – young homosexual men – who laid particular claim to the streets of Soho. Despite the visibility of lesbians on the February Parade (an annual Queer Valentine Carnival), it was a masculine perspective on public space which predominated, even though this masculinity was defined as irregular and transgressive. (1995: 581)

158

Entrepreneurs welcomed this spatial concentration of gay consumption although, as Mort noted, 'the absence of an accompanying residential population in Soho made it unlikely the district would foster the type of ethnically centred gay communities which had emerged in San Francisco's Castro district, or in New York's Greenwich Village' (p. 581). But its development was important, nevertheless, in making a gay identity visible and in involving gay men in planning issues in London.

Conspicuous consumption and spectacular cities

The significance of the city as an arena of consumption has been a continuing theme through urban history and not only in the development of what Mort termed a 'regime of gendered commerce'. I want to trace some of the history of conspicuous consumption by returning to Baudelaire, or rather to his influence on Walter Benjamin, a German critic writing between the 1920s and 1940s, to sketch a brief outline of some of the relationships between consumption, urbanization and gender relations over the twentieth century. Benjamin drew, in his work on shopping and display in what is now known as the arcades project (see Buck-Morss's book *The Dialectics of Seeing* (1991)), on Baudelaire's ideas of the city as a magical and mythical spectacular display. In his work on what we now term conspicuous consumption, Benjamin analysed the rise of the department store at the end of the nineteenth century, looking in particular at the significance of glass arcades where goods were displayed for the voyeuristic pleasure of the passing spectator. Benjamin also studied fairs and exhibitions such as the one held at Crystal Palace for Queen Victoria's silver jubilee in 1851. Here, too, fabulous arrays of exotic goods, and even 'exotic' people, were displayed before the curious gaze of the passers-by. In such exhibitions, Benjamin saw the origins of a pleasure industry in which advertising based on spectacle and fantasy manipulated the desires of the masses.

As the twentieth century progressed, the significance of consumption and advertising became a central aspect of economic and urban development, and in the 1960s the French social theorist Guy Debord wrote about the rise of 'a society of the spectacle' (Debord 1994). Later, postmodern theorists such as Baudrillard have pointed to the rise of hyperreality, where images have become even more important than reality as places are marketed through the construction of image and fantasy. Perhaps the extreme example here is Las Vegas where visitors may sit in a pastiche of a Roman forum and watch the sun rise and set every twenty minutes. In waterfront developments across the globe, consumers may eat in Italian tavernas or buy clothes in mock Parisian shops and streets. But as David Harvey

159

argued in his classic text *The Condition of Postmodernity* (1989), image and spectacle are the basis of more mundane urban economies near the end of the millennium. The mechanics of capitalist accumulation grind on as usual below the glittering surface of these displays and spectacles.

Almost all these theorists, however, have tended to underplay the significance of gender relations in the development of new urban spectacles. For women the rise of consumerism paradoxically not only rooted them in their place as consumers rather than producers, as frivolous not serious – as well as women actually being the consumers of the growing range of items, their images were used both to sell and display goods and as a metaphor for exotic otherness – but also led to the development of spaces of pleasure which women might visit without male escorts. I have already suggested that the department store is a location of great significance here. It is explored in more detail in the next section.

Shopping for pleasure: consumption as (partial) liberation

One of the most indispensable documents in the recent renewal of interest in the nineteenth-century shift to economies based on consumption is the novel *Au bonheur des dames* by Émile Zola, first published in 1882. A century later the University of California Press published a new edition *The Ladies Paradise*, with an introduction by the cultural critic Kristin Ross (Zola 1982). As Ross details, a number of technological and urban changes paved the way for Paris to lead the way in the development of department stores. The great public works of Baron Haussmann transformed the city's streets, and wide boulevards were carved through the heart of Paris. New pavements or sidewalks were laid down, allowing pedestrians to stroll and pause to gaze in the windows of the new stores. Developments in glass and iron technology permitted large windows to be inserted in shop frontages, and electrification enhanced the spectacular nature and theatricality of the displays that were constructed behind them. Changes in the internal layout of the new stores, too, combined with the great variety of goods assembled under one roof, increased the impression of shopping as a pleasurable leisure activity (see plate 6.1).

Ross argues that Aristide Boucicault, the French entrepreneur who took over the Bon Marché retail store in 1852 (it was later to become a major chain)

> could be called the inventor of "browsing": passers-by could, for the first time, feel free to enter a store without sensing an obligation to buy something.

160

Plate 6.1   Contemporary shopping spaces: Brent Cross, North London

Goods were rotated frequently, with a low mark-up in price; high volume and frequent rotation created the illusion of a scarcity in supply among what were in fact mass-produced and plentiful goods. (Ross in Zola 1982: vii–viii)

The consumers who were the clientele of these new shops were predominantly women. The net result, as Rachel Bowlby (1985) argued in her analysis of consumer culture in the novels of Dreiser, Gissing and Zola, was that for middle-class women the fantasy world created in department stores, those 'colossal phantasmagoric dream factories' (Ross in Zola 1982: ix), became a 'second' home and a place of escape from their everyday lives and domestic routines. Tea rooms, lounges and powder rooms were provided for the comfort and respite of the consumers. But as Zola observed in his own notes to the novel, the desires of these female consumers were manipulated by male entrepreneurs, owners and floorwalkers: this paralleled women's construction as consumers rather than producers in the developing social relations of capitalism. Douglas, quoted in Domosh (1996b: 259), notes that 'the lady's function in a capitalist society was to appropriate and preserve both the values and commodities which her competitive husband, father, and son had little time to honor or enjoy; she was to provide an antidote and a purpose for their labour'.

Thus women's participation in the semi-public arena of the store and the street reinforced rather than challenged the developing separate spheres of Victorian industrial societies. And yet Zola also noticed, in this and his other novels, the potentially transgressive aspects of women's presence on the streets of expanding cities. He emphasized the feminine and volatile nature of the urban crowd, its delirious and contagious energy, and threatening female sexuality, which might spill over into violence. Elizabeth Wilson (1991), recognizing this threatening aspect of the urban crowd, has even suggested that this fear lay behind the development of town planning, resulting in women's reconfinement in the suburbs. It was believed in the nineteenth century that ' "public" woman, unlike public man, who is a serene and rational figure, is a woman prey to savage and violent impulses' (Ross in Zola 1982: xviii). Susanna Barrows (1981) has also suggested that behind this particular portrayal of a threatening feminine urban crowd lay the shadow of an even more intimidating group of women: French feminists and their association with moments of revolutionary fervour. In Britain too, especially in the suffrage movement at the beginning of the twentieth century, the women who took public action, marching and protesting in the streets, were portrayed as a huge threat to civil order, as well as unfeminine traitors to their sex.

In contemporary feminist analyses, the centrality of advertising and consumption in the social construction of feminine identities continues to be an important research focus, and as Robin Dowling (1993) has argued, a more nuanced understanding of the significance of place than is common in cultural studies work distinguishes the recent geographical scholarship. As she suggests, 'the construction of femininity occurs as part of the creation of place, and the characteristics of a place have an impact on the meaning of commodities and their associated femininity. [Thus] retailing is uniquely suited to an analysis of the links between femininity, place and commodities' (p. 296). In her own empirical study of Woodwards, a department store in downtown Toronto, Dowling shows how contradictory discourses of familialism (women as wives and mothers) and modernity (the superiority of scientific rationality) led to a particular notion of the feminine consumer in changes in the design and management of the store's food section in the period between 1945 and 1960.

In Britain, there is a growing collection of studies in what has been termed the 'new retail geography' and by other social scientists looking at the construction of gendered identities, of both consumers and retail assistants (see, for example, Michelle Lowe and Louise Crewe's (1996) work on The Gap and Paul Du Gay's (1996) case studies of the construction of hybrid subjects in clothing stores), in which the distinctions between leisure and work are blurred. In the new work, however, the fluidity of gendered identities, rather than the differences between women and men, are explored in particular circumstances. Indeed, at the end of the twentieth century, consumption, advertising and shopping have become identified as the essence of postmodernity, in which spectacle and desire combine to produce fluid subjects who are ambiguously gendered. As Simpson (1994) and Mort (1996), among others, have shown, the idealized male body is now as much an object of the male (both homoerotic and straight) gaze as the female body, and shopping has become an ambiguously gendered activity. However, as Wilson pointed out and I noted earlier, the flâneur himself more than a century earlier was a decentred and irresponsible subject, perhaps the forerunner of the new postmodern subject that is coming into being at the turn of the millennium.

Out (of place) in the open

I want now to illustrate a different aspect of the relationship between place, femininity and leisure, by looking at women's relationship to the 'great outdoors'. As the social construction of gender has been so bound up with a public/private distinction, it raises questions about a woman's place in the countryside and in the semi-rural parks and other green spaces in cities and on the urban fringe. I have shown, in chapter 2, how women's participation in particular sporting activities tends to be based on assumptions about decorum and the lack of physicality in the construction of ideal feminine bodies. Here I want to change the emphasis and focus on active and physical pleasures, looking specifically at questions about the place of women in the British countryside and in recreational woodlands on the urban-rural fringe. First we turn to the work of the British geographer Jacquelin Burgess and her colleagues (Burgess 1996; Burgess et al. 1988; Harrison and Burgess, 1994) and then to the specific responses of women of colour to the British countryside illustrated by photographer Ingrid Pollard.

For a number of years Burgess and her colleagues have explored the social and cultural dimensions of attitudes to and the use of a range of open spaces in southern England, including urban parks and semi-wild areas such as marshlands and recreational woodlands on the urban fringe. Gender, age and ethnic differences were explored in their work. Both the men and the women whom they interviewed for their research expressed fears of sexual attack: the women were fearful for their own safety, the men for their women friends and family – although official Home Office statistics show that teenage boys are actually the group most vulnerable to personal assault in public spaces. At the same time, however, young men, especially when gathered in large numbers, are also seen as threatening by other people. Burgess found that for Asian and Caribbean women the fear of racial attack

163

from gangs of white men and/or youths inhibited their use and enjoyment of woodland areas even when they visited in family groups. So as we found in urban parks, like Tompkins Square in New York City, 'community' spaces are dominated by certain groups who exclude others, either by their actual behaviour or by the implicit threats that their presence poses.

While participation in rural activities such as woodland walks raises questions about safety for all women, for women of colour there is a further and more complex issue to explore, related to the representation and meaning of the British countryside, and to their exclusion from these representations. Although the meaning of landscapes is mobile and changing (think, for example, of the representation of the Lake District as barren and forbidding in the eighteenth century compared with its contemporary idyllic majesty), representations of the countryside are bound up with images of the nation. The protection of Britain's countryside is seen as part of the preservation of a national heritage. Indeed, the association is often specifically with an idealized version of England, rather than nation as a whole. One of the significant institutions in this field, for example, is the Council for the Protection of Rural England (CPRE). But as Paul Gilroy has pointed out, images of Englishness, of being British, exclude black British citizens: 'there ain't no black in the Union Jack' (Gilroy 1987). The celebration of, for example, 'Constable country' – rolling acres in rural Suffolk – or the greensward of 'Shakespeare's England' is based on a cultural heritage that denies slavery and racism (Malik 1992). (A more general discussion of the representation of nationality and its exclusions in literature may be found in Edward Said's *Culture and Imperialism* (1994), and I shall discuss the connections between gender and national identity in the next chapter.)

In Britain the black population is specifically urban-based, living predominantly in the larger cities of the UK: in 1991, according to the census, no less than half of all non-white people lived in Greater London. In an exhibition called *Pastoral Interludes*, first shown in 1984, the black artist Ingrid Pollard (1989) explored her relationship to the British countryside in a series of captioned photographs. Pollard was born in Guyana in the 1950s but came to England as a small girl. Phil Kinsman, a geographer at the University of Nottingham who is interested in the social construction of the countryside, interviewed Pollard in 1992 and has published both a working paper and an article, which I have drawn on here (Kinsman 1993, 1995). This is how Kinsman describes the exhibition:

> [It] consists of five tinted pictures of black figures, both male and female, in rural landscapes, accompanied by a text which speaks of a sense of dread in visiting the countryside, of not belonging, of a threat of violence, even death, and of the history of slavery which brought black people to Britain.

The title is of course ironic, and refers to the whole area of the pastoral ideal in English culture ... Pollard attributes *Pastoral Interludes* to her personal holiday experiences, a particular conversation with a black friend about black people confining themselves to some parts of England and the complex readings of some viewers of early showings of the pictures. They saw in them metaphors of exclusion – barbed wire and stone walls – which she had not at first intended to be their content. (1995: 301–2)

Pollard suggests that black people's experience of the British countryside is as 'a landscape of fear': a concept used by feminist geographers describing the general experience of women (Pain 1991) and lesbians in particular (Valentine 1990). Interestingly, however, both Pain and Valentine focused on urban rather than rural environments. Pollard's critique of the country-side depends on an examination of the social construction of black British identities. According to Kinsman,

She testifies that it is not considered to be part of the black experience to visit the countryside, and if it is to be visited, there are barriers of confidence to be overcome. She stresses that going to the countryside is a cross-cultural activity, that there is a country code that has to be learned, which proves to be a barrier to black people. Although there are also very material barriers preventing black people going to the countryside, much of what prevents them is indeed ideological, and a part of this is how black senses of identity are perceived in relation to the countryside. (1995: 307).

Stuart Hall, a renowned British sociologist, born in Jamaica, has argued that experiences of alienation from the land and a sense of not belonging, either to Britain or to the Caribbean, are a common experience for mi-grants. I shall discuss this experience in more detail in chapter 8 where questions of displacement and the formation of diasporic identities will be considered. Although Pollard concentrated explicitly on race in her work, in the reactions to the exhibition she recorded she noted that working-class people and white middle-class women found echoes of their own experi-ences in her photographs. This illustrates the complexity of the ways in which class, race and gender divisions both divide and unite groups in their experiences of different places.

Gendered beaches

The main alternative to the countryside as a public site of leisure is the seaside, and specifically the beach. With the rise in living standards and average wages, and improvements in mass transport during the twentieth century large numbers of people in the 'West' travel annually to the edge of continents to take a break from their regular routine. As I have argued in this and previous chapters, assumptions about sexuality – the appropriate relations between the sexes and their permitted visibility – are writ large in the built environment. Explicit and implicit rules and regulations about whose bodies are permitted in which spaces and the interactions between them are set into the nature and form of buildings, the spaces between them and their internal divisions. In all but exceptional cases and places, these regulations are based on heterosexual social relations and women's assured inferiority. Perhaps the most visible display of hegemonic sexuality in the public arena is on the beach and in its associated holiday developments. Here, in that liminal place between the land and the sea – literally a place on the edge – the sets of binary associations that structure Western social relations are made visible, and in some cases trangressed.

The beach is a place of freedom, where the usual (for holiday makers, at least) division of life between work and home is totally or partially disrupted. Here, in a space between land and sea, the boundary between nature and culture is also fluid. At low tide, the beach may be 'civilized' with chairs, rugs, food and games equipment, but this colonization is fragile and temporary and all signs of it are washed away twice daily. On this anomalous strip, other signs of the civilized side of the nature–culture divide are also challenged, as the temporary occupants strip away many of the signs of their class position with their clothes; they are reduced merely to bodies of various shapes and signs, and pleasure becomes primarily a physical, rather than cerebral, experience. Fiske, in a paper entitled 'Reading the beach' (in Fiske 1992), suggests that the following list of binaries is challenged by the anomalous categories of the beach (p. 57; 'bathers' in the list refers to swimming costumes):

A	*Anomalous category*	*Not A*
SEA	Beach	LAND
NATURE		CULTURE
NAKED	Topless/Bathers	CLOTHED
FUR	Tan	SKIN
SWIMMING	Surfboard	BOATING
FISH	Scuba	MAN
ANIMALS	Pets (dogs)	MAN

The use of 'man' is perhaps a little irksome in these divisions.

There is one binary category, however, which is not challenged on the beach. Gender differentiations, of course, loom even more significant on stripping, as the beach becomes a display of sexuality and a locus dominated by the gaze. Above all, beaches are arenas for looking (indeed doing more is often explicitly forbidden by notices of public by-laws): men look at women, women at women, men at men, women at men, and adults at children. In all but the exceptional locations, however, it is the heterosexual male gaze that dominates the displays, although beaches are often distinguished by the dominance of a certain group – the surfers' beach by young men, for example, or a family beach by adults and children. In his paper, Fiske, a sociologist working in Australia, perhaps not unsurprisingly chose to focus on the sexist nature of the surfers' culture.

> The surfboard is perhaps the perfect example of a category anomalous between nature and culture. It is carefully designed, with a scientific approach to the placement of fins and shape of the hull, yet it is also the most minimal object that enables man to float on the sea [that man again, but as we shall see in a moment, this time Fiske means exactly that]. . . . As befits its anomalous status, the surfboard is both sacred and taboo. To the surfie it is an object of near worship, and there are strong taboos that prevent girls, or the too young or the too old, from riding it.

Fiske continues:

> we are not interested here in a Freudian reading of the surfboard with male sexuality, but it is worth remarking on the sexist nature of most youth subcultures, where male and female behaviour is clearly distinguished, and where males are active and dominant and females passive and subordinate. Vans, motorbikes and surfboards are conventionally driven/ridden by males and the size, skill, decoration involved in them is part of the male status order. Females are passengers, spectators, there to be won, possessed, flaunted by the male. Surfers' writing mingles accounts of mastering waves with ones of easy mastery of girls. They have an exclusive language for each . . . but the key term is hunting, which applies equally to waves and females. Hunting is where man first denotes his mastery over nature: it is the prerequisite of cooking, which, in turn, becomes the resonant metaphor for the process of culturizing nature. And consequently it is seen as a natural activity – man hunting for food, hunting for females, hunting for waves is man behaving 'naturally' because he is acting according to his bodily needs. (1992: 60)

Thank goodness for the inverted commas round naturally. Fiske seems so taken with the masculinity of surfers in his discussion of their attitudes and language that I felt he almost believed their arguments about the 'naturalness' of women's passive and inferior position.

If you are interested in a further exploration of some of the reasons for the sexist rituals among youth subcultures, you might turn to my social geography reader *Undoing Place?* (McDowell 1997b), where I have reprinted studies of, among others, bikers and mods, and to the edited collection by Skelton and Valentine, *Cool Geographies* (1997).

Conclusions

In this chapter it has become clear that there is a series of complex relationships between gender, sexuality and space. The divisions and associations are more complicated than a simple binary division between the public and the private, where each sphere is associated respectively with men and with women. Instead there are complex and paradoxical associations between gender and locale, between identity and particular places, for men as well as women. For both sexes, the city and its public spaces are associated both with fear and with delight, with danger and heady freedoms, whereas the beach is an anomalous space. Definitions of gender, identity and place, as well as the relationships between them, have always been more fragmented, complex and fluid than suggested in some of the earlier feminist analyses and in conventional liberal theory. The particular division between the workplace and the home, the city and the suburbs, private family life and the public arena that was established in the industrial revolution in 'the West', made concrete in nineteenth-century cities – and which perhaps reached its apotheosis in the urban areas of the US and UK in the 1950s – was always cross-cut by a more fractured set of lines and divisions than has sometimes been recognized in theoretical analyses.

Further, urban space itself is not just the straightforward, legible or scientific space of the urban planners and cartographers. It is also constructed through sets of myths and representations which are given meaning by everyday spatial practices, as De Certeau (1988) and Lefebvre (1991) have suggested. Spaces have different meanings for different groups, and each space may, over the course of a day, a week or longer, be occupied by a series of different social groups whose practices imbue the same spaces with different meanings at different times. The street and the park, for example, in the day and in the evening, or the holiday resort in and out of season, are different spaces in practice, in the everyday experiences of those who live in and use them.

At the end of the twentieth century, the profound reorganization of space and time that is taking place, albeit unevenly, through the development of global communications and information technologies has, for some at least, prised social relations and gender divisions free from the hold of specific locales, recombining them across huge space-time distances in hitherto unforeseen ways. These changes, migrations and movements – of capital, people and ideas – have placed new questions about the spatialization of everyday life at the centre of contemporary social theory in a wide range of disciplines. Thus geographic concerns have become central questions for the millennium. In the penultimate chapter I shall turn to some theoretical and empirical questions about the effects of movement, travel and displacements, but first, in chapter 7, I want to leave the scale of the city and address some of the relationships between gender and the nation-state.

Further reading

Mapping Desire by David Bell and Gill Valentine (1995) was perhaps the first collection of papers by geographers that seriously considered the multiple geographies associated with different sexualities. It includes papers about lesbian and gay relationships in a range of locations, as well as discussions of strategies of resistance. Frank Mort's *Cultures of Consumption* (1996), drawn on in this chapter, is an excellent excavation of the history of Soho. The fictional portraits of the Castro district in 1980s San Francisco by Armistead Maupin (1980, 1984, 1986) that I mentioned in chapter 4 provide an insight into 'alternative' life in that city, whereas Frances Fitzgerald's discussion of the same area in her book *Cities on the Hill* (1986) is a more serious look at the same area. They are relevant to the material discussed here as well as that in the earlier chapter.

Lifestyle Shopping, a collection of papers edited by Rob Shields (1992), includes a range of chapters on different types of spaces of consumption and draws on ideas from Henri Lefebvre, Michel Maffesoli, Walter Benjamin and Mikhail Bakhtin; it might be useful for readers interested in the current relevance of the work of these 'great men'. On the lure and power of advertising, however, it is hard to beat Judith Williamson's journalism. *Consuming Passions* (1985) is a collection of her pieces from newspapers and journals such as *New Society* in the 1980s. David Bell and Gill Valentine's recent book *Consuming Geographies* (1997) is an interesting assessment of the relationship between location and eating. The collection edited by Rosa Ainley (1998) includes papers on a wide range of public spaces including open space in London, shopping centres in New Zealand, dance halls in Kingston, Jamaica, and real and virtual streets in California. Finally Neil Wrigley and Michelle Lowe's book *Retailing, Consumption and Capital: Towards the New Retail Geography* (1996) is, as the title indicates, a collection of papers by the 'new' retail geographers.

169

7

Gendering the Nation-State

Introduction

In one of the case studies in the last chapter, I showed how images of the land – in that case the English countryside – are bound up with representations of nationality. Here I want to focus in more depth on questions about the representations of nation-states and unpack the ways in which they are linked to gendered meanings and ideologies, as well as to rules about the inclusion or exclusion of certain groups of women and men. As in the previous chapter, the relationships between 'race' or ethnicity and gender become particularly significant here, as nations are usually defined in terms of the links between a particular space or territory and its peoples to the exclusion of 'others'. There is also a second set of issues about the nation-state that I want to address in this chapter and that is the way in which its institutions and regulations define women as different from men and treat them accordingly. It will not surprise you, at this stage in the book, to discover that 'difference' also implies hierarchy and the inferior, or less equal, treatment of women. In both cases – representations and rights – questions about eligibility for and the rights of citizenship are important.

Feminist scholars have devoted a great deal of attention to investigating the relationships between gender and the nation-state and have produced two interconnected literatures about nation-states and the ways in which their institutions and practices are based on a public/private distinction. In the main, the focus here is solidly on the public side of the dichotomy, although as I shall show in my discussion of state institutions, their actions also affect the relative rights of men, women and children in their so-called private lives, in, for example, the regulation of sexuality or health care. (As you may recall from chapter 2, Foucault argued that the regulation of the body was a key aspect of the development of biopower as a mechanism of control in modern societies.)

The first set of feminist literature about the nation-state that I shall introduce in this chapter revolves around the relationship between the state and civil society and the actions of the state as a judge between citizens in its distributional and coercive policies. We might divide this literature itself into two connected areas. The first one is primarily concerned with women's rights as citizens, especially their formal rights, of which the right to vote has perhaps received the most attention. In the development of state institutions from the Enlightenment onwards, participation in state decision-making and in party political actions – politics in the formal sense – was, in general, considered appropriate for men and less so for women. Women, as a group, have been regarded as inferior to men and have had to struggle, first for suffrage or formal representation, and later for the recognition of a whole range of issues relevant to their lives and needs as women as political issues. In these struggles a predominantly rights-based politics has dominated in which women demanded equal treatment compared with men.

More recently, and especially in the 1980s and 1990s, questions of citizenship or economic justice have been, to some extent, replaced by a politics organized around questions of identity rather than access to rights. Religious fundamentalism, cultural revival and ethno-nationalism within states, as well as the recognition of different interests among women based on, say, age, race or sexual preferences, have brought to prominence a set of discourses, political struggles and social movements centred on the question of identity. Older political divisions, especially those based on class interests and, although to a lesser extent, gender divisions, have been superseded and a politics of difference has replaced that of equality or assimilation. I shall discuss the philosophical basis of this politics in more detail below.

The second set of issues that falls into my first category of feminist interest in the formal institutions of the state concerns women and the welfare state. As women have traditionally taken the major responsibility for their families' health, since they give birth and also live longer than men, they are the major clients of health services and welfare benefits, and in addition are key workers, especially in the more menial positions, in health services. Through these welfare institutions and through the legal system, therefore, 'private' issues of sexuality, childbirth and the management of health are regulated and controlled.

The second major category of feminist analyses of the links between the nation and gender has a rather different focus. Unlike the two sets of studies in the first category, which draw on political theory and focus on social practices, this second category combines its political focus with more recent analyses in feminist and critical cultural and literary studies of

171

images, symbols and representations of the nation in text, pictorial form and of the iconography of the built environment. Issues such as the construction of national identities, and the symbolic meaning of homeland, the mother country and/or the fatherland – both at times of crisis and in the longer term – have been studied, examining the gendered imagery of nationality and the links between nationalities and sexualities (Parker et al. 1992; Radcliffe and Westwood 1996; Yuval-Davis 1997). Here some of the questions raised by identity politics merge into questions about the gendered symbolism of the state in the struggle of post-colonial and post-imperial peoples against their earlier histories. The recent resurgence of so-called religious fundamentalism and of ethnic nationalism also raise interesting questions for feminist scholars as they depend so heavily on gendered views of the state and the nation and on gender-specific social practices.

What is the nation-state?

The first task, however, is to attempt to define the state and the nation. Here too there is a large body of literature in which the definitions are linked to alternative theoretical perspectives. While there is general agreement that the state is a group of institutions comprising the legislative, judicial and executive arms of government, as well as the police and armed forces, there is disagreement about in whose interests the state acts. For Marxist political theorists the state is an institution acting in the interest of capital, although there is scope here for contested interests of different fractions of capital – between financial or industrial capital for instance. (Will Hutton, in his popular book about the British state, *The State We're In* (1995), argues, for example, that the British state favours the interests of finance capital at the expense of industrial capital, especially in comparison with the German state.) Pluralist theorists argue instead that the state represents the interests of a wide range of interest groups, differing only on their views of how conflicting interests are resolved by argument to achieve either a consensus or an alliance of interests. Others suggest that because the set of institutions embedded in the term 'the state' are so many and varied, it is impossible to actually define and theorize the notion of 'a state' at all and instead the diverse policies and practices of that wide set of institutions relevant to particular issues should be the focus of analysis.

For feminists the important issue to address is the extent to which these institutions act in the interests of men and masculinist power. Although this focus on a diverse set of institutions is the way that some of the research about gender and the state has proceeded in practice – examining suffrage campaigns, for example, or the impact of welfare payments on certain groups of women – I want to suggest that it is useful to retain an idea of the state, because it provides the link between state and nation and so allows us to address questions about the social construction of nationalism and nationality and the ways in which they draw on gendered ideologies, symbols and systems of representation. The state is, therefore, that set of institutions that governs a particular territory and the people who live within its boundaries, although there are stateless nations whose connection to a particular land or territory remains disputed. Palestine is the most obvious example at the present time, but there are also examples where new or emergent nations are disputing their rights of occupation. I shall turn to questions of statelessness and displacements of different kinds in the next chapter.

The boundaries of nation-states, of course, change over time and may or may not enclose a physically contiguous territory. In the same way, a nation-state is not a permanent and unchanging entity, as has been vividly demonstrated at the end of the twentieth century when the former Soviet Union and former Yugoslavia have fractured into numerous nation states. Nation-states themselves are multiple and changing entities, with diverse intentions which have varied effects. And, as Yuval-Davis and Anthias remind us in their introduction to an interesting collection of papers about gender and the nation-state, an explicitly feminist analysis of the role of the state 'involves looking at the specific political projects of states and the economic and social context within which they are articulated as well as the social forces that both construct and oppose them' (1989: 6).

In this chapter I focus first on the policies of the state, especially its welfare policies and the ways in which they construct, define and affect women's sense of themselves, their place in society and their lifetime opportunities. It is here – in welfare policies that, for example, define women's dependence on men, the regulation of sexuality for men and for women, women's rights to bear children and the responsibilities of different household members – as well as in legal or formal citizenship rights, that the clearest indication of gender relations in different nations is to be found, and as I indicated in the introduction, there is a large body of feminist research revealing their structure. I shall discuss some of this, and then turn to the work on national symbolism and gendered representations. The local state – those practices and institutions that operate at a subnational level – also affects gendered social relations, as I indicated in chapter 3 where we looked at the specific example of women's initiatives, and indeed, many of the policies and practices of the nation-state are administered locally. In this chapter, however, I want to focus on the level of the nation as a whole rather than its local institutions.

173

Defining citizenship: equality and difference

One of the most significant arenas of feminist theorizing and practical politics has been in struggles to extend citizenship rights to women and attempts to adjudicate the competing claims of equality and difference. As feminist historian Sally Alexander has argued, feminism has always revolved around a tension between 'the pleas for equality and the assertion of sexual difference' (1987: 162). For early feminists involved in suffrage campaigns, a commitment to women's equality with men was the overriding aim, although differences between the sexes were also recognized in, for example, campaigns around maternity and child health provisions. But however simple a statement of the desire for equality may seem to be, what still remains to be defined is exactly what form this equality should take.

In the late nineteenth century and the early part of the twentieth century, in suffrage campaigns in Britain, other West European countries and the US, it was taken for granted that equality with men was the aim. Women wanted access to the advantages they perceived were available only to men, and their view of the desired form of equality was women's equal representation and participation in the public arena – in the worlds of work and formal politics, for example. Full suffrage was finally achieved by women in the US in 1920 and in Britain by 1928 but this did not bring with it equality with men in all 'public' arenas. In Cambridge University, for example, women were not officially awarded degrees until 1948 and, as I argued in chapter 5, equal pay for women remains elusive in virtually all sectors of employment in all economies. The rate of change in women's acquisition of civil and political rights is spatially uneven between countries, and in several parts of the world women have yet to gain the vote or equal rights to participate in the formal or public political arena. The maps in the *Women in the World Atlas* (Seager and Olson 1986; Seager 1997) provide interesting comparisons of the status of women in different nation-states in the early 1980s.

The distinction between the public and private spheres is, as you are aware, a key binary division in Enlightenment thought and liberal theory, and one which feminist scholars and activists have taken great trouble to deconstruct and displace. It is a distinction that lies at the heart of arguments about formal equality and has been both a great strength for women in their achievement of the vote and *de jure* equality, as well as an obstacle in their struggles to achieve *de facto* equality. Let's examine this contradiction in more detail.

In the transition to the modern order in Western Europe during the Enlightenment, a whole range of conventional privileges were dismantled and the origins of the modern democratic state were established. Unevenly over time and space, the divine right of kings was challenged and individualism emerged as a theory of social life in which the equality of individual citizens was asserted. As Carole Pateman has argued, 'neither liberalism nor feminism is conceivable without some conception of individuals as free and equal beings, emancipated from the ascribed, hierarchical bonds of traditional society' (1987: 103), although, as she also shows, feminists have disagreed with liberals about the boundary between the public and the private, as well as mounting a more thoroughgoing critique of liberalism in their later work. If liberals asserted the primacy of the individual then some way had to be found to justify women's exclusion from equal rights and it is here that the public/private distinction was essential.

The theoretical basis was provided in John Locke's *Second Treatise* (see Laslett 1967), in which the family was distinguished from civil society (civil society is commonly defined to include those institutions and practices that are related to but distinct from the particular organizations of the state: the education system and organized religion, for example), and political power was defined to include the rule of husbands over wives, having a 'foundation in nature' as men are 'the abler and stronger'. This 'natural' subordination, Locke argued, is based on ties of sentiment, and blood. Thus ascription and affection distinguished the family from the public sphere, where associations between free individuals were, it was asserted, based on universal and impersonal characteristics, characteristics that seemed to be confined to men. Thus women, as wives and daughters, were excluded from the 'public world of equality, consent and convention' (Pateman 1987: 106), which, contrary to assertions in liberal theory, rested on patriarchal privilege or what, in modern liberal states, Carole Pateman terms 'fraternity'. In a fraternity, men rule over women in the private domain, but agree a 'contract' which provides for social equality between men in the public domain (Pateman 1988).

As I have shown earlier, the historical development of capitalism during the nineteenth century led to a visible sexual divide as women married and were excluded from the labour market. Locke's exclusion of the family from civil society, and so the exclusion of women from civil rights, remained unquestioned as it seemed so 'natural'. Although later liberals, John Stuart Mill among them, accepted that women were not lesser beings and should not automatically be excluded from participation in public affairs, a 'separate but equal ideology' was constructed. Civil society was defined as consisting of a public and a private domain; it was maintained that women chose their role in the latter as wives and mothers and so had power and fulfilment in this private arena. These arguments still have force today in some quarters.

175

Equality and equal rights for women

Liberal theory was clearly vulnerable to feminist assertions that women as rational individuals should have equal rights to participate in the public sphere. It was especially open to attack on the grounds of women's denial of the right to vote and here important arguments were mounted by the developing suffrage movements in Western democracies at the end of the nineteenth and into the twentieth centuries. Indeed, the establishment of formal equal rights for women and men remained an important organizing position in Western feminist movements in the postwar era; it lies behind such legislation as the Sex Discrimination Act and the Equal Pay Act introduced in Britain in the 1970s, and the Equal Rights Amendment passed in the United States in 1967, where previously the Civil Rights Act had referred only to racial difference.

A range of institutions in Britain from universities to local authorities, have adopted equal opportunities policies, and political parties have begun to bow before the demands from women for more equal representation. In 1997, 120 women were elected to the House of Commons, for example. However, the Labour Party's short-lived policy of women-only selection lists of parliamentary candidates in certain constituencies was declared illegal and abolished. This illustrates one of the most vexed issues raised by liberal equal opportunities policies. By what method is the aimed-for equality to be put in place? How is women's equal representation in a range of arenas to be achieved?

In the United States, positive discrimination in university entrance policies was introduced through the mechanism of quota systems to achieve the desired ratio between, say, women and men, or people of colour and white people within a reasonable timespan. In the 1990s, however, positive discrimination has been challenged in a number of US states, including Texas and California, and, significantly, in these states student recruitment to universities is again biased in favour of white people. The arguments used in both countries to challenge a quota system is that it is unjust not to appoint or recruit the 'best person for the job'.

Here we reach the second dilemma for liberals. What does 'best' person mean? How are criteria of judgement between people established? Are they fair? It is now well established that most evaluative schemes have built-in biases. As feminist analysts of job evaluation methods have pointed out those schemes that value assertiveness or decisive action tend to reward skills that are socially constructed as masculine. Similarly, if the sole basis for university entrance is examination scores, students who have attended 'good' schools in 'good' neighbourhoods often perform to a higher stand-

176

ard, leading to a bias towards students from middle-class backgrounds and, in many cases, private schools. As all geographers know, there are spatial associations between social class and income, residential location and school attainment scores, so that, as Harvey (1971) argued long ago and I outlined in chapter 4, cities are mechanisms for 'the redistribution of real income' in ways that exacerbate inequalities between the social classes.

The third, and related, dilemma for equal opportunity or liberal feminists arises when the question 'equality with whom?' is posed. As Anne Phillips noted, 'a commitment to sexual equality does not of itself tell us what shape that equality should take. Equal pay for the jobs men do or equal shares in the jobs done by men? Equal opportunities to compete with men or numerical equality in each sphere of life? Equal responsibilities for housework and child care or better conditions for women at home?' (1987: 1–2). Each of the policies I have mentioned, for example, is based on a different set of assumptions. A quota system assumes numerical representation, whereas Britain's Equal Pay Act was based on an assumption that the pay for the jobs that women did should be equal to that for jobs done by men. The Act has had a limited impact on pay differentials, however, because, as we saw in chapter 5, men and women are highly segregated in the labour market and do different types of work. A more appropriate way, therefore, to move towards greater equality might be to recognize the differences between men and women and the different jobs they do and take these into account.

Equality and sexual difference

The limitations of the liberal assumption that we are all ungendered individuals has long been recognized by feminist theorists. Indeed, that most radical difference, women's ability to bear children, has been adduced as (part of) the basis of women's inequality. Unless women's role in reproduction is taken into account in the policies and practices of institutions, then women will never be able to compete on an equal basis with men, if that is the desired policy aim. In certain arenas, of course, difference is taken into account: in, for example, the right to maternity leave and maternity pay for women. In Great Britain this is a right at present open only to women who have been continuously employed by the same employer for two years. In some countries, men too have a right to parental leave on the birth of their child. But, in general, issues about the family are ignored in traditional equal opportunities policies. In the labour market, in particular, it is assumed that women are able to fit themselves into slots designed for men. Thus in the university system, for example, promotion is based

177

primarily on the number of publications an individual produces each year, regardless of whether a woman academic may have given birth recently.

The recognition of differences between people, whether on the basis of gender, age, ability or disability, or some other distinction, has led to attempts to reformulate notions of equality and social justice. Here the work of the feminist political theorist Iris Marion Young has been extremely influential. I have already introduced some of Young's work in chapter 2, where I outlined her analysis of the pregnant body. A number of geographers, including David Harvey (1992, 1996), Glenda Laws (1994), and myself (McDowell 1994d) have found her notion of justice based on inequalities between groups rather than individuals extremely thought-provoking. In her book *Justice and the Politics of Difference*, Young constructs a multiple definition of injustice or oppression to replace the belief that inequalities in the distribution of material goods and resources are the basis of injustice. Young draws on earlier arguments but adds to them ideas about social prestige, physical power, and stereotypes about idealized bodies. She argues that injustice takes a multiple form, consisting of 'five faces of oppression' that involve 'social structures and relations beyond distribution' (Young 1990b: 9). The five dimensions create hierarchical divisions between people by 'othering' an inferior group, that is by defining it as different from and inferior to the 'norm', which is, as you know now, a familiar idea from the literature on the social construction of gender.

The first of the five faces of oppression that Young distinguishes is *exploitation*, which involves the appropriation of the value of one group's labour by another, for example that of workers by capitalists or women's domestic labour by men. The second dimension is *marginalization*, the exclusion of certain people from useful participation in society, for example the elderly, disabled or unemployed. The third is *powerlessness*, defined as the lack of respect accorded to groups other than professional workers. The fourth dimension is *cultural imperialism*,which is a form of double exclusion in which the stereotyping of the views and experiences of certain groups constructs them as 'others' – who are then excluded by the universalization of the dominant group's experiences and culture as the norm. And the fifth is *violence*, which Young defines as random and unprovoked attacks that have no basis other than to humiliate the person who is their focus.

Young's work provides political theorists and political geographers with a powerful tool to think beyond divisions which have their basis in the allocation of material rewards in a capitalist society – whether between the social classes or between women and men – and to connect these to inequalities that have their basis in what we might term cultural norms. Here her final two faces of oppression are particularly significant. Young argues that a key mechanism of cultural imperialism is the confinement of 'others' within their bodies. Thus 'dominant discourse defines them in terms of bodily characteristics and constructs their bodies as ugly, dirty, defiled, impure, contaminated or sick' (1990b: 123). For women, conventional and idealized notions of beauty and desirability simultaneously 'render most women drab, ugly, loathsome, or fearful bodies' (p.123) and construct them as nothing but a body.

Young's work has parallels in feminist scholarship and in work about the nature of citizenship and the welfare state. In the first area, think back to Walby's definition of patriarchy in which she distinguished six distinct facets of women's oppression, based both in economic structures and cultural practices. Similarly, in an analysis of inequality in postwar Britain, the social policy expert Richard Titmuss (1987) outlined a threefold structure of inequality, based on the distribution of income, welfare state benefits and 'fringe benefits' in the workplace, including material goods such as cars and pension entitlements and the status, prestige and power to make personal decisions that is accorded to some people. Titmuss's work, however, remains solidly within the distributional model of inequality, despite his recognition of the multiple axes of inequality.

In both Young's and Walby's work, questions remain about the distinction between the different axes of oppression, their analytical separation and their equivalence (is each dimension equally significant?). What it is important to understand about Young's theory of oppression, however, is that it leads to a different view of politics from liberal models. Whereas distributional models of (in)justice demand an egalitarian politics of redistribution, a 'difference' version of justice leads to an emancipatory politics of recognition. Here we see the same dichotomy that has divided feminist politics throughout the twentieth century. Young constructs a powerful argument that the purpose of political struggle is not to abolish differences between groups but to accept and celebrate differences, which she believes must not be hierarchized.

This leads us to that huge and fiercely contested debate within geography at present, and indeed in the social sciences and humanities at large. Does an acceptance (even celebration) of difference necessarily lead to a formless relativism; to an inability to make judgements about the bases of difference and discrimination and their relative significance? Postmodern theorists line up on one side with activists in identity politics (usually a motley combination of women, gays, ecologists, greens, road protesters and others) against the adherents of a modernist belief in progress and of a continued belief that class divisions are of overwhelming significance in contemporary capitalist societies. David Harvey is perhaps the most notable

179

adherent of the second position among geographers, for despite his serious reading of the work of feminists and poststructuralists, he remains convinced that a geohistorical materialist explanation is superior, and he is disturbingly dismissive of feminist politics in places in his long and complicated book, *Justice, Nature and the Geography of Difference* (1996) (but see Young's response to this in *Antipode* (1998)).

In the former camp, the difference adherents, there is a wide range of views but general acceptance that although there is no singular basis of inequality, some differences are more important than others. Many social scientists have long recognized that 'race', gender and sexuality are all structural dimensions of oppression and political struggles against racism, sexism and heterosexism do not detract from class-based struggles. As the feminist theorist Nancy Fraser has recently argued in her consideration of class politics and identity politics: 'I refute the view that we must make an either/or choice between them ... The most philosophically satisfying approach is to develop a more general overarching conception of justice that can encompass both distribution and recognition' (Fraser 1997b: 127, and see also Fraser 1995). As she suggests, each approach to social justice (the Marxist liberal and the difference perspective) must range across both economic and cultural aspects, since cultural differences are both affected by and affect the operation of the economy. Indeed, as I outlined in chapter 5, one of the successes of feminist work on the economy has been to show the crucial importance of gender divisions in economic processes. And for all 'others', transformative redistribution surely is an essential aspect of recognition. Full participation in public life demands adequate economic resources. Indeed, the feminist political theorist Carole Pateman (1989) has suggested that individuals find it impossible to be full citizens of a modern state if they are short of money. She argues that some form of waged work or a basic minimum income is a prerequisite of modern citizenship.

The personal is political

It hardly needs to be spelt out following the preceding discussion of the significance of cultural norms (about the body and the recognition that violence is part of power) that feminists have also disputed a second distinction between the public and private that is central in liberal theory: that is the division between civil society and the private sphere. The idea, expressed in a 1960s feminist slogan, that 'the personal is political' has challenged both the definition of what is political and the basis of participation in the political arena. In a move that is now seen as the forerunner of identity politics, from the mid-1960s onwards women began to organize around 'private' issues of health and reproduction, childcare and domestic violence. These are issues that never used to be defined as political and certainly were not visible in political geography as it was defined in universities in the 1960s and 1970s. As feminist geographers and others have argued, Castells's definition of 'collective consumption' (that is the state provision of urban goods and services) not only meant the neglect of women's work in providing these services 'for love' in their homes (remember the arguments in chapter 3); it also meant that the increased reliance of the state throughout the 1980s on women's voluntary work, both in the home and in the community, which was the basis for 'rolling back the state' and the inaptly named 'community care' policy, was not adequately analysed.

Sylvia Walby, in her recent book *Gender Transformations*, has recently provided a succinct recap of the problems with Castells's notion of collective consumption and his allocation of feminist struggles to the broader category of 'new social movements':

> [Castells] does not adequately deal with the gendered nature of so-called collective consumption. . . . [His] major error arises from conceptualising the production of labour power as consumption rather than production. The use of the concept 'consumption' implies a failure to recognize that the work that women do in the home as domestic labour is work. The term signals 'leisure', not work. This is misleading . . . Castells ignores the extent to which the issues which he names as collective consumption, as part of the circuit of capital, are part of a patriarchal system. What is for Castells a movement from individual to collective consumption within capitalism, is a movement which radically transforms certain aspects of gender relations: one from privatised labour within a patriarchal mode of production to socialised labour outside of the patriarchal mode of production. Castells' failure to appreciate the significance of this gender dynamic means that he gives an incorrect specification of the structural changes which generate the 'new social movements' in terms of capitalism, not patriarchy. Further, he does not analyse the gendered nature of the forces pushing for and against these transformations, and his account of the historical specificity of these changes is incorrect. (Walby 1997: 143)

While I disagree with Walby's complete separation of capitalism and patriarchy – the so-called dual systems approach – I strongly support her conclusions. As I have argued elsewhere (McDowell 1991a), there are important contradictions in the ways in which women's waged, domestic and voluntary work is increasingly being relied on in recent transformations of the

181

economy and the welfare state. Walby is also helpful in her reminder that the feminist struggles around 'consumption' (aka domestic production) identified as one example of 'new social movements' by Castells are not new at all.

> Feminist attempts to socialise women's domestic labour have existed since first-wave feminism. . . . First-wave feminists campaigned for public provision for education, for the public feeding of school children, for nurseries, for the public provision of health care . . . [and] I would argue that these efforts by feminists constituted an important political force behind the development of the welfare state. (1997: 143)

Gender divisions, state institutions and spatial differences

Without too much misrepresentation, it is possible to allocate feminist research into the practices and policies of the state to one of three spatial scales: the international, the national and the local. A wide range of issues has been investigated, from the ways in which discriminatory citizenship policies exclude certain groups of women, to local differences in eligibility for services, as well as studies focusing on women's struggles to assert their identities.

Let us first look at questions at the international level. Here the work of Cynthia Enloe is deservedly well known. She has written widely on international politics and gender relations, including analyses of the role of the military and studies of international economic divisions and gender relations. Here I want to draw examples from her book *Bananas, Beaches and Bases: Making Feminist Sense of International Politics* (1989). While Enloe's book deals with widely accepted and well-defined issues in international politics – nationalist movements, diplomacy, military expansion and international debt for example – she addresses them from an unconventional and feminist standpoint, focusing on women rather than men as the international actors in these arenas. Her book includes studies of sex tourism, the gendered travel patterns related to the military, to the diplomatic service and to domestic service, as well as analyses of the significance of gender in the production, advertising and consumption of agricultural and industrial goods such as bananas and blue jeans. Her pioneering work has stimulated a large number of studies of similar issues by feminist geographers in the last few years.

Let's begin with a statement from the preface to *Bananas, Beaches and Bases* where she explains the thinking that led her to place women at the centre of the book.

182

I began this book thinking about Pocahontas and ended it mulling over the life of Carmen Miranda. Pocahontas is buried in Highgate Cemetery in London and Carmen Miranda has a museum dedicated to her in Rio. Neither is the usual starting point for thoughts about contemporary international politics, but each woman made me think in new ways about just how international politics works.

Pocahontas was a Powhantan Indian, the daughter of a tribal chief who acted as an intermediary between her own people and colonizing Englishmen; she later married one of these English settlers and travelled to London, as if confirming that the colonial enterprise was indeed a civilizing mission. She never returned to her New World homeland, however, for she died of civilization's coal dust in her lungs.

Carmen Miranda lived three centuries later, but her life has remarkable parallels with her Indian foresister's. She was a Brazilian grocer's daughter who became a Hollywood star and the symbol of an American president's Latin American policy. She died prematurely of a heart attack, perhaps brought on by the frenzied pace of life in the fast lane of America's pop culture.

These women are not the sorts of international actors I had been taught to take seriously when trying to make sense of world affairs. But the more I thought about Pocahontas and Carmen Miranda, the more I began to suspect that I had been missing an entire dimension of international politics – I got an inkling of how relations between governments depend not only on capital and weaponry, but also on the control of women as symbols, consumers, workers and emotional comforters. . . . Here I consider women-as-consumers, in both industrialized and Third World countries, as global political actors. Furthermore, as tourism demonstrates, companies and their government allies are marketing things not usually thought of as 'consumer goods': tropical beaches, women's sexuality, the services of flight attendants. (Enloe 1989: xi–xii).

These are the women that Adrienne Rich referred to as 'in the back row of politics' (quoted by Enloe, p. xii) but who have become increasingly visible as feminists redefine what is meant by the term 'political' and insist that tourism and childcare are just as worthy of academic attention as international statesmanship, financial flows and wars. And, as Enloe argues, if feminist studies can reveal the ways in which international politics and economics are 'dependent on artificial notions of masculinity, we can show that this seemingly overwhelming world system may be more fragile and open to change than we have been led to believe' (p. 17).

Domestic servants and world politics

Although I have already discussed domestic work in chapter 3, here I want to look explicitly at Cynthia Enloe's study of the significance of domestic workers in the international arena. You will remember from the earlier chapter that domestic service employed several million women in the industrial nations at the beginning of the twentieth century. By the 1950s, however, it seemed to have become a residual occupation. Changes in the economy during the first half of the twentieth century opened up better-paying work for working-class women, whereas their more affluent sisters seemed to have succumbed to the idea that being an unpaid housewife was their ideal lot in life. From the 1970s onwards, however, middle-class women entered the labour market in growing numbers and began to experience the double burden of waged and domestic work that working-class women had never relinquished.

There were various responses to this change, on a collective and an individual basis. Women influenced by the feminist movement began to organize publicly and privately. In the public arena they organized campaigns for increased state provision, especially of childcare facilities, whereas at home those of them with live-in male partners tried to encourage their increased participation in domestic tasks and childcare. Other women swallowed the concept of 'superwoman' that was around in the 1980s, trying to 'have it all', whereas yet others made the traditional compromises, by refusing promotion, for example, or working part-time. Women who were feminists agonized over a different option – the longstanding bourgeois practice of hiring other women to do their housework and to look after their children. It seemed a denial of claims of sisterhood to employ another woman in their home, but cutbacks in the already meagre state provision of childcare in the 1980s and 1990s seemed to leave no acceptable alternative for many women.

A significant proportion of the women who are currently employed as nannies, cooks and cleaners in industrial nations are in-migrants, either from an ex-colony or from a poorer, sometimes adjacent nation. In the United States, for example, many domestic workers are from Mexico and Central America (Romero 1992); in Canada domestic workers in some cities are often women from the Caribbean (England 1997; England and Stiell 1997), whereas in others, women from the Philippines are an important group in this labour market (G. Pratt 1997). Here is Enloe exploring the reasons that push poor women to migrate for employment in domestic service:

> Women seek domestic-servant jobs outside their own countries for many reasons. Whilst those reasons may be the result of distorted development – elite corruption, dependence on exploitative foreign investors, refusal to implement genuine land reforms – the women who emigrate usually speak in more immediate terms. They need to earn money to support landless

parents or an unemployed husband. They are the sole supporter of their children. They are afraid that if they don't emigrate they will have no choice but to work as prostitutes. They cannot find jobs in the fields for which they were trained. Civil war has made life at home unbearable. They have sisters and schoolmates who have gone abroad and promise to help them find work. They may be private calculations but they help governments trying to balance their trade and pay off their international debts. (1989: 184)

Remittances from workers abroad are a significant element in the earnings from exports in many poorer countries: in Pakistan, whose people (men and women) often work in states of the Middle East, India, Sri Lanka, the Philippines, for example, money sent back home accounted for between 20 and 50 per cent of foreign earnings in the 1980s. The latter two countries are those most dependent on remittances from female migrant labour. The legal position of women domestic servants varies between industrial countries but the conditions under which these women work are often extremely exploitative. In Great Britain, for example, a family who moves to live in Britain on a temporary basis may bring a Filipina maid with them, but she has no independent right of residence in the country. This ties her to a single employer. Similarly in Italy, women who enter on a tourist visa but wish to acquire a longer-term guest visa are tied to a particular employer. In many countries, women with only tourist visas are often employed illegally. In other cases, women may have no papers at all. In California, for example, many domestic servants are undocumented workers who have entered the US illegally and so are extremely vulnerable to exploitation.

Because domestic workers by definition are employed in the home, and often work long hours, they find it difficult to organize on a collective basis to improve their circumstances. However Enloe documents a number of initiatives. 'In the 1950s Toronto's Negro Citizenship Association established a hostel and meeting place so that Caribbean women working as domestic servants could talk to each other and, if necessary, escape an intolerable household' (Enloe 1989: 189–90). Recently in Los Angeles, an advocacy campaign called Superdomestica has been launched with racy advertising and drop-in advice centres.

But as Enloe emphasizes, the relationship between a woman domestic worker and her employer is never simply a personal one: there is not only the 'false kinship' identified by Gregson and Lowe (1994), but the relationship is also affected by the government's immigration regulations and its administration of them. In Canada in the 1980s a group of Caribbean and Filipina women formed a coalition to change the immigration laws so that foreign domestic workers on temporary visas would be better protected under labour law. In 1988 the Aquino government actually imposed a ban on all recruitment of Filipinas outside the country but many women argued that this was inappropriate because it both reduced their employment opportunities and failed to recognize their need for protection in the 'host' country. In Hong Kong, for example, a group called United Filipinos Against the Ban was formed. Gradually, the government relaxed its total ban with country after country, influenced by its continuing need for foreign currency.

The position of Filipinas in many countries remains problematic. In Britain, for example, there have been several court cases where employers have been found guilty of inhuman treatment or cruelty. A British feminist sociologist and novelist Michelle Stanworth has used such a case as the basis for a fictional investigation by her protagonist Laura Principal in her novel *Running for Shelter* (1995) (published under the name of Michelle Spring).

As Enloe emphasizes,

> immigrant domestic workers' relationships with each other and their employers are shaped in large part by political debates over immigration. These debates, so indicative of a society's own national identity and what it thinks of its place in the international system, are usually riddled with assumptions about male and female citizenship. Broadly speaking, many governments since World War II have acted as if an "immigrant worker" was male. An "immigrant's family" was composed of the wife and children of that male worker. This portrait does not match the facts, for governments have depended on immigrant women to work in hospitals, to clean office buildings, hotels and airports, to mind children and to operate sewing machines during the decades of post-war economic expansion . . . The facts notwithstanding, this portrait of a masculinized immigrant workforce encouraged policy makers to see restrictions on women immigrants as a means of preventing male immigrant workers from putting down roots. If a worker's wife and children could be kept in their home countries, the worker himself could be sent home when his economic utility waned. (1990: 190–1)

Enloe concludes her study of the international flows of domestic workers by a salutary reminder not to simplify the geography of this process. It is not solely affluent First World women who employ their poorer sisters: 'Literally hundreds of thousands of women from Third World countries are cleaning the homes and minding the children of other, more affluent Third World women.' In China, for example, and in many Latin American nations, domestic service is a significant occupation for 'native' women. Fascinating geographies of domestic employment are being uncovered, including evaluations of the success of different political campaigns to improve women's lives (England 1997; England and Stiell 1997; Pratt 1997).

Gender and rights at the national level

Enloe's concern with international issues has parallels in the work of the feminist theorists Nira Yuval-Davis and Floya Anthias, who together (1989) and separately (Yuval-Davis 1997) have worked on a range of questions in different societies about the connection between women and the nation state. Like Enloe, these researchers are interested in the ways in which women are included in or excluded from the rights of citizenship, as well as in the ways in which women 'reproduce nations, biologically, culturally and symbolically' (Yuval-Davis 1997: 2). Here feminist work has been important in uncovering a complex set of relations between class, gender and ethnicity (Blunt and Rose 1994; Moghadam 1994; M. L. Pratt 1992; Ware 1992). In a wide range of historical circumstances, in colonial, postcolonial and industrial societies where in-migration is significant, the ways in which class aspirations and racist fears have been crucial in distinguishing between women, and in constructing certain groups as less eligible, has been documented. As Enloe argued:

> British, American, Dutch, French, Spanish, Portuguese women may not have been the architects of their countries' colonial policies, but many of them took on the roles of colonial administrators' wives, missionaries, travel writers and anthropologists in ways that tightened the noose around the necks of African, Latin American and Asian women. . . . Without the willingness of 'respectable' women to see that colonization offered them an opportunity for adventure, or a new chance of financial security or moral commitment, colonization would have been even more problematic. (Enloe 1989: 16)

This interesting and painstaking historical work provides a powerful support for recent feminist arguments about difference and diversity, as well as raising often painful questions about women's political involvement in movements that oppress other women.

As well as analyses of the welfare state, recent feminist research has focused on additional questions of gender and nationality as the nation-state begins to seem increasingly fragile. One of the most marked features of the political landscape of the 1990s has been the significance of a range of social movements that have grown up to challenge the authority and legitimacy of national states and their practices of group exclusion on the grounds of race, religion, language or ethnicity. These movements often challenge the territorial basis of nation-states and may be based on sub- or supranational alliances – for example ethno-nationalism in middle Europe has resulted in the break-up of former nations into smaller groups, whereas other movements such as Basque or Kurdish nationalism cross state boundaries. In many of these social movements based on what might loosely be termed identity politics, questions about the family, the position of women and gender relations loom large.

Gender and welfare

When we turn to examine state legislation and administrative practices, we find a large body of research about the ways in which the state controls women's rights, especially in what might be broadly termed the welfare sphere. Feminist scholars and activists have long recognized that the institutions and policies of the welfare state have a huge significance in women's lives. As Yuval-Davis (1997) has observed, 'the struggle of women for reproductive rights has been at the heart of feminist struggles since the inception of the movement' (1997: 22). Rights to abortion and contraception, but also the right to give birth, have been central areas for feminist pressure, and there have been noticeable geographical variations in the existence of these rights in this century, related to nationalist ideologies and to the power of organized religion in different countries. Population policies are often a key way in which the state enforces its definition of nationality. Yuval-Davis writes:

> A central dimension of these policies would usually be, to a greater or lesser extent, a concern about the 'genetic pool' of the nation. Nationalist projects which focus on genealogy and origin as the major organising principles of the national collectivity would tend to be more exclusionary than other nationalist projects. Only by being born into a certain collectivity could one be a full member of it. Control of marriage, procreation and therefore sexuality would thus tend to be high on the nationalist agenda. When constructions of 'race' are added to the notion of the common genetic pool, fear of miscegenation becomes central to the nationalist discourse. (1997: 22–3)

The population policies and marriage bans of Nazi Germany (Koontz 1986), and the South African apartheid state are among the most notorious examples in this respect, but there are other examples. These include religious rules and prohibitions – for example, Jewish identity must be passed through the mother – and rules determining citizenship. In contemporary Britain, the so-called patriality rule means that for in-migrants full citizenship is restricted to those with a British grandfather. Yuval-Davis (1997: 27) quotes the 1970s case where a Ghanaian man claimed British citizenship on the grounds that his African grandmother was legally married to his British grandfather. His case was rejected by a judge who argued that in the period in question no British man would have legally married an African woman (WING 1985). In other cases, controls have been based on the desire to restrict the rate of population growth. The single-child policy of the Chinese state since the communist revolution is the best-known example here. In other (now former) communist nations, however, where the state worked to increase the population by raising birth rates, motherhood was revered and women with large families were rewarded. In the former Soviet Union, women with ten children were designated 'heroine mothers'. In France after the Second World War and in modern-day Israel, child allowances and generous maternity leave have been used to encourage women to have larger families (Abdo and Yuval-Davis 1995; Ehrlich 1987).

An alternative way to increase the population is through in-migration (DeLepervanche 1989), but in these settler societies, as they are known, there may be explicit or implicit hierarchies of desirability of origin which affect the position of women from different parts of the world. The 'white Australia' policy in the period after the Second World War is one example, and even though this policy has now been abolished, an implicit ethnic hierarchy remains in place (Stasiulis and Yuval-Davis 1995), as is the case in Israel. In Britain, frequently expressed fears about the birth rate among minority communities, combined with rhetorical images of floods and swamps, commonly raised by right-wing politicians (Margaret Thatcher as well as Enoch Powell), are other examples of the connections between origins, natality and nationality which result in a hierarchy of more and less eligible groups.

For and against the state

Feminist scholars have had a long ambivalence about the role of the welfare state and women's position. Early work (see for example, Wilson 1977) tended to emphasize the oppressive role of national welfare policies, not only in the ways I have outlined above but also through the effects of a range of other policies based on the assumption that women are dependent on men and that their key role is as a wife and mother. The assumptions behind the postwar welfare provisions introduced by William Beveridge in Great Britain in the 1940s have been widely cited as evidence for this argument. Thus in the 1944 White Paper that laid the basis for the postwar welfare state, it was argued that the task of married women was to rebuild family life, rather than to enter the labour market.

In the 1980s and 1990s a more complex understanding of the relationship between the welfare state and gender inequality has been developed by feminists as the ways in which state support is essential (albeit at inadequate levels) for certain groups of women – single mothers in particular – have been investigated, as well as the significance of welfare state institutions as employers of women (Fraser 1997b; Pateman 1989). As welfare policies have come increasingly under attack since the advent in the early 1980s of right-wing governments in the US and Britain committed to 'rolling back the state', it is important that feminist analysts develop and defend new arguments about the significance of welfare policies for women as part of the establishment of greater equality between women and men.

The notion that women's key role is in the family remained the basis of welfare policies in industrial nations until the 1980s. It is based on what has been designated an old 'gender order', (McDowell 1991a; Fraser 1994) that has begun to crumble in the last two decades. As I argued in chapter 4, the movement of women in increasing numbers in many countries into the social relations of waged work altered their position in the family and challenged old patriarchal notions. Add to this large-scale migration from country to city and to 'Western' nations, the rise of racist attitudes and behaviour, and the growing antagonism of the better-off towards redistributive policies – radically altered by the election of a Democrat as President in the US and a Labour government in the UK respectively, and it is clear that the social assumptions that lie behind the welfare institutions are not only being challenged, but in some cases, have been swept away.

Nancy Fraser has argued that the old gender order was based on the ideal of the family wage system (whereby a male breadwinner was able to support his dependants with his income from waged labour), which was inscribed in the structure of most industrial-era welfare states. These welfare states had

> three tiers, with social insurance programs occupying the first rank. Designed to protect people from the vagaries of the labour market (and to protect the economy from shortages of demand) these programs replaced the breadwinner's wage in the case of sickness, disability, unemployment or old age. Many countries also featured a second tier of programs, providing direct support for full-time female home-making and mothering. A third tier covered the 'residuum'. Largely a holdover from traditional poor relief, public assistance programs provide paltry, stigmatized, means-tested aid to needy people who had no claim to honorable support because they did not fit the family-wage scenario. (Fraser 1997b: 41–2)

In post-industrial capitalism, however, the nature of the family wage system has changed irretrievably, as has the structure of gender relations and the family. Casual, temporary and part-time work does not provide the basis of family support that old industrial, male work did, and at the same time women's position in the labour market and in the family has altered (McDowell 1991a). Families and households are also increasingly diverse (Stacey 1990).

For all these reasons, Fraser asserts, it is crucial that feminists engage in 'systematic reconstructive thinking about the welfare state' (1997b: 42). She demands hard thinking by feminists about the principle of gender equity that should lie behind the post-industrial gender orders that are coming into being in different ways in different nation-states, and about the various institutions of welfare that might support greater equity. Fortunately for us, she also proceeds to deconstruct two existing feminist responses to such a demand and to substitute a third alternative, albeit in my view (as I shall show in what follows) an extremely optimistic, but important, vision of the future.

Fraser suggests that, so far, it is possible to distinguish two alternative visions of future welfare provision in what might be broadly regarded as feminist literatures and practices in contemporary social democracies. These she terms the *universal breadwinner* model and the *caregiver parity* model. Fraser argues that the first vision is implicit in the current political practice of most US feminists and liberals, and, I would add, it is the view that informs the early statements of the British Labour government that was elected in 1997. In this model, gender equity is fostered through women's employment and employment-enabling welfare policies, such as day care for children. In the second model, on the other hand, more prominent in Western European countries other than the UK, improving women's status and achieving gender equity is aimed for through policies to establish the importance and parity of informal carework with waged labour. The major policy instrument is financial allowances for caregivers. These alternative models map on to the equality/difference distinction I outlined above.

While both models have their adherents, the implications, and costs, are large. The universal breadwinner model is impossible while gender inequalities in wages remain so pronounced, and the costs of establishing alternative care provisions to that of individual women's labour are huge. Similarly, unless the gender distribution of caregiving is challenged, it will remain a female 'ghetto' and parity of esteem will be difficult to establish, so undermining the caregiver parity model. Fraser's answer to this is a compromise or third alternative which she terms the *universal caregiver* model. In this model the best features of the other two are combined and both women and men are encouraged to do primary carework at different times in their careers. The aim is to 'induce men to become more like most women are now' (Fraser 1997b: 60). Greater gender equity would result

191

through measures which would 'make women's current life-patterns the norm for everyone' (p. 61). These would include a shorter working week than for current full-time jobs; employment support services provided not only in the family but also by the state and voluntary agencies in which all men, and not just those with dependants, would be encouraged, through incentives, to work.

The aim is to eliminate the gender coding of waged work and caregiving. As Fraser recognizes, this would entail 'subverting the existing gender division of labour and reducing the salience of gender as a structural principle of social organization. At the limit, it suggests deconstructing gender' (p. 61). Here we see an interesting convergence with arguments that are more common among feminists looking at cultural policies and body politics than at the welfare state.

Clearly, Fraser's aims are utopian in the current political climate. They require not only large-scale socioeconomic restructuring, and greater political control over private corporations, many of them operating in a global economy, but also new progressive taxation on incomes and wealth to fund new welfare provisions. At the current time, at the end of the twentieth century, when almost all industrial nations are attempting to cut their welfare spending and when punitive versions of workfare programmes are being considered in attempts to force individuals off their reliance on benefits and into the labour market, the prospect of such progressive restructuring looks extremely unlikely.

But Fraser is persuasive in her arguments that feminists must reclaim their ability to formulate utopian visions of gender equity appropriate to a post-industrial gender order, especially in the climate of tentative and provisional thought that seems to encapsulate the postmodern era. This is why her is work so stimulating; it reclaims some of the ground that socialist feminists attempted to make theirs in the earlier analyses of second wave feminism at the end of the 1960s, when the political climate seemed more hopeful. Feminism surely must continue to be differentiated from other variants of current theorizing by its recognition of the desire to change the current relationships between individuals and social collectivities in a more progressive direction.

Welfare provision and spatial variations

Despite the commonality of an assumption of the existence and desirability of a family wage system that informed postwar welfare reform in industrial capitalist nations, significant variations remain between and within nation-states, as Fraser's dual model of welfare provision makes clear. She is not alone in devising models of welfare provision and it is interesting to compare her work with that of Gosta Esping-Andersen (1990). While his model is not an explicitly feminist one, he does point to the significance of family values and religion in distinguishing between what he terms welfare regimes. He points out a range of differences between nation-states which have been significant in the ways in which their welfare policies have developed. These include the role of religion, the size and degree of centralization in the country, the extent of a middle class and of the power of workers' organizations, as well as the role of socially conservative institutions such as the church.

Esping-Andersen identifies three regimes. The first is the 'liberal' welfare state with its reliance on strict eligibility criteria for mainly means-tested benefits for low-income clients, and its encouragement of market provision. Here welfare is seen as a safety net and no more. The US, Canada and Australia, and increasingly Great Britain, fall into this category. The second is the 'updated corporatist-statist regime' with state provision to supplement family resources. Here women are clearly defined as dependants, encouraged to become mothers through some provision of family benefits, but day care for children is not usual. This model is common where religious observance remains important, and includes Austria, France and Italy. The third regime is the 'social democratic' model with universal provision of high-quality services. The aim is to socialize the costs of child-rearing and to cater for individual dependence. Here the distinction between welfare and work is fused and women are encouraged to work. Indeed it is a model that is dependent on full employment to fund the huge costs of welfare provision. Sweden is the state that most closely approached this model in the 1970s but it has since withdrawn from the full commitment to universal, non-market provision.

Although these regimes do not map exactly on to Fraser's threefold model – partly as her third option is an optimistic proposal which is still in the future – Esping-Andersen's second regime has some features of the caregiver parity model, and his social democratic regime is similar to the universal breadwinner ideal. There are also interesting parallels with Walby's distinction between private and public patriarchal regimes, the caregiver model emphasizing the continuing importance of care in the home, for example.

Geographers, however, in their research so far, have tended to focus in more detail on spatial variations within states, at the regional or local level, than on these differences between nation-states. Questions of the location of facilities and their accessibility from different catchment areas have been the focus of a great deal of work and sophisticated measures of accessibility which combine not only geographical but social distance have been developed. In an interesting study of state welfare provisions for the elderly in the US, for example, Glenda Laws examined the links between age, gender relations and spatial mobility, showing how state policies institutionalize restrictions on people's movement. As she notes:

> Unlike other forms of of social apartheid, segregation on the basis of age is formally (under the rules of law) recognized and enforced in the United States and many other parts of the world. Children cannot begin school until a certain age. Young adults cannot enter the spaces of bars and taverns until they reach an age determined by state legislation. A driver's license similarly requires that the holder has reached a legally defined minimum age. Criteria for entry into some forms of housing are based on age. So, while we condemn discrimination on the basis of a whole range of characteristics, discrimination on the basis of age continues to be protected by state-sanctioned legal statutes that are both cause and effect of social attitudes toward people of different ages. These statutes place restrictions on where an individual can go and, in the case of driver's licenses, on how one might get there. (Laws 1997: 47)

It is important to recognize, however, that these restrictions are often for the protection both of the individuals to whom they apply and for the wider community.

Laws unpicks the ways in which the sexed body, age and bodily appearance, restricted physical mobility and reduced eyesight, gender and income intersect with welfare policies based on particular views of 'the citizen' and 'normal' family life to produce gendered patterns of spatial mobility over the life course. Doreen Massey (1998) has also developed a similar argument through a moving case study of the increasing spatial restrictions that affected the daily lives of her elderly parents in a Manchester suburb.

Imagined communities and gendered images of the nation

So far in this chapter I have considered the material ways in which the various institutions of the state have both constructed and used gender divisions in ways that discriminate against women. I want now to turn to a brief discussion of how the nation-state itself is often rendered as gendered, embodying images of masculinity or femininity in its representations and symbols. In this section, therefore, the focus shifts from the material practices of the state and its differential treatment of men and women to the ways in which gendered language, imagery and artefacts are drawn on to construct a particular version of nationalism and national identity. The separation is not, of course, as clear-cut as I present it here. We have already seen how ideas about femininity and nationality affect, for example, the treatment of immigrant workers.

In *Imagined Communities*, a book first published in 1983 that has had a significant impact on geographical scholarship, Benedict Anderson argues that the modern nation-state is an ' "imagined political community" . . . imagined because the members of even the smallest nation will never know most of their fellow members, meet them, or even hear them, yet in the minds of each lives the image of their communion' (1991: 6). This communion was made possible by technological change, especially the development of the printed word, enabling the majority of the population to consume the texts and maps which construct this imagined nationhood. According to Anderson, all nations are *limited*,with finite if elastic boundaries (even the most expansionist states stop before wanting to dominate the world); *sovereign* (the concept itself is one from the age of Enlightenment and revolution which destroyed the idea of a divine right to rule); and a *community*, because 'regardless of the actual inequality that may prevail in each, the nation is always conceived as a deep, horizontal comradeship' (p. 7). Thus, in short, a nation is a cultural artefact, constructed through maps, flags, buildings, monuments, common customs, sport and political rhetoric in order to include its citizens in a common project.

While Anderson reveals many of the facets of how this imagined community is constructed and maintained, enabled to demand supreme sacrifices from its people, he ignores the significance of gender in his analyses. The very term horizontal comradeship, although theoretically gender-neutral, brings with it connotations of masculine solidarity. While I want to remedy Anderson's exclusion of gendered imagery and social relations, it is important to emphasize that class-based and ethnically differentiated images and languages are also part of the social construction of national identity, acting in the same ways as gendered symbolic structures to include certain groups and exclude others. Thus, as many fine analyses of the colonial and postcolonial state have shown (Bhabha 1990, 1994; Said 1978; Spivak 1987, 1988; R. Young 1995), the ways in which nations are represented and imagined are fluid and are made and remade under different historical circumstances.

I want to look at two examples here: first nationality and nationalism among Irish women living both in Ireland and on the British mainland, drawing from the work of Bronwen Walter (1995), Catherine Nash (1993) and Nuala Johnson (1995), and secondly, and more briefly, at national identities in contemporary Latin America, through the work of Sarah Radcliffe and Sallie Westwood (1996).

In work on ethnicity and identity in the United Kingdom, white migrants to the UK are often ignored. As we noted earlier Gilroy (1987) has asserted that, 'there ain't no black in the Union Jack.' But the social construction of Britishness, 'characterised as male, middle class, Home Counties, Anglican Protestant and white' (Walter 1995: 35), also racializes and excludes a range of other 'Others', including the Irish in Britain. Further, as Walter explores, the experience of gender cross-cuts nationality, so that not only 'are representations of Irishness and Britishness highly gendered constructions, but the material experiences of being a man or a woman within the Irish community or an Irish woman or an Irish man within British society are very different' (p. 35). In the construction of ethnic identities and material differences within and between groups, place makes a difference. Ethnicity is not an unchanging social characteristic but is rather fluid and context-dependent. As Stuart Hall noted, 'Far from being eternally fixed in some essentialised past, they [ethnic identities] are subject to the continuous "play" of history, culture and power' (1990: 225). Many Irish people in Britain are 'invisible' in the sense that their numbers are difficult to assess from official statistics in the census and because their whiteness means they are not immediately distinguishable as different from the majority British population. This invisibility is reinforced as the Irish in Britain are widely regarded as a 'suspect population' associated with acts of terrorism and so many people of Irish origins are anxious not to draw attention to themselves.

Irish identity is inextricably linked to religion, and two religio-ethnicities – Protestant and Catholic – are constructed and maintained through myths, stories, poetry and events that celebrate shared pasts and futures. In both cases, masculinity is an integral part of the construction of national identity through its associations with war and death. Women seldom appear as individuals: the statues and names on war memorials are almost always those of men. Women are not, of course, absent from the discourse of nationalism but are

> confined to the world of metaphor rather than active participation, [and to] forms of representation that confirm their disempowerment. The trope of the family is widespread in the figuring of national narratives – homeland, motherland, fatherland, daughters and sons of the nation. This imagery serves to naturalise a social hierarchy within an apparent unity of interests so that its gendered formation is unquestioned. (Walter 1995: 37)

As we saw earlier, this naturalization of the association of women with families and homes is also evident at the small-scale level of individual homes and urban land-use planning. The symbolic representation of the Irish nation as female is particularly strong: 'Mother Ireland' as a protective and suffering figure is a potent image in response to British imperialism. Yet public representations of female figures are often seen as transgressive or highly destabilizing (Loftus 1990), and as we have already noted, the association of women with the streets is often read as immoral.

In an interesting exploration of statues and monuments in contemporary Eire, Nuala Johnson (1995) drew this conclusion. In her survey she found that mythical and fictional figures of women outnumbered 'real' political and cultural figures. In Dublin, for example, a statue of a female character from James Joyce's *Finnegan's Wake*, Anna Livia Plurabella, was erected to symbolize the city and its river. This is how Johnson explains its reception: 'After its unveiling the statue underwent a series of renamings – "the floozie in the jacuzzi", "the whore in the sewer", "the skivvy in the sink" – a strategy by Dubliners to deflate the high-art pretensions of the monument itself, to cut it down to size so to speak' (1995: 57); but also a strategy which Johnson, quoting from A. D. Smith (1991: 11), argued reveals a ' "male role-shift from that of slave to master" in a postcolonial context'. The female figure of Plurabella 'invokes gender-coded stereotypes of woman in public space as whore, temptress, pollutant and [she is] scaled to virtual anorexic proportions as she bathes in the waters of the city' (Johnson 1995: 58). And as Johnson, like Walter, emphasizes,

> although allegorical figures of woman as motherland and protector of the private sphere of home and family enjoy acceptance in nationalist discourse, in the city woman's role in public space, as suggested by the renaming of Anna Livia Plurabella, is confined to that of prostitute or seductress strolling streets normally occupied by men. (p. 58)

Thus statues of women are concrete representations of the gender dichotomies that run through earlier chapters (see plate 7.1).

In her work on Irish nationalism, Catherine Nash (1993) ties together the themes that have run through this book so far in an exploration of the work of Kathy Prendergast, an Irish artist. Through a detailed look at Prendergast's drawings, Nash shows how the artist produces images of nationalism mapped on to the female body that avoid the essentialism of both a natural and organic intuitive association of woman and nature in some feminist work and the assumption of a native or racial closeness to nature found in some postcolonial studies of identity, place and landscape.

In the work on ethnic identity in Ireland, opposition to colonial and imperial power is a continuing theme. For postcolonial nations in many parts of the world, of course, this is a uniting theme, and a great deal of exciting work is being undertaken about representations of identity in art, text and landscape in many emerging nations. Sarah Radcliffe and Sallie

Plate 7.1   The Broadgate Venus, London: feminine, semi-naked and black.
Does she signify Empire or slavery?

Westwood (1994, 1996) have begun to unpack the long and complex history of nation-making in Latin America and its specificity in different nation-states. They argue that 'with [their] early colonisation and early independence, Latin American countries have a long history of post-coloniality and nation-building projects marking differences in timing and context in comparison with Europe, Asia and Africa' (1996:10). Through conquest, colonialism and indentured labour, a complex mix of peoples had to be forged into a single nation, into *el pueblo* (the people), as independence movements emerged in various Latin American countries in the nineteenth and twentieth centuries.

In these movements, print capitalism, as identified by Anderson, had its place, but so too, in later movements, did the popular media (films, radio and later television), which were also channels for official propaganda. Oral narratives had a place too. Flags and other national symbols incorporating images of women, gender-specific national costumes, national calendars, holidays and festivals are potent images of the nation, and as Radcliffe and Westwood show in their work, 'powerful discourses of nationhood link men and women to the nation in highly gendered ways, simultaneously fractured through complex relations of sexuality' (1996: 134).

Among the most important symbols of a newly emerging nation is its money – the coins and notes of a new regime – and here allegories of the female form are a common image in representations of the nation (Hewitt 1994). Women tend to appear on banknotes and coins either as symbols and allegories or as more realistic portraits. Among the symbols images of beauty and virtue, liberty, justice and plenty are common ones. Femininity represents either culture or impartial justice – womanhood as above the mundane struggles engaged in by mortal men – or is associated with nature, fertility and plenitude. In the notes issued by former colonies, the culture/nature distinction is often found in the same image. 'Native' women appear unclothed, next to their clothed, 'civilized' sisters from the West. This was a common image on French colonial notes, for example. The image of a 'dusky native maiden' linked with tropical fruits, lush vegetation and, if dressed, exotic costumes is a classic representation of colonial or oriental 'otherness' (Said 1978; Spivak 1987), stirring both desire and anxiety or guilt about imperial exploitation.

One of the ironies of these female representations or allegories – whether statues, friezes, faces or figures on flags or banknotes – is that the symbolic images of women often bear little or no relation to the position of women in those societies at particular times. As Marina Warner noted in her historical analysis of women as *Monuments and Maidens*:

> Justice is not spoken of as a woman, nor does she speak as a woman in mediaeval moralities or appear in the semblance of one above City Hall in New York or the Old Bailey in London because women were thought to be just, any more than they were considered capable of dispensing justice. Liberty is not represented as a woman, from the colossus in New York to the ubiquitous Marianne, figure of the French Republic because women were or are free. In the nineteenth century, when so many of these images were made and widely disseminated, the opposite was conspicuously the case . . . Often the recognition of a difference between the symbolic order inhabited by ideal, allegorical figures, and the actual order, of judges, statesmen, soldiers, philosophers, inventors, depends on *the unlikelihood of women practising the concepts they represent.* (1985: xix–xx, emphasis added)

But as Warner (1985), Nash (1993) and G. Rose (1993) have documented and as I discussed in chapter 1,

> the body is still the map on which we mark our meanings; it is chief among metaphors used to see and present ourselves, and in the contemporary profusion of imagery, from news photography to advertising to fanzines to pornography, the female body occurs more frequently than any other: men often appear as themselves, as individuals, but women attest the identity and value of someone or something else. (Warner 1985: 331)

And as we have seen here, the 'something else' is often a longed-for and struggled-over sense of national identity.

Conclusions

In this chapter we moved to a different scale of place – the nation-state – to examine some of the relationships between gender and nationality, in both the practices of the nation-state and in its representations and symbolic identity. The ways in which men and women are differentially treated as individuals and as members of social collectivities, as well as the ways in which gender ideologies and symbols are part of the social construction of nationality and nationalism have been examined. The chapter has also drawn on a range of social theories, from the political to the social and cultural, from liberal individualism to postmodern theories of justice. In the last few years, geography has become more 'theory conscious' than in previous decades, as the links between human geography, economic sociology, politics and cultural studies have become closer. The relationship has not been all one way. The key concepts of our discipline – space and place, connection and distance, migration and globalization – have become important concepts and foci of research and theorizing in the other social sciences.

In this chapter, as previously, the central linking theme has once again been the notion of dichotomies and their deconstruction: between men and women, masculinity and femininity, individuals and symbols, disembodiment and female bodies, between the public and the private, and the corresponding association of men with the first attribute in these pairs of terms. I have shown here how these dichotomies were naturalized and influenced the ideals of politics and the nation-state, as well as the ways in which their naturalization has been broken down and latterly challenged by the recognition of the complexity and diversity of the social construction of gender and the social relations between men and women, women and women, men and men.

As I think the length of this chapter indicates, the arena of the nation-state is a fascinating one for geographic research. At the end of the twentieth century the nation-state, a key social formation of the modern era, is itself being challenged by socioeconomic and political forces working out and interrelating in complex ways at the sub- and supranational levels. The effects on gender relations are complicated and diverse. In too many cases it seems that the splintering of former nation-states and their reformation into new nations have had an adverse impact for women, as the narratives of nationhood constructed by these new countries tend to hark back to a former, perhaps mythical, era when traditions reinforced male dominance. Where these trends are reinforced by a coincidence of the state and religion, women's position seems to be particularly parlous. It is, however, difficult to generalize here, as it is at the level of supranational trends. In Europe, it seems as if the extension of the European Union, and the gradual introduction of the programme of the Social Chapter of the Maastricht Treaty, may enhance women's civil rights and increase the formal equality they achieved at different dates in the twentieth century through suffrage campaigns. In too many parts of the world, however, in practice civil and political rights are still denied to women and it seems as if constant struggle is essential to extend the rights and privileges of citizenship to women as well as to men.

Further reading

Nira Yuval-Davis has been a key person in the construction and explication of feminist analyses of the state. Her work includes an edited book with Floya Anthias, *Women-Nation-State* (1989), and more recently the sole-authored book *Gender and Nation* (1997). Anne Phillips's analyses of feminist political theory are unsurpassed, in my view, in their clarity and lucidity. The introduction to her edited collection *Feminism and Equality* (1987) provides an extremely clear outline of the debates about rights within feminism, followed by an interesting collection of short essays by some noted feminist scholars, including Carole Pateman, whose own work in this area is worth exploring in more detail. Try her edited collection *The Disorder of Women* (1989) and the more complex but fascinating *The Sexual Contract* (1988). Phillips has also jointly edited an interesting collection of essays *Destabilizing Theory* (Barrett and Phillips 1992), which not only includes papers on feminist political theory but also deals with lesbian identities, power and bodies and feminist painting.

Iris Marion Young's *Justice and the Politics of Difference* (1990) is an important book in thinking through the implications of a postmodern definition of social justice, to which Nancy Fraser's new book *Justice Interruptus: Critical Reflections on the 'Postsocialist' Condition* (1997) provides a response and an alternative view. Zillah Eisenstein in *The Colour of Gender* (1994) shows how to take the language of universal democratic rights and reconceptualize them to include women of colour. All of these books are well worth reading.

If you are interested in Latin America, you might look at Sarah Radcliffe and Sallie Westwood's (1996) book on which I have drawn here and at Sarah Radcliffe's (1996) paper on Ecuador. Jo Sharp's essay in *BodySpace* (Duncan 1996b) provides a useful survey of arguments about the gender of nationalism, illustrated with examples from Eastern Europe. Anne McClintock's *Imperial Leather* (1994), which I mentioned in chapter 2, is also relevant here as she deals with questions about national identity in colonial and postcolonial societies. Jane Jacob's *Edge of Empire* (1995) is an excellent study of the ways in which colonial and imperial ideologies influence the construction and meaning of the built environment in the metropolitan centre, that is London. Issue 2 of *Gender, Place and Culture* includes several interesting papers about national identity and the use of space, and the special issue of *Feminist Review* (no. 44, 1993) on 'Nationalisms and national identities', as well as containing the paper by Nash referred to here, also has a number of other excellent articles. There is an interesting feminist literature about Ireland. As well as the papers referred to in the chapter, look for Catherine Nash's historical analysis of masculinity (1996a) and Loraine Dowler's (1998) study of women involved in struggles in Northern Ireland. There are a number of feminist analyses of war: see for example the books by Cynthia Enloe (1983, 1993), Barbara Ehrenreich (1997), Jean Elshtain (1987) and Tamar Mayer (1994). And for further ideas for teaching geopolitics from a feminist perspective, see Heidi Nast's (1998) recent discussion of the links between heterosexuality and geopolitics. Finally, a selection of some of the articles mentioned in this chapter is to be found in *Space, Gender, Knowledge* (McDowell and Sharp 1997).

8
Displacements

Introduction

In this penultimate chapter, which is the final substantive one, I want to turn to a specific consideration of movement and travelling. Although the implications of migration within and between nations and the rise of postcolonial and post-imperial movements have already been mentioned in earlier chapters, travel has not yet been the key focus. As many commentators have pointed out, however, travel is one of the key terms and metaphors in a great deal of recent writing influenced by postmodern ideas (see, for example, Clifford 1997 and Kaplan 1996). The significance of travel and migration, of geographical movement between places, has, of course, been an important part of our discipline since its origins. A wide range of specialist studies of the reasons for migration, the 'push' and 'pull' factors that persuade or force people to move between places, have been carried out by geographers, as well as analyses of the impacts on both the migrants and the 'receiving' population. In particular, studies of the effect of migration on inner city areas have a long tradition in urban geography.

While the causes and consequences of migration and the impacts on the receiving and donating communities have been relatively well documented, until recently far less attention has been paid to the journey itself. Studies of travellers, gypsies and nomads are perhaps an exception, but here the geographic literature remains small (Sibley 1981). Further, travel, migrancy and movement tend to have been analysed as if they were exceptional and temporary phenomena, especially in so far as settled peoples have been involved. But in many parts of the world at the end of the twentieth century – in Rwanda and Burundi, in Bosnia-Herzogovina and Serbia, for example – unsettled conditions, destabilization and forced movement seem to have become a more 'normal' part of life than a fixed and permanent existence.

It is important, however, not to exaggerate the novelty of the scale of movements at the end of the millennium. At the end of the nineteenth century and the beginning of the current one, millions of people left Eastern and Western Europe to settle in North America; in the inter- and postwar eras, the tragedy of the Holocaust saw the enforced shipment of hundreds of thousands of Jews, gypsies and homosexuals to their deaths, as well as movement to other parts of Europe, to North America and Israel, and that of apartheid saw the uprooting of millions of blacks and resettlement in the so-called Homelands in South Africa, as well as the migration of millions of men to single-sex mining camps and to urban hostels on a temporary or permanent basis.

One of the most interesting academic impacts of globalization and the movement of peoples around the world (whether for pleasure or in response to famine, disease, war and persecution – or to a feeling that the last frontiers of exploration, at least on earth, are being reached) has been the development of a new focus of analysis in the social sciences on travelling, on journeys and on extended periods or multiple chains of movement. As the anthropologist James Clifford has noted, in his discipline the idea of selecting a traditional fieldsite – often a rural village – to study 'untouched' or 'primitive' cultures has been challenged and to a large extent overturned by the pace of interconnections and cultural contacts in the twentieth century, although he also suggests that some earlier anthropologists underestimated the significance of movement. In a vivid image reminiscent of Augé's arguments with which I began this book, Clifford suggests that anthropologists should reimagine their traditional fieldsites. They should think of 'the traditional rural village as a transit lounge. It's hard to imagine a better figure for postmodernity, the new world of mobility, of rootless histories' (1997: 1). But, as he also cautions, 'not so fast' . . . for none of this is new. It is, rather, a rethink by Western anthropologists who had been too ready to see 'tradition' and 'stability' in worlds other than their own, counterposing the supposed pace of modernity with what they designated traditional societies.

Clifford's note of caution about trumpeting the newness of contemporary global change is echoed by others who also question the extent to which the current phase of globalization is significantly different from earlier periods (see, for example, Hirst and Thompson 1996, a book by a political scientist and an economist respectively). Indeed the new focus on travel and movement may reflect an academic or a disciplinary crisis as much as material changes. Thus it has been suggested that the current notion of globalization and its correlates (creolization, hybridization, translation, for example: concepts which I shall discuss in more detail later in this chapter) is more a reflection of the condition of the theorizers and the state of theory than anything else. Its Western bias, for example, is evident in the categorization of the classifiers, those Western theorizers who see themselves as cosmopolitans, but define others, the classified, as creoles. Jonathan Friedman (1997), an anthropologist like Clifford, has linked changes in his discipline to the desires of its practitioners.

> Global culture was in some sense a new object of anthropological investigation. This was a means, at least, to carve out a niche for cultural experts (anthropologists) in the more general trend toward the study of global systemic processes. If the economists and economic historians and sociologists have their world systems, anthropologists could have their cultural world system or world system of culture. (Friedman 1997: 270)

I wonder whether the same argument might be constructed for geography and geographers? Certainly for some the increasing penetration of capitalist globalization and forms of democracy has increased the command of the world systems approach. However, the new focus on movement and globalization has had a more interesting impact on geographic theorizing. As we saw in an earlier chapter, Doreen Massey's powerful arguments that in the late twentieth century localities are 'global' (see Massey 1991, the introduction to Massey and Allen 1984 and chapter 1 in Massey and Jess 1995) have shown geographers a way to combine the local and the global in order to reassert the significance of place. This emphasis on the interrelationships between scales producing the specificity of particular places has been enormously influential in reorienting geographical scholarship since the early 1980s. It might be argued that anthropological scholarship has also taken a similar path, as Friedman recognizes:

> Globalization is not about the flow or movement of culture. Culture does not move. It is not a substance. Rather we must investigate the relation between global social processes and the practices of social reproduction, and identification/representation of the world, the processes by which meaning is attributed in specific social contexts distributed in the global arena. (1997: 270)

The emphasis on interconnections means, I believe, that we have to rethink some of our traditional foci and emphases as geographers, turning to new ways of studying people who are in transit, whose identities are unfixed, destabilized and in the process of changing. For feminists, used to challenging fixity and essentialist, unchanging notions of what it means to be a woman, this move is long anticipated and welcome. It is here, in the analysis of flux and fluidity, in ways of becoming rather than being a woman, in the making and remaking of identities, that some of the most interesting recent work by feminist scholars is being undertaken.

It is also creating exciting opportunities to make visible the exceptional rather than the habitual and to reveal the historical importance of women who 'broke the rules' and stepped out of place. Feminist historiographers are now uncovering the significance of the thousands of 'ordinary' and extraordinary women who were travellers to and explorers of what were to them 'foreign lands', but who have been written out of history and geography. They include women who travelled with men, as wives and companions, and on their own, as refugees and tourists, as wage labourers, explorers or pilgrims. Indeed, as Clifford has recently noted, 'women have their own histories of labour migration, pilgrimage, emigration, exploration, tourism and even military travel – histories linked with and distinct from those of men' (1997: 6). Before I look at some of this work, I first want to pursue the implications of a focus on travel for geographic theorizing.

Travelling theory

Travel, even the idea of travelling, challenges the spatial association between home and women that has been so important in structuring the social construction of femininity in the 'West', in Western social theories and institutional practices. Because it was taken for granted for so long that a woman's place was in the home, the history of her movement was ignored. As Domosh has pointed out, the heroic history of geographical exploration as well as the histories and philosophies of the discipline have excluded women (see Domosh 1991a and b, and Stoddart's 1991 aggressive reply, as well as Livingstone's *Geographical Tradition* (1992), which writes women out of the history of geography). Although it is now widely accepted that many women were travellers (and I shall discuss this further below), the recent emphasis on vocabularies of travel in contemporary social theory has the effect, according to the cultural critic Janet Wolff, of continuing to privilege masculine experiences.

In a thought-provoking paper, Wolff outlines the currently popular metaphors in cultural criticism – 'nomadic criticism, traveling theory, critic-as-tourist (and vice versa), maps, billboards, hotels and motels' – and argues that

> these metaphors are gendered, in a way which is for the most part not acknowledged. That is they come to critical discourse encumbered with a range of gender connotations which have implications for what we do with

206

them *in* cultural studies. My argument is that just as the prac
ideologies of *actual* travel operate to exclude or pathologize wom
use of that vocabulary as metaphor necessarily produces androc
dencies in theory. (1992: 224, original emphasis)

In Wolff's view, the language of travel is too heavily compromised to be
an appropriate metaphor for rethinking subjectivity and identity.

She illustrates her argument by evaluating a number of strands in recent
theory construction in different disciplines, including anthropology,
postcolonial criticism, postmodern and poststructuralist work. As she points
out, travel as a metaphor or the notion of travelling theory is used by,
among others, Edward Said (1983), Fredric Jameson (1991) and James
Clifford (1988). Wolff accepts that this work has been important. She
suggests that 'Clifford is one of a number of cultural theorists who have
recently revolutionized the methodologies and conceptual frameworks of
cross-cultural study, at the same time demonstrating and deconstructing
the entrenched ideologies of self and other on which such study has been
based' (Wolff 1992: 226). In the new work, both theory and subjectivity are
retheorized as fluid and provisional. While Wolff recognizes that 'it is easy
to see why notions of mobility, fluidity, provisionality and process have
been preferable to alternative notions of stasis and fixity' (p. 228) she is
pessimistic about its relationship to feminist theorizing. As she points out,
feminism and feminist scholarship are based on 'a fundamental commitment to a critique which is premissed on the existence of systematically
structured, actual, inequalities of gender' (p. 228). The masculine celebration of travel and provisionality tends to deny these fixed structures.

Wolff's argument is part of a wider feminist critique of certain versions
of a postmodernist stance (see Bondi 1991; Mascia-Lees et al. 1989;
McDowell 1991b; Soper 1990), where the embrace of difference makes it
more difficult to make general political claims for a redistribution of power
and resources. Caren Kaplan (1996) also has some reservations about travel
as a metaphor, and as a social practice. Interestingly, she reminds us that
travel as an activity to 'broaden the mind' and to give 'perspective' has a
long association with modernity. In this case it was not the fluidity of
travel and its challenge to ethnocentric viewpoints that was emphasized
but rather it was seen as an activity to add to the cultural capital of the
traveller – usually a white bourgeois Western man. Thus Kaplan suggests
that her study of travel and travel writing has produced for her 'a profound
scepticism towards the terms in which travel is described' (1996: x).

I find that I share Kaplan's scepticism as I read some of the recent travel
writing. As well as work on metaphors of travel in critical theory, there has
been a huge expansion in writing about travel. Some of the texts are

'academic' in nature, but the increase is especially evident in the last few years in popular writing, in the main, but not only, by men – Bruce Chatwin (1979, 1987, 1988), Redmond O'Hanlon (1996), Paul Theroux (1979, 1990, 1992) and Jonathan Raban (1980, 1986, 1995) come to mind. These authors tend to construct themselves as popular heroes, struggling, resisting and overcoming hardship and temptations. It is clear that their greatest fascination is with themselves and not with the 'others' they encounter on their travels. These are boy's own adventure stories for a restless and more sophisticated age.

Like Wolff, I find it hard to come to any other conclusion than that these are men running from commitment, denying or rejecting 'feminine' values of immobility, care and nurturance provided at home by wives and mothers. Stories of resistance through escape also ignore the ways in which struggle and commitment to change are possible among those who remain static. It is important to recognize that localism does not necessarily imply a narrow view of the world, nor travel a broad one. I think that this assumption is one which parallels the more general point made by Doreen Massey (1992) when she challenges the idea that whereas time is seen as fluid and provisional, space and location tend to be theorized as stasis and fixity.

It seems clear to me, however, despite these worries, that there are several advantages of rethinking concepts of place and culture through the metaphor of travel. A focus on travel permits, for example, the destabilization of a singular view of history, and here feminists as well as postmodern and postcolonial theorists have been united in recent decades. That teleological view of history that dominated our own discipline for so long – that progress was a single road towards modernization, westernization and urbanization – is challenged by a focus on multiplicity, on travel and intersecting movements, and, crucially, by decolonization.

Here is Clifford reflecting on his efforts to rethink the notion of culture:

> *travel* emerged as an increasingly complex range of experiences: practices of crossing and interaction that troubled the localism of many common assumptions about culture. In these assumptions, authentic social existence is, or should be, centred in circumscribed places. . . . Dwelling was understood to be the local ground of collective life, travel a supplement; roots always precede routes. But what would happen, I began to ask, if travel were untethered, seen as a complex and pervasive spectrum of human experiences? Practices of displacement might emerge as *constitutive* of cultural meanings rather than their simple transfer or extension. The cultural effects of European expansionism, for example, could no longer be celebrated, or deplored, as a simple diffusion outward – of civilization, industry, science or capital. For the region called 'Europe' has been

constantly remade and traversed, by influences beyond its boundaries. And is not this interactive process relevant, in varying degrees, to any local, national or regional domain? Virtually everywhere one looks, the processes of human movement and encounter are long-established and complex. Cultural centres, discrete regions and territories, do not exist prior to contacts, but are sustained through them, appropriating and disciplining the restless movements of people and things. (1997: 3, original emphases)

This description of places as constituted by connections and movement exactly parallels the earlier arguments of Doreen Massey (1991) in her well-known paper (reprinted in, for example, two recent readers, Daniels and Lee 1996 and Barnes and Gregory 1996) about how geographers must theorize a 'global sense of place'. So while a focus on a locality may remain, a set of movements at a variety of spatial scales needs to be analysed to understand how the particularity of any place is constructed. Clifford's term for this new conceptualization of place is 'translocal': places where the 'culture' is a complex articulation of 'local and global processes in relational, non-teleological ways'. He rejects older ways of theorizing 'mix' – acculturation (where one group conforms to another) or syncretism (with an image of two clear systems overlaid). Instead, he argues, 'the new paradigms begin with historical contact, with entanglement at intersecting regional, national and transnational levels. Contact approaches suppose not sociocultural wholes subsequently brought into relationship, but rather systems already socially constituted relationally, entering new relations through historical processes of displacement' (1997: 7). Let's look in more detail, through an example, at how this argument implies a different way of theorizing the links between identity and place or, in Clifford's terms, understanding translocal culture.

Changing identities

In chapter 3 we began to address questions about the ways in which the terms migrant, culture and community have become connected in a discourse that sets apart people of colour as different from the majority population. In an excellent study of migration into Southall in West London, Baumann has illustrated the implications of different ways of theorizing travel and in-migration. He argues that 'simplistic equations between ethnic identity, culture and community have congealed into a hegemonic discourse about any and all ethnic minorities' (1996: 22). Further, as Paul Gilroy suggests, this dominant discourse assumes 'cultures supposedly sealed from one another forever by ethnic lines' (1987: 55). Compared to white Britons, ethnic minorities are constructed as 'traditional' and often as social problems. A static conception of unchanging cultural values which are assumed to unite all migrants from a particular area of origin is remarkably strong and is common in Britain, for example in both left- and right-wing debates. Baumann illustrates the commonality as follows:

> The right-wing version of the dominant discourse envisages people from the former colonies who migrated to Britain for a better life. Yet their ethnic and cultural distinctiveness sets them apart from an equally reified British or English culture. They thus live in disadvantaged communities which, viewed almost as societies within society, create 'social problems'. Classic recent examples are 'the black community' and its putatively problematic family structure and 'the Asian community' and its 'problem of arranged marriages'. Classic examples among migrants from the past are 'the Irish' and their supposed collective drinking problem.
>
> Liberal versions of the dominant discourse shun any reference to problems in a community's culture. Instead they envisage immigrants, or more politely migrants, who are excluded from full civic equality by social disadvantages. These handicaps, an almost natural consequence of migration, keep them living in their insulated communities, captive of their reified 'cultures', often specified as 'traditional'. The remedies envisaged are gradual, and they need to be directed at both sides of the equation, the 'host population' and migrants alike. . . . The left-wing version of the dominant discourse replaces cultural reform with cultural revolution, yet it, too, endorses the equation between 'communities' and their reified cultures. Rather than judging community cultures as an obstacle to social mobility within the system, it validates them as a necessary and progressive form of resistance against racism. (1996: 24)

In more sophisticated, and more interesting, recent work, Baumann's study of Southall included, these oppositional dichotomies are rejected completely. It is argued instead that migration changes individual and group identities, affiliations and cultural attitudes and practices, among both the mobile population and the 'hosts'. As soon as it is recognized that cultures are fluid and temporary social constructions, made and remade over time – Clifford's translocal culture – it is apparent that movement involves the remapping of cultural identities and practices for *all* those involved.

This brings us straight to recent arguments about 'translocal' identities from postcolonial literatures in particular. Here the key concepts used to refer to translocal culture and identities include hybridity, diasporic identity and cultural translation.

Plate 8.1   Diasporic Chinese women in the US

Theorizing translocal identities: hybridity, diaspora and translation

In the growing number of studies that have begun to examine the effects of travel and movement in different locations – in the borderlands straddling the US/Mexico boundary, in the Caribbean, in global cities of the West where Third World peoples live in significant numbers – a variety of terms have been used to capture the transformations that have taken place in the sense of self and belonging. Creolization is a common Caribbean term, whereas metizo or border identities are referred to in the south-west US, for example. The term hybrid or hybrid identity is a more widely used term, as is that of diaspora or diasporic identity. (The term diaspora means the dispersal and scattering of a population, the most typical example being the Jewish diaspora; whereas hybridity, a term originally from biology, refers to the result of breeding two plants or species, and became used to refer to people of mixed origins.) These terms are what are often known as contested concepts, especially that of hybridity, with its connotations of inferiority/impurity, and so they have to be carefully defined. They are sometimes used in association with each other, as in the following definition, which is from the important work on British identities by Stuart Hall:

211

'The diaspora experience as I intend it here is defined, not by essence or purity, but by the recognition of a necessary heterogeneity and diversity; by a conception of "identity" which lives with and through, not despite, difference, by hybridity' (1990: 223).

So, for Hall, the idea of a diaspora experience or hybridity includes both movement and change, whereas for some scholars the maintenance of a previous cultural identity is a significant part of the definition of a diaspora (see plate 8.1). For Orthodox Jews, for example, their sense of themselves as Jewish and belonging to a common nation, albeit scattered, depends on their cultural separation from other social groups and the maintenance of a belief in their eventual re-establishment and regrouping within their home-land.

Crossing spaces: making connections

So hybridity, as used by cultural theorists such as Stuart Hall, merely means that identities and cultural forms are a product of intermingling and fusion, a product of movement. The term has, however, been used in a range of somewhat different ways. It has been used in association with images that suggest an identity between two competing worlds: to refer to those who seem to live on the borders or in the margins, and here Chicana/o and Latina/o scholars have made a significant use of the term hybridity, betweenness and borderlands (Anzaldua 1987). Alternatively, it may be used to signify a third identity that replaces the two that construct the hybridity. Here the terms border crossing, betweenness or third space (Bhabha 1990, 1994) are also sometimes used to imply the same concept. In fact the terms are not so different from each other, as the concept of living in the margins or betweenness is not meant to imply marginality but rather the transcendence of identities that are either Mexican/Central American or US (I return to Anzaldua's work below). A group of Indian scholars working on identities of resistance in imperial and post-imperial India (Spivak 1987, 1988) have also claimed this 'between' hybrid identity as one to celebrate. In their work the idea of a subaltern identity parallels that of hybridity.

In his analyses of the black diaspora in the United States, Paul Gilroy (1993) has identified a new form of hybrid culture which he terms a *Black Atlantic* identity. Stuart Hall (1990) in his parallel work on British cultures prefers the term 'translation', whereby the 'native' population cast off their 'little Englander' attitudes and the 'black' population their appeals to difference, to mutually embrace their hybrid or translated identities. But as Friedman has perceptively pointed out, 'hybridity is only socially significant if it is practised, that is if people actively identify as such' (1997: 290). Hybridity or translation has to be seen as a positive *political* choice of identity, leading to a more inclusive notion of what it means to be 'British'. As Hall himself has argued, translation is an optimistic assertion of diversity and change, and its development is far from certain. Instead both 'minority' groups and 'natives' may withdraw into an exclusive and conservative reassertion of their 'roots'. Thus in Britain, the rise of ideas of black nationalism or of Rastafarian identity have been important ways of asserting pride in cultural origins, whereas elements among the white population cling to ideas of white Britishness, little Englander, the bulldog breed and so forth, which have unpleasant fascist associations among the extreme right-wing.

Robert Young (1995), a postcolonial literary theorist, has argued that the term hybridity should not be used at all as it carries with it the racist baggage of inferiority and miscegenation. Hybrid animals, for example the mule, are sterile and it used to be assumed that cross-racial unions had similar results. However, in the rapidly expanding literature of cultural geography, the term hybridity is widely used. For Homi Bhabha, a key exponent of the notion of hybridity, also in the literary field:

> the importance of hybridity is not to be able to trace two original movements from which the third emerges, rather hybridity . . . is the 'third space' which enables other positions to emerge. This third space displaces the histories that constitute it, and sets up new structures of authority, new political initiatives, which are inadequately understood through received wisdom. . . . The process of cultural hybridity gives rise to a something different, something new and unrecognisable, a new area of negotiation of meaning and representation. (1990: 211)

Although Bhabha's work has been criticized by Gillian Rose (1995b) as a disembodied – or a gendered – approach, as she believes that his emphasis on an ungendered (post)colonial subject ignores the particularity of women's and men's experiences, I find his work provocative in its insistence on transformation, the possibility of new identities beyond current binary distinctions and so the prospect of political change. For geographers, as I suggested above, all these terms are particularly interesting as they separate the notion of identities from specific places and force a reconceptualization of both place and identity.

The politics of location

In the last few years, there has been an exciting coincidence of work on the theorization of place in geography and in literary and cultural studies. In this work spatial metaphors and concepts have a key role (Gregory 1994;

213

Kaplan 1996; Nash 1993; Smith and Katz 1993). As Caren Kaplan has argued:

> Maps and borders are provocative metaphors, signalling a heightened aware-
> ness of the political and economic structures that demarcate zones of inclu-
> sion and exclusion as well as the interstitial spaces of indeterminacy.
> Topography and geography now intersect literary and cultural criticism in a
> growing interdisciplinary inquiry into emergent identity formations and so-
> cial practices. Geographers who believe that all modes of description and
> analysis follow narrative conventions and are, therefore, highly constructed
> and historically contingent articulate various versions of 'geographic imagi-
> nations'. (1996: 144)

Thus, through analyses of materiality and of metaphor and meaning, the multiple ways in which place and identity are constructed and the connec-tions between them are revealed. In these analyses, we need to examine together, as Derek Gregory has suggested, 'maps, landscapes, and spaces *and also* images of location, position, and geometry' (1994: 7, original em-phasis), and it also behoves us to remember that 'different people in differ-ent places are implicated in space-time colonization and compression in different ways' (1994: 414). There is, in other words, a spatial politics to uncovering the ways in which identities and places are being transformed and reconnected, positioning people within new patterns, or geometries, of inclusion and exclusion.

In an influential paper, the feminist political theorist Chandra Talpade Mohanty (1991) has begun to explore some of the political realignments that may result from the new patterns of place identities. She has shown how the movement of many Third World women from the 'South' be-cause of poverty or ambition has opened a space for a powerful realign-ment of Third World feminism and the development of what she terms a new 'cartography of struggle' which unites Third World women 'in situ' as it were with the women who have moved to the North. The politics of location may also take new forms as links between women in different places are forged through political struggles, music or film, and through a reimagined sense of place or nationality. In Mohanty's sense, a politics of location does not depend on a territorially based identity but rather on the development of networks between members of an imagined community of Third World women. The common interests of these women are constructed by the ways in which capital positions them in marginal spaces, exploiting them as the new proletariat of the emerging global economy (Afshar 1991; Chant and McIllwaine 1995; Fuentes and Ehrenreich 1983; Nash and Kelly 1983; Ward 1990).

Rethinking difference

Perhaps one of the most interesting implications of the retheorizing that has come about through the conceptual centring of metaphors of travel, movement and boundaries in several disciplines is the challenge that is being mounted to the concept of difference, which itself has been so crucial in challenging the phallocentrism and universalism of Western discourse. As I have argued in many of the earlier chapters, the theoretical and political implications of recognizing multiplicity and difference – on the basis of gender and many other dimensions – have been a key element in postmodern and feminist theory. Theorists interested in hybridity and translation are now arguing, however, that we must jettison the term 'difference' itself, with its connotations of fixity and difference from the One: that singular bourgeois masculinity against which all the other 'Others' are defined and measured as lacking in different ways. (The parallels between this argument and Young's rejection of the use of the term hybridity are interesting, I think.) Instead of the identities of 'oppositional' or 'minority' groups being constructed as different from a 'norm', it is now asserted that all identities are a fluid amalgam of memories of places and origins, constructed by and through fragments and nuances, journeys and rests, of movements between. Thus, the 'in-between' is itself a process or a dynamic, not just a stage on the way to a more final identity. As Preis has argued, 'The idea of a boundary or of traits, with an inside and an outside, a here and a there, seems insufficient. It is the space in-between which imposes itself as a reception place for differences at play' (1997: 98).

These arguments echo the important earlier work by, in the main, feminists in the United States who were part of the migration from Central America. Gloria Anzaldua, for example, has written in similar terms about the development of what she termed a 'mestiza consciousness', which is a consciousness of the borderlands, developed from the collusion of Mexican and Anglo cultures. Anzaldua demands the rejection of dualistic thinking and argues that a mestiza consciousness comes from 'being on both shores at once. . . . A massive uprooting of dualistic thinking in the individual and collective consciousness is the beginning of a long struggle, but one that could, in our best hopes, bring us to the end of rape, of violence, of war' (1987: 80).

Before I end this chapter with an attempt to assess the implications of these debates about provisionality and fluid identities, I want to turn briefly to some empirical examples of current work on travelling and movement, by geographers and by other scholars, looking at gender divisions among travellers.

215

Let's first look at some recent research on journeys and then at mobility as a way of life.

Gendered journeys: the gender of travelling and travellers

One of the most interesting developments in recent geographical work in this area has been the combination of an interest in travel and travel writing with historical geographies of colonial and postcolonial states. The development of colonial empires by modern Western powers led to millions of lives being uprooted and transferred to other places, on a temporary or more or less permanent basis. Whereas the history of these movements of men is well known, the impact on women's lives has been less well explored. For the Western soldiers and colonial administrators – the vast majority of them men – their journeys were connected to their working lives and their sense of often missionary zeal to bring 'civilization' to another, and inferior, people. For the thousands of women who went with them, in the baggage of the empire, as wives, mistresses and camp followers, their purpose was different. These women had to comfort their menfolk and recreate an image of home in a foreign land, and their thoughts and feelings are recorded not in official documents and treaties but in letters home and in diaries. And even for the redoubtable women who went to Africa, to India, to Egypt and elsewhere as nurses, missionaries and explorers or combinations of these roles, the historical record is less certain than for their male counterparts.

In their collection *Writing Women and Space* (1994), Alison Blunt and Gillian Rose have begun to provide a counterbalance to the official stories of travel, unpicking different histories and geographies of, among others, British women in India at the time of high Empire, travels in West Africa by Mary Kingsley (and see also Blunt 1994) and others, and colonial politics in Australia. Through these studies, the history and geography of colonialism are made more complicated. Not only do imperial women become visible but the singular perspective of colonization as mapping and conquest is challenged, and so too are stories of struggle and resistance, as colonial women are often both complicit in and resistant to strategies of domination (Ware 1992). In her splendid book *Imperial Eyes* (1992), Mary Louise Pratt examined the role of travel writing as part of the ideological apparatus of empire. Her work is more nuanced than either the outright celebration of much earlier accounts, but less condemnatory than some analyses. Drawing on evidence from the 1750s to the 1980s, Pratt shows

216

how through travel writing the otherness of empires and their inhabitants was constructed for readers in the metropolitan core, as well as how the peoples of the 'periphery' received, appropriated and challenged the representations of themselves.

In the twentieth century, diplomatic wives are the counterpart of the Victorian women who accompanied their menfolk to imperial fields. Cynthia Enloe, whose work has already been discussed, has argued that although women are still seldom diplomats in their own right, they play a key role in foreign policy. 'If managed correctly, women as wives can help a government achieve its international objectives. If they aren't controlled effectively, however, they can do serious damage to a government's global interests' (1989: 9). As Enloe observes, diplomatic wives are essential in the 'hostessing' that has become an indispensable part of diplomacy. Not all women did, or do, it willingly. Enloe quotes from the letters Vita Sackville-West wrote to her new friend Virginia Woolf from Tehran in 1926. Sackville-West had joined her diplomat husband Harold Nicolson there and wrote to complain that 'I don't like diplomacy, though I like Persia.' As Enloe records,

> despite her forceful resistance to playing the dutiful wife in either private or public, by the 1920s Vita had encountered role expectations she couldn't avoid: 'She paid calls, attended and gave luncheons and dinners . . . she even gave away hockey prizes.' Yet her heart wasn't in it . . . and within a few months she was heading back to England, leaving Harold to cope with diplomatic rituals on his own. (1989: 97)

Vita, indeed, never settled down as a conventional wife and the story of her troubled relationship with Harold is told in fascinating detail in *Portrait of a Marriage* (1973) by their son Nigel Nicolson.

As Enloe documents, many diplomatic wives found their unpaid work thankless and while not running away like Vita, women married to Swedish, Canadian, British and American diplomats began to organize and lobby for recognition from the 1970s onwards. Making 'public demands for services, jobs, alimony and even salaries', Enloe records, 'they were joined in their political lobbying by military wives' (1989: 95). For these women, like the women gypsies studied by Okely and whose lives I outline below, travel tended to reinforce their subservience rather than challenge conventional gender relations. These empirical examples add to theoretical arguments about the particularity of gendered experiences and warn us to look carefully at claims about the significance of travel as a central metaphor of postmodernity.

217

Mobility as a way of life

While the travel of the men and women discussed above is seen as purposeful and valuable by the wider societies of which they are members, the lifestyle and behaviour of other mobile groups are constructed by the wider society either as deviant or problematic, or as a remnant of an earlier way of life. Gypsies, Romany peoples and travellers are an example, often despised as outsiders in many European countries.

Judith Okely is a British anthropologist who has done ethnographic work over many years with British gypsies, or travellers as they prefer to be known by outsiders. She argues that travellers have often – but incorrectly – been seen as a marginal group that will vanish with economic development (Okely 1975a), as their 'traditional' livelihood as dealers and traders, hawkers and casual workers disappears. According to Okely, this assumption is misleading, although the definition of their status as marginal is certainly accurate. Despised by many settled people, travellers themselves reject conventional norms. Okely found, for example, that gypsy men had no desire to hold a regular job. They despised the wage labour relationship, regarding farmwork, for example, as 'women's work' and endeavouring wherever possible to be self-employed in small, family-run enterprises such as scrap metal dealing.

Okely found that there are strong gender divisions in all areas of life among gypsies in Britain. One of the most interesting differences is the extent to which men and women chose to 'pass' in the broader society. Unlike many ethnic minorities who are recognizably different from the wider society, gypsies in the main are not physically distinct, despite stereotypes about dark hair and dark eyes among the 'real Romany' peoples. Although membership of the group depends on having one gypsy parent, it is 'way of life and commitment to certain gypsy values' (Okely 1996: 51) that confirms it. The lack of physical distinctiveness, however, means that gypsies can choose whether to conceal or reveal their ethnic identity and here gender differences are evident.

Okely argues that there are four ways in which ethnicity or ethnic images are performed by gypsies. These are an exoticized, a concealed, a degraded and a naturalized image. The exoticized image is more commonly adopted by women, who use romantic stereotypes and dress (scarves and gold jewellery for example) to capitalize on the image of gypsies as fortune-tellers with second sight. Men, however, are more likely to profit from concealing their ethnicity, wearing suits or ties to arrange the hire of halls for sales, for example, or using printed cards to advertise their tarmacadam business (Okely 1975a). Occasionally, however, both sexes, but more typically men, will degrade their image, wearing rags or acting foolishly to beg or scavenge. Some pretend non-literacy to evade official requests. Finally, in some relationships of trust between gypsies and 'mass' society, usually based on individual contacts and exchanges, ethnic identity is irrelevant.

These four ploys or performances are similar to the notion of gender identity as performance or image discussed in earlier chapters, and Okely's work is now regarded as an early recognition of the arguments about fluid and mobile identities. The self-ascribed image of gypsies changes over time, as does their definition by the 'host' society. As Okely concludes, in the nineteenth century gypsies were more likely to be seen as depraved than deprived, whereas the latter view is more common now. The host society's image of the gypsy woman, however, has remained more stable over time. If she is a young woman, she is typically viewed as sexually promiscuous, sensual, provocative and exciting; if she is an older woman, she is seen as a bad mother or a threatening crone. Just as women as a group are Othered, so minority women are doubly othered, often seen as closer to nature and more sexually available than the more civilized 'white' woman. This is a common thread that runs through the discursive construction of women of colour as well as gypsy women.

Within gypsy society, however, there are strongly prescribed rules of sexual conduct and purity, and gender divisions between the sexes are rigid. Gypsy women are strongly hedged by conventions and are expected to be faithful and subservient to their husbands in the camps, despite the evident need for independence and aggression in their relations with gorgios (the gypsy word for non-gypsies). One of the ways in which women are controlled is through the erection of a set of beliefs and fears about ritual pollution, in which certain parts of the body, the washing of clothes and of utensils and the preparation of food are the subject of strict regulation. Gypsy men are seen as innately pure, whereas women are a source of pollution and can only aspire to purity through careful attention to their behaviour, and particularly their sexuality. Thus many of the most essentialized stereotypes of femininity seem to be found in their strongest form among a people with a mobile way of life. This is perhaps paradoxical for feminist theorists now turning to metaphors of fluidity and travel in their theoretical reconstruction of gendered social relations.

Conclusion: transgressions and transformations

In the conclusion to this chapter I want to return to the idea of a politics of location and examine the implications that flow from the coincidence of feminist, geographical and cultural theorizing about travel and mobility, and the idea of identity as fluid and transitional, based on fragments of place memories, on desires and experience. I want to assess whether there are liberatory or conservative conclusions to be drawn from the insistence that all claims are contextual and situated, and that a politics develops from an understanding of common location. One of the questions to be raised in an assessment of the possibilities of a new form of politics is the relationship between location and place. As Michel Foucault argued, the history of spaces (space is the term used by Foucault rather than place) also involves a history of power. For the new political demands of, say, the Third World women in the 'West' to be taken seriously, these demands (on which their cartography of struggle is based) have to be heard. But as the feminist critic Elsbeth Probyn has argued, the politics of location depends on 'where we speak from and whose voices are sanctioned' (1990: 178). At present not all 'Others' have equal voices.

It is also apparent that a politics of identity is not automatically progressive. Stuart Hall has reminded us that movement and travel, and the dissolution of boundaries which is engendered by postmodernity (through the global reach of capitalism and enforced migration, as well as desired movement), may result in the reformation of exclusivist and defensive enclaves. Migration may lead to a clinging to old notions of identity and a desire to reject the new experiences as often as to a progressive transformation of identity through the breaking down of old binary distinctions. In many cases – and I briefly discussed the revival of ethnic nationalism in the previous chapter – movement entails the reassertion of old gender relations as well as their transformation.

I want to conclude, therefore, with some questions about the possibilities of overcoming oppositional gender identities. To what extent are opportunities currently opening up for women, and for men, to find new ways of becoming – to be neither female nor male, at least as we presently understand those terms? Is there another way or multiple ways of 'doing gender', which allow the construction of a range of multiple femininities and masculinities, even, perhaps, a way to move beyond binary gender divisions? To what extent will women be able to resist and evade subordination, instead of being 'apprenticed' to it?

It is now some time since feminism was solely a campaign for 'equality'. The work I have introduced here brings with it the prospect of something different: of new sets of social relations and forms of representation. It seems possible to envisage a future that will not depend on binary, hierarchical distinctions: a future that is neither the white, male, colonial, capitalist world we have to endure at present nor solely a struggle against it, but is instead a more complex and fluid world with possibilities of evading and transgressing old divisions. Indeed, perhaps even the word transgression is the wrong one: what is being constructed now is not only an oppositional politics of gender that stands outside conventions – as the term transgression implies – but new ways of doing gender that extend the possibilities of more liberatory ways of being gendered. Stuart Hall has referred to 'new ethnicities' in his work on cultural translation. We might perhaps extend this term to refer to 'new genders', where through translation both the transgressors and those that stand against them are altered. As Grossberg has argued, in the context of a discussion about how cultural studies as a discipline might be transformed, it is time

> to move beyond models of oppression, both the 'colonial' model of the oppressor and the oppressed, and the transgression model of oppression and resistance. Cultural studies needs to move towards a model of articulation as 'transformative practice', as a singular becoming of a community. Both models of oppression are not only inappropriate to contemporary relations of power, they are also incapable of creating alliances; they cannot tell us how to interpellate various fractions of the population in different relations of power into the struggle for change. For example, how can we involve fractions of the empowered in other than a guilt-ridden way? My feeling is that an answer depends on rearticulating the question of identity into a question about the possibility of constructing historical agency, and giving up notions of resistance that assume a subject standing entirely outside of and against a well-established structure of power. (1996: 88, and also quoted by Thrift 1997: 150)

The Marxist echoes of Grossberg's language (fractions and articulation) may not chime with recent feminist work on identity politics, and neither have feminist scholars assumed a (female/feminist) subject standing outside and against patriarchal power (indeed throughout this book I have shown how the female subject is defined by her position within dominant structures of power), but the overall argument of the passage is a powerful one. For the purpose of feminist scholarship and politics is surely not only to challenge the fictions and limits of available notions of femininity, but those of masculinity too.

Grossberg also emphasizes the importance of combining a historically situated understanding of the construction of identity with a progressive hope for a better future, replacing the anxieties of analyses of ambiguity, disjunction and displacement that pervade so much of the current work about identity. It is, of course, important to recognize how liberatory this work was for those excluded from the 'norm' (be it the masculine norm of class politics or the norm of the white middle-class woman of a great deal of early feminism), and to recognize the importance of all that scholarship

221

that pointed out the differences between women, in their desires and hopes as well as the divisions created along race or class lines. But a future open to the emancipatory prospect of transformation and translation, albeit multiple, fluid and provisional, seems more hopeful than not just the recognition of, but the insistence on difference.

In some recent work on gender and sexuality, especially in the scholarship by queer theorists, there is an indication of how to move beyond binaries. The work of the geographers David Bell, Jon Binnie, Julia Cream and Gill Valentine on gender/sexual performances that I introduced in chapter 2 is one example. Similarly Mark Simpson in *Male Impersonators* (1994), his book about gay men, has also shown how multiple performances of masculine identity are destabilizing conventional ideas of hegemonic masculinity. He examines, for example, the trend in advertising to use male bodies to advertise a range of goods aimed at straight as well as gay men, and suggests that making male bodies rather than female bodies the object of the male gaze disturbs traditional notions of masculinity. If straight men enjoy looking at each other, then gay men may no longer be defined as different or 'other', at least in this limited example. Gay men can only be gay if straight men are determinedly straight. Deborah Cameron, a linguistic theorist, has noted in a parallel argument that 'men can be men only if women are unambiguously women' (1985: 156). It is quite clear nowadays that as many women are actively challenging previous definitions of femininity – in their looks, actions and achievements – they are beginning to do exactly that: stop being 'women'. This destabilizes the category of 'men' and 'masculine', clearly causing great anxiety among many men at present.

It seems then that there is some evidence (and a great deal of further scope) for change but its direction still seems undetermined. Anthony Giddens, a British sociologist, has recognized the extent of the uncertainties that currently face men 'doing masculinity', as women refuse to occupy their traditional places. In his book *The Transformation of Intimacy* (1992), he suggests that there is both a negative and a positive response by men to contemporary challenges to gender difference. He argues that evidence of increased levels of male abuse and violence constitutes a negative response, whereas the development of new ways of negotiating gender relations and greater personal intimacy between men and women is a more positive sign. His argument is contentious, however, with inadequate empirical evidence to make it incontestable, but it does support the arguments of other theorists about the uncertainties that lie behind new forms of identity and the possibilities of political transformation that are involved in their emergence.

It seems as though we are at a crossroads at present, where the prospects of a politics of difference have to be weighed against a new form of transformative politics that would be necessary to challenge the oppositional construction of masculine and feminine identity. I suggest, however, that we still have to face up to that long dilemma of feminist politics. To claim a position from which women may speak seems to entail holding on to some notion of womanhood or femaleness, rather than its deconstruction and ultimate dissolution into a shifting and unstable network of multiple differences. Nancy Fraser has argued that a transformative politics demands that 'all people be weaned from their attachment to current cultural constructions of their interests and identities' (1997b: 31). This seems to me to be an impossibility in the current social and economic circumstances, where stark material inequalities between men and women remain. Indeed, Fraser herself recognizes that such a politics – what she terms a 'deconstructive feminist cultural politics' – as well as older and more conventional forms of socialist feminist politics (campaigns in the workplace for example) are still 'far removed from the immediate interests and identities of most women' (p. 32). I believe, however, as Fraser does, that there is still a great deal to be gained from the notion of deconstructing identities. It gives us a vision of the future to work towards, when binary constructions of gender difference will no longer be so important, trapping women into becoming 'Woman'.

Further reading

There has been an exciting explosion of work about travel, displacement, migration, diasporas and border identities in recent years within and outside the boundaries of geography. On the importance of travel, Mary Louise Pratt's book *Imperial Eyes: Travel Writing and Transculturation* (1992) is a fascinating book drawing mainly on travels in the Americas. The geographers Alison Blunt and Gillian Rose have edited an interesting book about travel writing, mainly but not entirely about the former British Empire, called *Writing Women and Space: Colonial and Postcolonial Geographies* (1994). Rosi Braidotti's book *Nomadic Subjects* (1994) is a more theoretically challenging book. Nancy Fraser's political arguments are to be found in her recent book *Justice Interruptus: Critical Reflections on the 'Postsocialist' Condition* (1997). The collection of papers by anthropologist Ulf Hannerz *Transnational Connections: Culture, People, Places* (1996) looks at some of the implications of long-distance movement and cultural flows for ideas about the local and community. Finally, Kate Soper's book *Troubled Pleasures: Writings on Gender, Politics and Hedonism* (1990) is, as the title implies, a reflection on how to think about achieving political change and still have some fun.

9

Postscript: Reflections on the Dilemmas of Feminist Research

Introduction

In this final chapter, there is a shift of emphasis, as here I want to reflect on the dilemmas of doing feminist research within geography, looking at the changing debates through the lens of my own research interests. Although I have introduced a large number of different pieces of empirically based work in the preceding chapters, I have not directly addressed the question of how the feminist geographers represented there actually did and do their research. For many years, the issue of whether or not there is a specific way of doing research that makes it explicitly feminist has been hotly debated and there is a sizeable literature from a range of disciplinary perspectives about how to go about research to uncover gender differentiations, raising questions about appropriate feminist research methodologies. Many geographers have participated in these debates (see, for example, (Dyck 1993; England 1994; Gibson-Graham 1994; Gilbert 1994; Katz 1994; Kobayashi 1994; McDowell 1992c; Nast 1994; G. Pratt 1993; D. Rose 1993; Staeheli and Lawson 1994).

The Professional Geographer in 1995 included a set of particularly interesting papers from a number of geographers whose academic careers at the time had begun relatively recently. These women, most of them teachers in US and Canadian universities, worked within an environment where feminist research was at least tolerated and even encouraged. My own career as a feminist geographer began some two decades before theirs, when feminist approaches were less well established and some of the ground work that is now taken for granted had not been laid. It is important to note how relatively recent it is that feminist scholarship has even been tolerated let alone encouraged in geography. To give some flavour of how things have changed, I decided to end this book with a more personal look at feminist research, drawing both on my own experiences and on the reflections of others who were working in geography and related disciplines at much the same time.

I intend this chapter not to be an egocentric indulgence, but rather a contribution to the reflexive turn in recent geographical writing. In the second book authored by members of the Women and Geography Study Group (1997), there are some parallel explorations of their own histories and positions by feminist geographers writing at present. Like the *Professional Geographer* contributors, many of the women writing there became geographers more recently than I did, and you may like to compare their self-assessments of their careers with this chapter.

In the early 1970s, just as I was finishing my first degree, it was difficult even to think, let alone formally conceptualize, many of the things that we now take for granted within our discipline. I left Cambridge University in 1971 with a solid background in quantitative methods and techniques – the quantitative revolution was in ascendance in the department then – but also with a mixed bag of regional geographic knowledge. I doubt that the words politics or the state had been mentioned in the entire three years I was there and I am certain that the word feminism was never uttered.

In 1989 Caroline Ramazanoglu wrote a paper reflecting from a feminist standpoint on the MA dissertation she had written in the early sixties, not so long before my career began. She argued that the new feminist scholarship that had developed in the 1970s and 1980s enabled her to rethink that earlier fieldwork, realizing the significance of gender, subjectivity, emotion and power in its execution.

> In 1960–61, I carried out a sample survey of married women who were working full-time shifts as bus conductresses, canteen workers or sugar packers. This research was written up as an MA thesis in the tradition of post-war British empiricism, within the framework of an implicitly positivist methodology. While the knowledge generated by a positivist methodology can be validated within the terms of that methodological position, comparison with knowledge produced within the framework of other methodologies enables one to judge it 'inadequate' . . . . I want to consider in what respects a comparable study of shiftworkers from a feminist standpoint would constitute improved knowledge.
>
> In 1960 it was generally assumed that objective knowledge could be produced from survey research. I proceeded according to the hypothetico-deductive method, and took for granted that men were at the centre of the social world. Women were defined in relation to men. . . . [This] male-centred scientific standpoint within which I was working, constructed

225

married women shiftworkers as 'abnormal'. Shiftwork cut across women's 'normal' obligations to their husbands and children. Women were effectively defined in terms of these obligations, rather than as workers . . . . My first problem was to find a link between theories of society and married women shiftworkers. Since these women were defined as socially abnormal, I never found a satisfactory link.

My other problems were not specified in the sociology texts of the time and there was nothing in my education which enabled me to cope with them. These were all problems which were rooted in various ways in unacknowledged power relations. My age was a problem as it denoted (accurately) inexperience, but the main areas of silence in the thesis are those of gender and sex, class, race, control and objectivity . . . I also lacked consciousness of the research process and the research context as part of the research. I did not, therefore, have either concepts or methods which would have enabled me to produce much knowledge of what was happening in the lives of the women, in the organisation of work and domestic life, or in the research process. (Ramazanoglu 1989: 427–8).

This would have been a common experience among putative feminist scholars in the 1960s and 1970s. In 1993 I interviewed Susan Hanson (Professor of Geography at Clark University, in Worcester, Massachusetts, an important place for women and for feminist scholarship) about her career as a geographer. She explained how the development of feminist theories helped her clarify a growing interest in women's unequal circumstances that were revealed in the time budget analyses she began as a post-doctoral researcher in a period dominated by positive and quantitative analyses (see McDowell 1994a). She started graduate work towards the end of the 1960s and this is how she remembered that period of her life:

I started out doing research on travel patterns in Uppsala in Sweden. Behavioural geography was just beginning when I was at grad. school. It was the first chink in the armour of the positivist story. It was the first rumour of the idea that everybody's view is partial and it depends on your location and all those sorts of things. I developed an interest in gender in the 1970s as I used the Uppsala data to look at activity patterns of women and men. One thread of my work was an interest in multipurpose trips and 'trip chaining', which relates to the complexities of women's lives, to the combination of all sorts of activities in the daily space-time path. I was arguing against the transportation planners who thought the journey to work was the main sort of travel you needed to plan for and who thought of it as a simple, single-stop trip.

I wasn't at all influenced by feminism then. I just knew women had more complicated lives. I was unblissfully ignorant of feminism at that point. Where did the questions come from? At some point in the 1970s I became influenced by feminism but then a lot of the questions came from behavioural geography. (McDowell 1994a: 21)

And Janet Townsend, a British geographer of a similar age and standing, has told me how feminism altered her view of her research focus. Commenting on her own gender blindness in her early work, she is now amazed that in her doctoral work in a Spanish-speaking area of the Andes, she ignored the relations of power between men and women. With hindsight and a decade or more of writing by feminist geographers behind her, she realized that the same data, the same circumstances, were open to a very different interpretation. Her reanalysis of the evidence, the envisioning of the particular social context and behaviours, from a feminist perspective gives it a different meaning: a vivid illustration of a more contemporary acceptance by geographers that 'facts' are theory specific.

When Susan, Janet and I began our research careers there was still a dominant view in the discipline that research must be based on an ideal of scientific objectivity, denying personal experiences and personal interactions between a researcher and her informants. But these brief examples make it clear that research findings are not fixed nor immutable but subject to different interpretations as disciplines change and are influenced by different perspectives, be they Marxist, feminist, postmodernist or whatever, and the methodologies commonly employed within each perspective. For geographers, the sets of socio-spatial relations and the meanings of places that we uncover, and the explanations for them, are neither permanent nor constant but rather are multiple and varied. They are constructed by researchers whose outlooks differ, who may or may not have experiences of the phenomena under consideration, whose depth and breadth of reading, of imagination varies, and whose interpretation of similar events will change over time, both as her or his own knowledge and life experiences broaden and deepen and as the nature of geography as a discipline changes.

While this recognition has been and still is deeply contested in certain parts of the geographic discipline, there is now an acceptance by many that places and events have multiple meanings and multiple interpretations, and that these may be considered at different scales. Those geographers who have been influenced by what has become known as 'the cultural turn' in parts of the social sciences and humanities have begun to see places as a sort of spatial text that may be interpreted by 'readers', positioned and differentiated from each other by their gender, class, ethnicity, age and life's experiences (Barnes and Duncan 1992; Duncan and Ley 1994; Duncan and Duncan 1988; McDowell 1994b). So, it is argued, a place is perceived differently through the eyes of different people. Extending this argument, all academic writing should, as Gerry Pratt noted in her reflections on feminism and the influence of postmodern thought, 'be seen as a process rather than a product' (1993: 51).

While this is still contested and is often attributed to adherents of a 'postmodern' outlook, the claim that women see the world through different eyes has always been a central tenet of feminist scholarship. From the early days of feminist geography almost three decades ago, it has been argued that women and men are positioned differently in the world and that their relationship to the places in which they live is thus different too. These differences are the outcome of that particular structured set of inequalities that result in women's inferiority to, and oppression by men in different places at different times. While, as I have shown in this book, it is now clearly recognized that the forms taken by women's oppression are historically and geographically varied, and further that the simple binary distinction between women and men is too polarized a view of the world, the insistence on changing relationships of power and inequality based on a gendered division is what distinguishes feminist from postmodern analyses of difference. In this sense, feminist scholarship remains a modernist project with political and progressive aims.

Women studying women?

In the beginning, feminist geographers, including Susan Hanson, Gerry Pratt, Janet Townsend and me, took it for granted that our research subjects were women. While this may seem a trite or obvious statement, reflect for a moment on the differences between these terms: women, men, femininity, masculinity and gender relations. While the first two words encourage us to investigate the spatial behaviour, attitudes or whatever of women and men, taking for granted their gender and its associated characteristics, the second two encourage us to question the association of the *social* characteristics of femininity (docility, passivity, nurturing or emotional behaviour and so forth) and masculinity (aggression, rationality, controlled emotions, etc.) with biologically distinguished women and men and ask whether and how these attributes map on to bodies. And by posing questions in terms of gender *relations*, it became clearer that in order to come to conclusions about women, we need also to ask questions about men. This relational understanding, while always implicit in the early research which was basically designed to ask a set of geographical questions about why are women different from men, was not explicit in the earliest body of geographical research where the focus was firmly on women.

Now, however, it is accepted that in order to understand the position of women as the subordinate 'other' to men, and the social construction of femininity as inferior to an idealized version of masculinity, it is important to undertake research about men and masculinity, as well as about women and femininity. As Alison Scott argues in considering her own specialist interest, gender segregation in the workplace, this now seems such an obvious point, but in the early years the eyes of feminist researchers were focused almost without exception on women. She writes:

> During the last decade or so, research on women and employment has increasingly focused on gender segregation, that is the fact that women tend to work in jobs and occupations that are dominated by women and men in ones that are dominated by men. It has proved to be one of the most profound dimensions of labour market inequality and one of the most enduring. Yet the sex ratio of a job has only recently come to be taken seriously as a labour market variable, and then only in studies of women and employment. . . . It is [however] an essential datum for the analysis of employment whether or not the research is specifically concerned with gender.
>
> [The book is concerned with] methodological innovation [in several aspects. One is] the inclusion of men. . . . The inclusion of men might seem obvious to many working in this field today, but we should remember that gender segregation is still popularly perceived as a 'women's problem'. Moreover, early studies of gender segregation were mainly concerned with women, and, perhaps as a consequence of that, there have been few data available for men. Studies of men's employment – which dominated industrial relations and labour market studies for so long – were not specifically concerned with gender segregation . . . systematic comparisons between men and women – which are essential to the analysis of relative inequality – could not be made. (Scott 1994: 1–3)

The implications for research design and the selection of informants is clear. We must include men in our samples in future research designed to elicit the comparative position of women. Thus in my own work on occupational segregation in merchant banks, I compared a sample of women and men in the same occupations in order to address questions about differential rewards for similar tasks, qualifications, work histories and promotion patterns and prospects (McDowell 1997a).

But the initial focus on women was important and had a number of interesting implications. For many feminists it was a political decision to study women, a strategy to make us visible, to reveal our previous exclusion from the corpus of geographical research (one of the earliest papers, for example, was called 'On not excluding half of the human in human geography' (Hanson and Monk 1982, and see the extract below). There has been a long debate since then about the political significance of the difference between naming this research women's studies or gender studies, with anxieties about the possibility of co-option by men of something called gender studies. But the focus on women, and the designation

229

women's studies, brought dangers with it. Within geography, there developed too easy an association of the 'geography of women' with women academics and students. It was assumed by many that this new type of work was only for and by women and that once a small beginning had been made in a corner of a course, a journal or a department, then women could be left to get on with it. The rest of geographical research might go on as usual, untouched by questions of gender divisions and power relations, and with almost no recognition that the ungendered, disembodied individuals that appeared as the subjects of this research were, in the main, men. But note in the extract below that Hanson and Monk were aware of this danger and rejected this separation in their 1982 paper.

> Our purpose here is to identify some sexist biases in geographic research and to consider the implications of these for the discipline as a whole. We do not accuse geographers of having been actively or even consciously sexist in the conduct of their research but we would argue that, through omission of any consideration of women, most geographic research has been passively, often inadvertently, sexist. It is not our primary aim to castigate certain researchers or their traditions, but rather to provoke lively and constructive criticism on the ways in which a feminist perspective might be incorporated into geography.
>
> There appear to us to be two alternative paths to this goal of feminising the discipline. One is to develop a strong feminist strand of research that would become one thread among many in the thick braid of geographic tradition. We support such research as necessary but not sufficient. The second approach, which we favour, is to encourage a feminist perspective within all streams in human geography. In this way issues concerning women would become incorporated in all geographic research endeavours. (p. 11)

If you look at the list of authors who were involved in the early years of putting women's lives on the geographical agenda you will see that almost without exception they have been women geographers. In the early stages, our male colleagues seemed to assume either they were ungendered or that women were not worth studying. In these years, feminist researchers insisted that a wide range of new areas, often at the finest spatial scale, should be opened up for investigation. These included childcare provision, domestic power relations, housework, women's life-cycle stages (single parenthood, widowhood, etc.) and their relationship to spatial behaviour, women's fear of urban violence, women's workplace trips, women's access to resources such as healthcare, women's friendship networks, women's (lack of) social mobility, women's informal and community work at different stages of economic development, in advanced industrial societies as well as in 'Third World' societies. Because the subjects were new or previously unrecognized, it was often a major challenge to assemble appropriate information and data sets.

Collecting the data

One of the first methodological issues, therefore, was to establish whether there were any existing data sources that were useful. Joni Seager and Ann Olson began this task on a cross-national basis and produced a wonderful and innovative atlas *Women in the World* (1986), which is now available in a third edition produced by Joni Seager (1997). Janet Townsend (1991) has drawn up a useful table showing the types of information that are needed to do comparative work and to construct what she terms a regional geography of gender, that will reveal the extent variations in the lives and opportunities of women and men. I have reproduced it here to show what still remains to be done just to describe gender-based inequities (see table 9.1).

The issue of the lack of accurate statistics is, of course, often inseparable from conceptual questions. Unless, for example, unpaid labour is classified as 'work' and so counted as the subject matter of economic geography, in the same way as waged work is, then statistics about unpaid work will not be collected. And while the 'informal' economy has long been a focus of interest among geographers working in 'developing' countries, the assumption that in 'advanced' societies waged work in the 'formal' economy has replaced other forms of work militates against the collection of accurate statistics about other forms of work, which until recently were dominated by women. Here feminist geographers have interests in common with feminist economists in their arguments that, for example, the statistics for the gross national and gross domestic products are inaccurate without including domestic labour (see, for example, Marilyn Waring's arguments in her book *If Women Counted* (1989)). But remember too that, as I reported in chapter 5, the British government as recently made a gesture in this direction.

Thinking about feminist methods

In beginning the task of making women's lives in different parts of the world more visible to geographers, feminists began to ask themselves whether there might be different ways of doing things. This question seemed particularly important in areas of development, urban and social geography where the questionnaire survey, the interview and the case study were established methods. Perhaps there was a specifically feminist way to

231

Table 9.1   Extensive data for a regional geography of gender

---

These variables could in theory be mapped at all scales from the local to the international, but the data are often not available. (The majority are in use somewhere, but only those asterisked are widely available on an international basis, and the quality and comparability may still be poor.) The classification of variables is of necessity coarse, with much overlap between classes. Intra-gender differentiation is often as important as inter-gender.

The gendering of spatial divisions of labour: who does what, when where and how? (All data by gender)

Time budgets
Unpaid work: participation rates, kind of activities, share of the work
Paid work: full time: participation rates*, share of the labour force*, unemployment
Paid work: part time and/or casual: participation rates, share of the labour force
Paid work: participation rates of single, married and divorced people, and by parents by age and number of dependent children
Occupational and industrial concentration and segregation
Length of working life
Incomes, income distribution, wages/earnings
Trade union membership
Proportion covered by social security or insurance schemes
Proportion dependent on state support
Ownership of property, usufruct rights, access to credit
Leisure time, leisure activities

The gendering of the sexual contract

Rates of different sexualities
Legal age and average age of first marriage by gender
Marriage rate, divorce rate
Prevalence of common law marriage, arranged marriage
Per cent of adults who are: single, ever married, divorced, widowed by age and gender
Births to unmarried women, births to teenage women, rates of childlessness, adoption
Household structures, percentage of woman-headed households, proportion living alone
Rates of prostitution by gender and age
Violence: the incidence of marital rape, the incidence of homicide, assault, incest, child abuse, by gender of perpetrator and victim
Genital mutilation (excision or infibulation of girls, castration of boys) by gender

The gendering of space

Personal space, activity space (daily and lifetime), use of transport (public and private), and migration by gender and age
Urban and rural sex ratios, by gender and age
Marital residence and marriage distance
The incidence of purdah, seclusion and the veil
Non-marital sexual harassment, rape, assault, homicide: incidence in the home, workplace and public space by gender of perpetrator and victim
Gendering by the state

Formal political power (all data by gender)

Suffrage*, registered voters, membership of political parties
Office holders at different levels of government, legislature and executive

Legal rights

Individual rights by gender
Entitlement to equal opportunity, equal pay etc., if any*
Gay rights
Maternity and paternity rights, rights to abortion
Parental and marital rights; rights to divorce by gender
Inheritance

Gendered state policies e.g. conscription, maternity benefit, censorship

The gendering of well-being (all data by gender)

Life expectancy*, median age
Mortality (by cause and age, including maternal* and infant* mortality
Morbidity, including incidence of infertility, rates of sexually transmitted diseases
Defined disabilities
Health care, e.g. immunisation
Nutrition, age at puberty
Suicide rates, crime rates, alcoholism, etc.

The gendering of biological reproduction

Sex ratios* (age-specific and overall)
Contraception (type, availability, level of use*), rates of abortion*
Total fertility rates (females*; rarely available for males)
Fertility ratio* (number of children under 5 per thousand adult women)
Son or daughter preference, infanticide by gender

Table 9.1 contd:

Table 9.1 *contd*

The gendering of the reproduction of society

Care facilities for children

Education (all data by gender and where possible by age)

Rates of literacy*
Rates of enrolment* and attendance
Levels of attainment and specialisation
Numbers of teachers by rank, subject, and level of pupils

Religion

Religious adherence: significance for gender identity, activity space and
    opportunity

Gendered customs

Gendered organisation e.g. clubs
Media representation of gender and sexuality
Attitudes to rape and wife-battering
Dowry or brideprice
Kinship systems

Diversity in the locality, region or country

Ethnicity

Resistance: the gendering of change

Organisations seeking to change the existing construction of gender
Refuges for battered spouses, rape victims

Source: J. G. Townsend, 'Towards a regional geography of gender', *Geographical
Journal*, 157 (1991), pp. 26–7, table 1

'administer' a questionnaire, for example? Indeed the very word administer grated, as did the advice from conventional texts on methods in human
geography to remain distant from the research 'subject', to strain for objectivity and lack of involvement for fear of bias or contaminating the
evidence by personal interaction. This went against the grain of the emphases in the women's movement about participation, empathy with women,
and support for our 'sisters'.

Table 9.2 is taken from a discussion in the early 1980s of the differences

Table 9.2   Contrasting claims of research methods

Mainstream methods claim to be	An alternative method would acknowledge that it is
Exclusively rational in the conduct of research and analysis of data	A mix of rational, serendipitous and intuitive phenomena in research and analysis
Scientific	Accurate but artistic
Oriented to carefully defined structures	Oriented to process
Completely impersonal	Personal
Oriented to the prediction and control of events and things	Oriented to the understanding of phenomena
Interested in the validity of research findings for scholars	Interested in the meaningfulness of research findings to the scholarly and user communities
Objective	A mix of objective and subjective orientations
Capable of producing generalised principles	Capable of producing specific explanations
Interested in replicable events and procedures	Interested in unique although frequently occurring phenomena
Capable of producing completed analyses of a research problem	Limited to producing partial discoveries of on-going events
Interested in addressing problems with predefined concepts	Interested in generating concepts in vivo, in the field itself

Source: S. Reinharz, 'Experiential analysis: a contribution to feminist research', in G. Bowles and R. Duelli-Klein (eds), *Theories of Women's Studies*, London: Routledge and Kegan Paul, 1983, p. 168, table 11.1

between conventional research methods and alternative methods by a feminist sociologist, but her table is equally applicable to the geography of the time (although it is interesting to compare the similarities of the characteristics of the alternative method with geographers' discussions in the 1980s of the advantages of case studies, see Sayer and Morgan 1985 for example).

There was a general agreement that collaborative methods must be part of a feminist research strategy. Any woman interviewing women must, it was argued, recognize and build on their commonalities of experience and become part of a mutual exchange of views between the researcher and her collaborators. Hence the assertion in the title of an influential paper by Ann Oakley, a British feminist sociologist: 'Interviewing women: a contradiction in terms' (1981). Recognizing our humanity, or rather our common femininity, and drawing on women's documented attributes of interactive rather than interrogational conversational and interview styles, feminists were encouraged to share their experiences with other women, and to produce research findings that were for as well as about their subjects. The desirable attributes of a feminist style of research, compared with conventional ways of doing research are laid out in table 9.3, which extends the series of contrasts in table 9.2.

The most common strategy advocated by feminists in the search for a collaborative and non-exploitative relationship with the participants has been some variant of a qualitative methodology, either based on in-depth interviews, or on participant observation and ethnographic research methods. Thus it is often argued that qualitative, detailed, small-scale and in-depth case study work is particularly well suited to women studying women. Such methods use to best advantage skills of listening, empathy and the validation of (shared) personal experiences. Case study work, in particular, is seen as allowing the development of a less exploitative and more egalitarian relationship between a researcher and her participants than is possible using other methodological approaches and tools.

The interconnections and relationships that build up over time between an interviewer and her respondents are thus seen as a valid part of the research process, rather than something to be guarded against. Intersubjectivity rather than objectivity is the ideal to strive for in feminist case study work and should be recognized as part of the research output rather than excluded from the final product. Many feminist methods texts of the 1980s saw interactive forms of participant observation, in particular, as the ideal method for the achievement of feminist ends. As Duelli-Klein argued, 'a methodology that allows for women studying women in an interactive process will end the exploitation of women as research objects' (1983: 95).

Looking back this seems an over-optimistic view and in more recent exchanges about research methods it is increasingly recognized that relations of power, and even exploitation, are not insignificant just because we are all women. We need to think about our own position, especially the power we may have. In 1992, Helen Callaway, a feminist anthropologist suggested that 'the project of "engendering knowledge" requires that the study of other societies, including their gender relations and their ideologies, be carried out with scrupulous examination of ourselves as gendered identities. This means continuing scrutiny of the submerged

Table 9.3   A comparison of conventional and feminist research methods

	Conventional or patriarchal	Alternative or feminist
Units of study	Predefined, operationalised concepts stated as hypotheses	Natural events encased in their ongoing contexts
Sharpness of focus	Limited, specialised, specific exclusive	Broad, inclusive
Data type	Reports of attitudes and actions as in questionnaires, interviews and archives	Feelings, behaviour, thoughts, insights, actions as witnessed or experienced
Topic of study	Manageable issue derived from scholarly literature, selected for potential scholarly contribution, sometimes socially significant	Socially significant problem sometimes related to issues discussed in the scholarly literature
Role or research:		
in relation to environment	Control is desired, attempt to manage research conditions	Openness, immersion, being subject to and shaped by it
in relation to subjects	Detached	Involved, sense of commitment, participation, sharing of fate
as a person	Irrelevant	Relevant, expected to change during process
impact on researcher	Irrelevant	Anticipated, recorded, reported, valued
Implementation of method	As per design, decided a priori	Method determined by unique characteristics of field setting
Validity criteria	Proof, evidence, statistical, significance: study must be replicable and yield the same results to have valid findings	Completeness, plausibility, illustrativeness, understanding, responsiveness to readers' subjects' experience; study cannot be replicated

Table 9.3 *contd*

The role of theory	Crucial as a determinant of research design	Emerges from research implementation
Data analysis	Arranged in advance, relying on deductive logic, done when all data are 'in'	Done during the study, relying on changing ideas as the research is in progress
Manipulation of data	Utilisation of statistical analyses	Creation of gestalts and meaningful patterns
Research objectives	Testing hypotheses	Development of understanding through grounded concepts and descriptions
Presentation format	Research report: report of conclusions with regard to hypotheses stated in advance, or presentation of data obtained from instruments	Story, description with emergent concepts including documentation of process of discovery
Failure	Statistically insignificant variance	Pitfalls of process illustrate the subject
Values	Researchers' attitudes not revealed, recognised or analysed, attempts to be value-free, objective	Researchers' attitudes described and discussed, value acknowledged, revealed, labelled
Role of reader	Scholarly community addressed, evaluation of research design, management and findings	Scholarly and user community addressed and engaged; evaluate usefulness and responsiveness to perceived needs

Source: S. Reinharz, 'Experiential analysis: a contribution to feminist research', in G. Bowles and R. Duelli-Klein (eds), *Theories of Women's Studies*, London: Routledge and Kegan Paul, 1983, pp. 170–2, table 11.4

power relations in the discourses of our own society as well' (see Callaway 1992: 30).

It may seem to be the easiest thing in the world, once you have decided whom to study, to talk to other women, gain their confidence and discover all sorts of things about their lives, even given the differences in age, class and, sometimes, nationality that divide us from each other. Janet Finch remarked, in a reflection on her own study of clergy wives and playgroup mothers, on 'the extreme ease with which, in my experience, a woman researcher can elicit material from other women' (1983: 71). But this easy establishment of a rapport with other women does not free us from exploitative social relations between researcher and researched (although these are not always biased in favour of the researcher) or even from the dangers of betraying our subjects.

Judith Stacey (1988, 1990), a self-identified feminist sociologist, found that in her work on family relationships in California's Silicon Valley, she came to question the assumption that qualitative methods reduce the distance between a researcher and her subjects. She found that in the course of her own detailed ethnographic fieldwork with two extended families, she was more, not less, likely to become bound to her informants in a network of exploitative relationships, abandonment and betrayal than in her earlier work. Thus, she argued, 'precisely because ethnographic research depends upon human relationship, engagement and attachment, it places research subjects at grave risk of manipulation and betrayal by the ethnographer' (Stacey 1988: 22–3). She described several situations (a lesbian affair, a secret paternity case and illicit activities) the knowledge of which she felt placed her 'in situations of inauthenticity, dissimilitude, and potential, perhaps inevitable, betrayal, situations I now believe are inherent in the fieldwork method' (p. 23). In my own PhD work with the deprived tenants of private landlords in inner London, I faced similar problems, as individuals either told me things about their lives that I would much rather not have been privy to, or, more problematically, expected or hoped that I would be able to advise or assist them in tenant–landlord disputes.

Daphne Patai, in a reflection on the possibility of interactive and empowering research methodologies – in her case in fieldwork with 'Third World' women – recognized similar issues. There are dangers when, as she puts it, 'feminist researchers are unconsciously seductive towards their research subjects, raising their expectations and inducing dependency' (1991: 143). Women studying women are quite likely to find themselves in circumstances where they are more knowledgeable, more powerful, more affluent or with greater access to a range of resources than the women they are studying. It is too easy to inadvertently raise expectations of positive intervention on behalf of the women being studied, leading to feelings of disappointment or betrayal, often on both sides.

Whether or not it is possible to be both field researcher and political/ feminist activist is discussed by Nancy Scheper-Hughes who worked in a shantytown in Brazil as a health worker and later went back as an academic anthropologist. Her book, *Death without Weeping* (1992), is a moving account of her long involvement there. Her first encounter with the settlement was as a Peace Corps volunteer. Scheper-Hughes was in her early twenties and she was a public health/community development worker. When she returned fifteen years later with a doctorate in anthropology, she tried to relate to the same women she had known from the previous visit in an 'academic' rather than personal sense, keeping her distance from them and their everyday demands. But in a final visit five years later, Scheper-Hughes realized that separating her academic role from her previous role as a friend and an activist was neither possible nor appropriate. In the extracts, she explains her shifting position.

> Lordes, Tonieta, Biu, and their families and friends were my immediate neighbours when I first lived and worked in the hillside shanty town from 1964 through the end of 1966, and their life experiences serve as a kind of divining rod that pulls me back always to a phenomenologically grounded anthropology. My experience of this small and tormented human community now spans a quarter of a century. And this ethnography has its origins not in certain theoretical conundrums (although these are found here too) but in practical realities and dilemmas. (p. 4)

> During this first encounter with Brazil, I confess to viewing the occasional anthropologists I ran into as remote individuals, overly preoccupied with esoterica and largely out of touch with the practical realities of everyday life in Brazil. . . . Nevertheless by the time I returned, fifteen years had elapsed, and it was anthropology, and not political or community activism, that was the vehicle of my return. . . . As for Lordes, Biu, and Tonieta, they had joined my other former neighbours and coworkers to become – and I fear there is no good word for it – key 'informants', research 'subjects', and assistants . . . at least initially. (p. 14)

During that visit, Scheper-Hughes was determined to separate academic work from political activism.

> Each time the women approached me with their requests, I backed away saying, 'This work is cut out for you. My work is different now. I cannot be an anthropologist and a companheira at the same time.' I shared my new reservations about the propriety of an outsider taking an active role in the life of a Brazilian community. But my argument fell on deaf ears. (p. 17)

> When I returned again five years later [I divided] my time not always equally between fieldwork and community work, as it was defined and dictated to me by the activist women and men of the town. If they were 'my' informants, I was very much 'their' despachante (an intermediary who expedites or

240

hastens projects along) and remained very much 'at their disposal'. I have had to occupy a dual role ever since 1985, and it has remained a difficult balance, rarely free of conflict. (p. 18)

In this examples, the researcher is more powerful, at least in certain senses, than her subjects, but clearly there are circumstances where the inequalities of power and prestige are weighted against the researcher. And in my own work on occupational gender segregation in merchant banks I was the supplicant, wanting access to busy, powerful people, with little to offer in return. What sort of methods are appropriate in these or similar circumstances? As Finch remarked, it is often easy to get other women to talk to us, although I found that powerful women are often more reluctant to reveal their feelings and information about their lives than women in other circumstances. But women researchers often find that it is also comparatively easy to get men to open up to them, used as they are to a sympathetic female listener – although the relations between male informant and female researcher are very different from relations when the researcher and her subjects are the same sex.

How ethical then is it to use one's femininity (even feminine 'wiles') to extract information from male respondents? And what sorts of images of femininity, which particular versions of ourselves should we and do we present to different interviewees? Although facilitating an interview may be relatively easy for a woman interviewing a man, it may also prove a frustrating experience as it is often difficult to break the conventions of powerful male/submissive female, talking man/listening woman dichotomy. I have undertaken too many interviews when men in powerful positions have told me what they assume I want to hear without listening to me.

Clearly interviewing men, if one is a woman, challenges the methodological assumptions that have informed feminist research. Those dominant ideas about common life experiences, at least in gender terms, and the development of empathetic relations with the researched no longer hold true. This does not mean, however, that the feminist critique of conventional methods should be dismissed. Whether it is men or women who are being interviewed or doing the interviewing, Callaway's comment, should be taken seriously: 'A deepening understanding of our own gendered identities and the coded complexities of our being offer the best resources for gaining insights into the lives of others' (1992: 30).

We are all gendered subjects and research interactions between us are affected by the assumptions about gender – about status and authority, about being in or out of place – that are related to our gendered identity. Reflexive research methods and styles of writing that take these personal relationships into account rather than attempting to ignore them are equally valid whether our subjects are women or men or the relations between them. These methods, as Ramazanoglu argued, 'improve' our research.

But there are other difficult ethical questions, too, facing all researchers who rely on qualitative methods. Is it ethical, for example, to reveal our research aims, and perhaps our politics, to those we know to be sympathetic to our views, but to disguise our purpose from informants we know would refuse to speak to us if they could read our minds? And how should we react to views that we ourselves might find offensive – sexist or racist comments perhaps – but that interviewees, feeling that they might trust us, feel able to express? In the extract below, Carol Smart outlines some of the problems she faced when interviewing lawyers and magistrates:

> The scope for employing feminist research practice when interviewing lawyers and magistrates is limited. I could open doors for myself or decline assistance with my coat but such practices are hardly revolutionary. In fact in my experience interviewing the legal profession and the magistracy gives very few opportunities for feminist practice to emerge. One important reason for this was the presumption in almost all the interviews that the interviewer and interviewee shared the same values and probably politics. This meant that in order to express a dissenting view the interviewer not only had to find an opportunity but would have, in the process, shattered the inferential structure within which the interview was carried out. In other words the interview would have become impossible. (1984: 155–6)

That these ethical issues are not particular to women or to feminist-inspired work is made evident in the next extract where Michael Keith, a geographer involved in political work around anti-racist policies, discusses his PhD fieldwork and the issues it raised for him.

> My own participant observation work with the police ... was arguably deceitful, unrepresentative, undemocratic, and perhaps indefensible. (Abstract)

> I am interested in ... the ethical conflicts that necessarily arise in ethnographic reportage. ... In blunt, issue-specific terms, how does the ethnographer respond to racism, sexism, and other manifestations of bigotry by the researched subject? Conventional protocols might suggest that it is improper to be overtly judgemental about such displays, a breach of ethnographic trust.

> Sitting in an area car in one of the police divisions of the Metropolitan Police most notorious for confrontation between the police and black communities I had spent eight hours giving tacit approval to the policing judge-

ments of the two officers in the car through my own failure to challenge several comments I had found offensive. Several, though by no means all of these comments could be readily classified as racist, but when I eventually did fall out with my 'informants' it was over more general, and, I had thought, barely contentious politics. (1992: 553)

And while holding our tongues or biting our lips may be permissible, even advisable in certain circumstances if we do not want to jeopardize the interaction, a much more difficult question is raised by not speaking out, or by undertaking our research 'under cover'. Is it permissible, ethical, to deceive our informants about our true status?

A number of researchers who have identified themselves as feminist have, for example, taken jobs in order to do research on the gender relations of workplaces and have covertly recorded the words and actions of their co-workers. Here is the feminist geographer Pamela Moss reflecting on her doctoral research and the reasons why she decided to disguise her identity as a student and a researcher.

> I undertook a four-phase research project for my doctoral programme at McMaster University. [In the first phase] I was employed for three and a half months as a maid in a housekeeping franchises service. . . . Though it was a difficult decision, I went into the employment situation covertly. I figured that this type of complete immersion would allow me particular insights into the labour process that could be gained no other way. I also thought by being inside the process, I would be able to set effective goals for myself as well as participate in setting emancipatory goals for effective social and political change collectively from within. (1995b: 83).

> Of course, I had concerns . . . [they] lay with my relationships to the women employed at the franchise, my co-workers. Would I gain the same experiences of being a maid in relation to power and labour and its regulation had I gone in, announced I was a feminist marxist doctoral student doing a project on what it was like to be a woman working as a maid in a post-fordist organisation of waged domestic labour and seeking ways to organise women in spatially fragmented labour processes? I exaggerate the case to make a point: I wanted the experience of being a maid in a housekeeping services franchise, not of being a student wanting that experience – even though I knew I couldn't have it. (1995b: 84)

Pamela Moss found that differences between her experiences and attitudes and the other women meant that in many cases she didn't 'fit in': she watched different television programmes, for example, ate different things for her lunch, but she felt that these differences were overcome as she trod a fine line between dishonesty and openness.

243

I was always honest. I didn't lie about my situation, nor did I mislead anyone by volunteering false information. But, and it is here that openness kicked in, I waited to be asked. Although difficult, I felt my own conscious-ness as a woman would override the uncomfortable feelings, which, for the most part, it did. (p. 86)

But in her paper, Moss did not reveal whether she came clean to her co-workers about who she 'really' was, or whether she managed to become involved in campaigns to improve the lot of these working-class women. I was left feeling uneasy about her claims.

An extremely difficult ethical dilemma that is sometimes raised in covert research is what to do in circumstances when the 'undercover' status of the researcher leads to knowledge of, or even participation in, illegal activities. In his fascinating book *In Search of Respect: Selling Crack in El Barrio* (1995), the anthropologist Philip Bourgois documents the decisions facing him as he went on the streets with crack dealers and had to negotiate keeping his informants' confidences while not actually being arrested him-self. He also found his marriage under some strain as the young men he took home were, at times, distinctly anti-social in their behaviour.

There is no simple answer to these ethical dilemmas posed by the adop-tion of qualitative, in-depth and interactive research methods. As the ex-amples I have chosen show, they are not unique to feminist methods. Arlene Daniels, in a paper on self-deception and self-discovery in fieldwork, has argued:

It is in the nature of ethical problems that they are not generally clear-cut, readily or finally resolvable. It is in the nature of fieldwork that you are likely to find yourself up to the waist in a morass of personal ties, intimate experiences and lofty and base sentiments as your own sense of decency, vanity or outrage is tried. (1983: 213)

While no general guidance about how to deal with these difficult issues is possible, it seems to me that you must hold on to your own standards of ethical behaviour and decency, and treat others as you would be prefer to be treated yourself if the relationship between the researcher and researched were to be reversed.

Deconstructing women

In the early and heady years of adding women into geographical scholar-ship, we were perhaps guilty of taking the difference between men and women for granted and of assuming that women had interests in common.

244

In more recent research, both these assumptions have been challenged. There has been a changing emphasis in feminist research – away from the automatic assumption that women should be the primary focus of our work, towards an emphasis on the social construction of femininity and masculinity, and studies of the construction and maintenance of multiple gendered identities in a range of places, circumstances and geographic scales, from the home and the workplace to the nation. This refocusing has also entailed greater attention to questions of symbolism and meaning, to representations of gender relations in art, the media, high and popular culture in addition to the more usual interest of (feminist) geographers in material social relations. As I argued in the introductory chapter, this refocusing is part of the more general turn to questions of meaning and representation in social and cultural geography as a whole.

A related change of emphasis revolved around the often painful recognition that women themselves are situated within networks of unequal power relations. This recognition challenged earlier ideas of commonalities between women as women and it became clear that women's common interests could now longer be assumed but rather that their extent and bases had to be investigated. As women of colour had long pointed out, their position in Western societies riven by racism is different from that of white women. Women are also positioned differently by their social class, their age and family status, by their sexual inclination, by whether or not they are able-bodied (Chouinard and Grant, 1995). In different circumstances and places these social divisions divide one group of women from another, resulting in cross-cutting lines of difference. In particular circumstances, then, their interests may conflict or cohere. So for feminist researchers in the 1990s, the first step is to challenge the assumption that women *per se* are a self-evident group to investigate and ask which women, in what circumstances and why, are the focus of my work. What is it that constitutes a particular group of women as a suitable category to investigate? In retrospect, as Alison Scott noted about the inclusion of men in feminist research, it now seems so obvious that women are different from each other.

The attention to difference and to the multiple voices of women has had an interesting effect on the ways in which feminist researchers present their results. As was made clear by tables 9.1 and 9.2 from Reinharz's paper, now published many years ago, feminist scholars have long been attentive to ideas of the provisionality of their research findings and the ways in which the 'results' are represented. In recent work, however, there has been a noticeable and welcome attempt to deconstruct the authoritative nature of the academic authorial voice. In telling the provisional stories of different women's and men's lives, the author often becomes a participant in her own research. The ways in which her own experiences and life course lead to certain questions being posed to the participants of a research project become a valid part of the process, no longer disguised as academic 'objectivity'. Increasingly, academic research is recognized as one story among many, even as 'fiction'. Here work on rewriting colonial histories and geographies is instructive, counterposing the singular view of earlier geographers – often white men – to more recent reinterpretations of the 'evidence': the letters and documents of empire to which are added other sources such as women's journals and the letters of women who were 'only' wives, to tell a more complex and multidimensional story, as I argued in chapter 7.

When this recognition of multiple voices became part of the understanding of gendered identity itself, however, a serious challenge to the fundamental basis of feminist research seemed to have arisen. The deconstructive turn in postmodern philosophy has combined with recent developments within the scholarship of feminism to depose the rational centred subject of previous eras. This raises difficult questions for feminist research methodologies that assume or take as self-evident the distinction between men and women, and the status of each as a coherent identity. The interconnections between gender, ethnicity and class, for example, meant that the automatic privileging of gender divisions had to be questioned and, as Gerry Pratt argued in her own retrospective analysis of her work, 'we began to unravel gender . . . [and] to tell a nuanced and expanded story . . . a tale of ambiguity, contradictions, diversity, interwoven dimensions of class and gender power, resistance and change' (1993: 55).

For some this recognition of complexity and ambiguity led them to question whether an explicitly feminist research had any future at all. Reflecting on the implications of the 'postmodern turn' for feminist research in geography, in a pessimistic paper entitled 'Stuffed if I know!', J. K. Gibson-Graham pondered:

> If we are to accept that there is no unity, centre or actuality to discover for women, what is feminist research about? How can we speak of our experiences as women? Can we still use women's experiences as resources for social analysis? Is it possible to do research for women? How can we negotiate the multiple and decentred identities of women? (1994: 206)

As this quotation indicates, Gibson-Graham (actually two feminists Julie Graham and Kathy Gibson whose combined identity is a gesture towards destabilizing individual authorial authority) is still committed to the emancipatory ideal of research *for* women and to the construction of gender as a binary division – women and men. But in recent work, the binary division has been unravelled, as has the distinction between gender, the body and sexuality, as I indicated in earlier chapters. And as I argued in chapter 1, gender is theorized by some scholars as fluid and open to change through self-reflexive practices.

The coincidence of feminist and postmodern thought in an insistence on the constructed, discursive nature of identity, on ideas about spectacle and performance, has led to a pronounced shift in the nature of feminist research in geography into what we might broadly define as the cultural arena. Work examining the ways in which notions of masculinity and femininity are affected by and reflected in texts, symbols and material artefacts, ranging through film and literature, high and popular culture, monuments and the landscape, is growing in volume. This means that as geographers we are having to learn ways of looking and doing research that have been less common in past decades. Textual and visual analysis, for example, is now being added to the portfolio of skills taught in many graduate schools of geography, complementing, even supplanting, the social survey methods of an older social science-influenced feminist method.

Indeed, Michelle Barrett suggested some years ago that 'academically the social sciences have lost their purchase within feminism and the rising star lies with the arts, humanities and philosophy' (1992: 204–5). An examination of the papers published by *Gender, Place and Culture* is instructive here, and other geography journals certainly publish many more illustrations than they used to. As long as the significance of material structures of inequality continues to be recognized, I find this move to examine the symbolic structures of gender differentiation liberating and exciting.

Conclusion

So finally, at the end of a book introducing you to a range of feminist geographical scholarship, let us end with these questions: does gender still matter? Is the category of gender now so fluid as to be meaningless? Is feminist research still possible? Indeed is a feminist politics still necessary if we have deconstructed the category 'Woman'?

I expect, if you have arrived at the end of the book with me, you already know what my answer is. Yes, I believe feminist research and politics are still important. Although it is possible to deconstruct all experiences and argue that one is never *just* a woman (or a man) (and throughout each chapter I have tried to show how gender cannot be separated from age, class, race, and even appearance, for example), it is also clear that we live in societies that are structured by relations of power. In contemporary industrial societies, capitalist social relations divide people by class position. Working-class men and women may have interests in common that working-class women do not share with middle-class women or white women with black women. But in these societies rampant sexism continues to unite women. Over time and in different societies, the relative significance of different dimensions of power will change as power relations are differentially structured. The significance of race, class, gender and caste in India, for example, is different now from earlier periods. Power relations are variable and the analytical categories that structure our research must reflect this variability. But this is not to accept that there are endless divisions between us, or that they are so fluid as to be subject to rapid change. Our lives are structured by a small number of crucial relations of power and gender is one of them. As Susan Bordo recognized, 'like it or not, in our present culture, our activities *are* coded as "male" and "female" and will function as such within the prevailing system of "gender-power relations" ' (1990: 152, original emphasis).

Feminist geographical research has an important task here: to uncover the variation in these gender-power relations, the ways in which they are maintained and the ways in which they might be undermined. In this way, we can join in the project of overturning the currently limited ways in which we are forced to be either a woman or a man.

Further reading

There are numerous books about feminist methods, although few of these are directed to geographers, and the geographical methods texts tend to ignore feminist research. I still find Helen Robert's *Doing Feminist Research* (1981) helpful, although it was published a good number of years ago now. S. Gluck and D. Patai's *Women's Words: The Feminist Practice of Oral History* (1991) is also good, and Judith Stacey's article 'Can there be a feminist ethnography?' (1988) raises some important and difficult questions that have not lost their salience. The papers on feminist research by geographers collected in *The Professional Geographer* 1994 and 1995, *The Canadian Geographer* 1995 and *Antipode* 1995 are a good place to start if you are thinking about research and research methods, but I think that the most useful way to think about the different ways of doing research is to read empirically based papers and books published by feminist scholars. The journal *Gender, Place and Culture* is one place to start, and increasingly many of the main journals in our discipline are publishing excellent feminist research papers.

References

Abdo, N. and Yuval-Davis, N. 1995: Palestine, Israel and the Zionist settler project. In D. Stasiulis and N. Yuval-Davis (eds), *Unsettling Settler Societies*. London: Sage.

Acker, J. 1990: Hierarchies, jobs, bodies: a thory of gendered organisations. *Gender and Society*, 4, 139–58.

Adler, S. and Brenner, J. 1992: Gender and space: lesbians and gay men in the city. *International Journal of Urban and Regional Research*, 16, 24–34.

Afshar, H. (ed.) 1991: *Women, Development and Survival in the Third World*. London: Longman.

Ainley, R. (ed.) 1998: *New Frontiers of Space, Bodies and Gender*. London: Routledge.

Alcoff, L. 1988: Cultural feminism versus post-structuralism. Signs, 3, 404–36.

Alcoff, L. and Potter, S. (eds) 1993: *Feminist Epistemologies*. New York: Routledge.

Alexander, S. 1987: Women, class and sexual differences. In A. Phillips (ed.), *Feminism and Equality*. Oxford: Blackwell.

Allen, G. and Crow, G. (eds) 1989: *Home and Family: Recreating the Domestic Sphere*. Basingstoke: Macmillan.

Allen, J. and McDowell, L. 1989: *Landlords and Property*. Cambridge: Cambridge University Press.

Allen, J., Massey, D. and Cochrane, A. (eds) 1998: *Rethinking the Region*. London: Routledge.

Amadiume, I. 1987: *Male Daughters, Female Husbands: Gender and Sex in an African Society*. London: Zed Books.

Amott, T. and Matthaei, J. 1991: *Race, Gender and Work: A Multicultural Economic History of Women in the United States*. Montreal and New York: Black Rose Books.

Andermahr, S., Lovell, T. and Wolkowitz, C. 1997: *A Glossary of Feminist Theory*. London: Arnold.

Anderson, B. 1991: *Imagined Communities* (1983) (rev. and extended edn). London: Verso.

Anker, R. and Hein, C. (eds) 1986: *Sex Inequalities in Urban Employment in the Third World*. Basingstoke: Macmillan.

Anzaldua, G. 1987: *Borderlands/La Frontera: The New Mestiza*. San Francisco: Aunt Lute.

Appadurai, A. 1990: Disjuncture and difference in the global cultural economy. *Theory, Culture and Society*, 7, 295–310.

Ardener, S. (ed.) 1981: *Women and Space: Ground Rules and Social Maps*. London: Croom Helm.

Ashcroft, B., Griffiths, G. and Tiffin, H. (eds) 1995: *The Post-Colonial Studies Reader*. London: Routledge.

Atwood, M. 1996: *Alias Grace*. London: Bloomsbury.

Augé, M. 1996: *Non-places: The Anthropology of Super Modernity*. London: Verso.

Auster, C. 1996: *The Sociology of Work: Concepts and Cases*. Pine Thousand Oaks, Calif.: Pine Forge Press.

Bachelard, G. 1969: *The Poetics of Space* (1957). Boston: Beacon Press.

Bahloul, J. 1992: *The Architecture of Memory: A Jewish-Muslim Household in Colonial Algeria, 1937–1962*. Cambridge: Cambridge University Press.

Barnes, T. and Duncan, J. (eds) 1992: *Writing Worlds: Discourse, Text and Metaphor in the Representation of Landscape*. London: Routledge.

Barnett, C. 1996: 'A choice of nightmares': narration and desire in *Heart of Darkness*. *Gender, Place and Culture*, 3, 277–91.

Barrett, M. 1992: Words and things: materialism and method in contemporary feminist analysis. In M. Barrett and A. Phillips (eds), *Destabilizing Theory: Contemporary Feminist Debates*. Cambridge: Polity Press.

Barrett, M. and Phillips, A. (eds) 1992: *Destabilizing Theory: Contemporary Feminist Debates*. Cambridge: Polity Press.

Barron, R. and Norris, G. 1976: Sexual divisions and the dual labour market. In D. Barker and S. Allen (eds), *Dependence and Exploitation in Work and Marriage*. London: Longman.

Barrows, S. 1981: *Distorting Mirrors: Visions of the Crowd in Late Nineteenth Century France*. New Haven: Yale University Press.

Baudelaire, C. 1963: The painter of modern life (1864). In *The Painter of Modern Life and Other Essays*, ed. J. Mayne. Oxford: Phaidon Press.

Baumann, P. 1996: *Contesting Culture: Discourses of Identity in Multi-ethnic London*. Cambridge: Cambridge University Press.

Becker, G. S. 1975: *Human Capital*. Princeton: National Bureau of Economic Research, Princeton University Press.

Beechey, V. 1977: Some notes on female wage labour in capitalist production. *Capital and Class*, 3, 45–66.

Beechey, V. 1987: *Unequal Work*. London: Verso.

Bell, D. 1995: [Screw]ing Geography: guest editorial. *Environment and Planning D: Society and Space*, 13, 127–31.

Bell, D. and Valentine, G. 1995: *Mapping Desire*. London: Routledge.

Bell, D. and Valentine, G. 1997: *Consuming Geographies: We Are Where We Eat*. London: Routledge.

Bell, D., Binnie, J., Cream, J. and Valentine, G. 1994: All hyped up and no place to go. *Gender, Place and Culture*, 1, 31–48.

Best, S. 1995: Sexualizing space. In E. Grosz and E. Probyn (eds), *Sexy Bodies: The Strange Carnalities of Feminism*. London: Routledge.

Beynon, H., Hudson, R., Lewis, J., Sadler, D. and Townsend, A. 1988: 'It's all falling apart here': coming to terms with the future in Teesside. In P. Cooke (ed.), *Localities: The Changing Face of Urban Britain*. London: Unwin Hyman.

Bhabha, H. 1990: The third space: interview with Homi Bhabha. In J Rutherford (ed.), *Identity: Community, Culture, Difference*. London: Lawrence and Wishart.

Bhabha, H. 1994: *The Location of Culture*. London: Routledge.

Blee, K. 1991: *Women of the Klan: Racism and Gender in the 1920s*. Berkeley: University of California Press.

Blomley, N. 1996: 'I'd like to dress her all over': masculinity, power and retail space. In N. Wrigley and M. Lowe (eds), *Retailing, Consumption and Capital: Towards the New Retail Geography*. Harlow: Longman.

Blunt, A. 1994: *Travel, Gender and Imperialism*. London: Guilford.

Blunt, A. and Rose, G. 1994: *Writing Women and Space: Colonial and Postcolonial Geographies*. New York: Guilford.

Bondi, L. 1990: Progress in geography and gender: feminism and difference. *Progress in Human Geography*. 14, 438–45.

Bondi, L. 1991: Gender divisions and gentrification: a critique. *Transactions of the Institute of British Geographers*, 16, 190–8.

Bondi, L. 1992: Gender and dichtomy. *Progress in Human Geography*, 16, 98–104.

Bondi, L. 1998: Gender, class and urban space: public and private space in contemporary urban landscapes. *Urban Geography*, 19, 160–85.

Booth, C., Darke, J. and Yeandle, S. (eds) 1996: *Changing Places: Women's Lives in the City*. London: Paul Chapman.

Bordo, S. 1990: Feminism, postmodernism and gender scepticism. In L. Nicholson (ed.), *Feminism/Postmodernism*. London: Routledge.

Bordo, S. 1992: Review essay: postmodern subjects, postmodern bodied. *Feminist Studies*, 18, 159–75.

Bordo, S. 1993: *Unbearable Weight: Feminism, Western Culture and the Body*. Berkeley: University of California Press.

Bourdieu, P. 1977: *Outline of a Theory of Practice*. Cambridge: Cambridge University Press.

Bourdieu, P. 1984: *Distinction: A Social Critique of the Judgement of Taste*. London: Routledge.

Bourdieu, P. 1989: Social space and symbolic power. *Sociological Theory*, 7, 14–25.

Bourgois, P. 1995: *In Search of Respect: Selling Crack in El Barrio*. Cambridge: Cambridge University Press.

Bowlby, R. 1985: *Just Looking: Consumer Culture in Dreiser, Gissing and Zola*. London: Methuen.

Bowles, G. and Duelli-Klein, R. 1983: *Theories of Women's Studies*. London: Routledge and Kegan Paul.

Boys, J. 1984: Is there a feminist analysis of architecture? *Built Environment*, 10, 25–34.

Boys, J. 1990: Women and the designed environment. *Built Environment* 16, 249–56.

Bozzoli, B. 1991: *The Women of Phokeng*. London: Currey.

Bradley, H. 1989: *Men's Work, Women's Work*. Cambridge: Polity Press.

Braidotti, R. 1994: *Nomadic Subjects*. New York: Columbia University Press.

Breitbart, M. M. and Pader, E.-J. 1995: Establishing ground: representing gender and race in a mixed housing development. *Gender, Place and Culture*, 2, 5–20.

Brewer, R. M. 1993: Theorizing race, class and gender. In S. M. James and A. P. A. Busia (eds), *Theorizing Black Feminisms: The Visionary Pragmatism of Black Women*. London: Routledge.

Brion, M. 1994: Snakes and ladders? Women and equal opportunities in education and training for housing. In R. Gilroy and R. Woods (eds), *Housing Women*. London: Routledge.

Bristow, J. 1997: *Sexuality*. London: Routledge.

Brydon, L. and Chant, S. (eds) 1989: *Women in the Third World: Gender Issues in Rural and Urban Areas*. London: Edward Elgar.

Buck-Morss, S. 1991: *The Dialectics of Seeing: Walter Benjamin and the Arcades Project*. Cambridge Mass.: MIT Press.

Burgess, J. 1996: Focusing on fear. *Area*, 28, 130–5.

Burgess, J., Harrison, C. and Limb, M. 1988: People, parks and the urban green: a study of popular meanings and values for open spaces in the city. *Urban Studies*, 25, 455–73.

Butler, J. 1990a: *Gender Trouble*. London: Routledge.

Butler, J. 1990b: Gender trouble: feminist theory and psychoanalytic discourse. In L. Nicholson (ed.), *Feminism/Postmodernism*. London: Routledge.

Butler, J. 1993: *Bodies that Matter*. London: Routledge.

Cain, M. 1986: Realism, feminism, methodology and the law. *International Journal of the Sociology of Law*, 14, 255–67.

Callaway, H. 1992: Ethnography and experience: gender implications in fieldwork and texts. In J. Okely and H. Callaway (eds), *Anthropology and Autobiography*. London: Routledge.

Cameron, D. 1985: *Feminism and Linguistic Theory*. London: Macmillan.

Campbell, B. 1984: *Wigan Pier Revisited*. London: Virago.

Campbell, B. 1988: *Unofficial Secrets: Child Sex Abuse – the Cleveland Case*. London: Virago.

Campbell, B. 1993: *Goliath: Britain's Dangerous Places*. London: Methuen.

Carsten, J. and Hugh-Jones, S. (eds) 1995: *About the House: Lévi Strauss and Beyond*. Cambridge: Cambridge University Press.

Casebourne, J. 1997: Lesbian gentrification in San Francisco. Unpublished dissertation, Department of Geography, University of Cambridge.

Casey, C. 1995: *Work, Self and Society: After Industrialism*. London: Routledge.

Cassady, S. 1990: *Off the Road*. London: Black Spring.

Castells, M. 1978: *The Urban Question*. London: Arnold.

Castells, M. 1983: *The City and the Grassroots*. London: Edward Arnold.

Cavendish, R. 1983: *Women on the Line*. Basingstoke: Macmillan.

Chant, S. 1991: *Women and Survival in Mexican Cities: Perspectives on Gender, Labour Markets and Low Income Households*. Manchester: Manchester University Press.

Chant, S. and McIllwaine, C. 1995: *Women of a Lesser Cost: Female Labour, Foreign Exchange and Philippine Development*. London: Pluto.

Chatwin, B. 1979: *In Patagonia*. London: Picador.

Chatwin, B. 1987: *The Songlines*. London: Cape.

Chatwin, B. 1988: *Utz*. London: Cape.

Chauncey, G. 1995: *Gay New York: The Making of the Gay Male World 1890–1940*. London: Flamingo.

Chouinard, V. and Grant A. 1995: On not being anywhere near 'the project'. *Antipode*, 27, 137–66.

Christopherson, S. 1989: On being outside 'the project'. *Antipode*, 21, 83–9.

Clifford, J. 1988: *The Predicament of Culture*. Cambridge: Harvard University Press.

Clifford, J. 1997: *Routes: Travel and Translation in the Late Twentieth Century*. Cambridge: Harvard University Press.

Cockburn, C. 1983: *Brothers: Male Dominance and Technological Change*. London: Pluto Press.

Cockburn, C. 1986: *Machinery of Dominance*. London: Pluto Press.

Cockburn, C. 1991: *In the Way of Women: Man's Resistance to Sex Equality in Organisations*. Basingstoke: Macmillan.

Collinson, D. and Hearn, J. 1994: Naming men as men: implications for work, organisation and management. *Gender, Work and Organization*, 1, 2–22.

Colomina, B. (ed.) 1992: *Sexuality and Space*. Princeton: Princeton Architectural Press.

Connell, R. W. 1987: *Gender and Power*. Cambridge: Polity Press.

Connell R. W. 1995: *Masculinities*. Cambridge: Polity Press.

Cosgrove, D. 1993: Commentary: On 'The reinvention of cultural geography' by Price and Lewis. *Annals of the Association of American Geographers*, 83, 515–17.

Cosgrove, D. and Daniels, S. 1988: *The Iconography of Landscape*. Cambridge: Cambridge University Press.

Cowan, R. S. 1983: *More Work for Mother: The Ironies of Household Technology from the Open Hearth to the Microwave*. New York: Basic Books.

Coward, R. 1983: *Patriarchal Precedents: Sexuality and Social Relations*. London: Routledge and Kegan Paul.

Coward, R. 1984: *Female Desire*. London: Paladin.

Craig, C., Rubery, J., Tarling, R. and Wilkinson, F. 1982: *Labour Market Structure, Industrial Organisation and Low Pay*. Cambridge: Cambridge University Press.

Craig, S. (ed.) 1992: *Men, Masculinity and the Media*. Newbury Park, Calif.: Sage.

Crang, P. 1994: It's showtime. *Environment and Planning D: Society and Space*, 12, 675–704.

Crompton, R. and Sanderson, K. 1990: *Gendered Jobs and Social Change*. London: Unwin Hyman.

Daniels, A. K. 1983: Self-deception and self-discovery in fieldwork. *Qualitative Sociology*, 6, 195-214.

Davidoff, L. and Hall, C. 1987: *Family Fortunes: Men and Women of the English Middle Class*. London: Hutchinson.

Davies, M. L. 1978: *Maternity: Letters from Working Class Wives* (1915). London: Virago.

Davis, A. 1981: *Women, Race and Class*. New York: Random House.

Davis, K. 1991: Remaking the She-Devil: a critical look at feminist approaches to beauty. *Hypatia*, 6, 23–34.

Davis, M. 1989: *City of Quartz*. London: Verso.

de Almeida, M. V. 1996: *The Hegemonic Male: Masculinity in a Portugese Town*. Oxford: Berghahn.

de Beauvoir, S. 1972: *The Second Sex* (1949). Harmondsworth: Penguin.

Debord, G. 1994: *The Society of the Spectacle*. New York: Zone Books.

De Certeau, M. 1988: *The Practice of Everyday Life*, trans. S. Rendall. Berkeley: University of California Press.

DeLepervanche, M. 1989: Women, nation and the state in Australia. In N. Yuval-Davis and F. Anthias (eds), *Women-Nation-State*. London: Macmillan.

Dennis, N., Henriques, F. and Slaughter, C. 1956: *Coal is our Life*. London: Tavistock.

Dex, S. 1985: *The Sexual Division of Labour*. Brighton: Wheatsheaf.

Di Leonardo, M. 1991: *Gender at the Crossroads of Knowledge: Feminist Anthropology in the Postmodern Era*. Berkeley and Los Angeles: University of California Press.

Diprose, R. and Ferrell, R. (eds) 1991: *Cartographies: Poststructuralism and the Mappings of Bodies and Spaces*. Sydney: Allen and Unwin.

Domosh, M. 1988: Geography and gender: home, again? *Progress in Human Geography*, 22, 276–82.

Domosh, M. 1991a: Toward a feminist historiography of geography. *Transactions of the Institute of British Geographers*, 16, 95–104.

Domosh, M. 1991b: Beyond the frontiers of geographical knowledge. *Transactions of the Institute of British Geographers*, 16, 488–90.

Domosh, M. 1996a: *Invented Cities: The Creation of Landscape in Nineteenth Century New York and Boston*. New Haven and London: Yale University Press.

Domosh, M. 1996b: The feminized retail landscape: gender, ideology and consumer culture in nineteenth century New York City. In N. Wrigley and M. Lowe (eds), *Retailing, Consumption and Capital: Towards the New Retail Geography*. Harlow: Longman.

Donaldson, M. 1991: *Time of our Lives: Labour and Love in the Working Class*. Sydney: Allen and Unwin.

Donaldson, M. 1993: What is hegemonic masculinity? *Theory and Society*, 22, 643–57.

Donzelot, J. 1979: *The Policing of Families*. London: Hutchinson.

Douglas, M. 1966: *Purity and Danger*. London: Routledge and Kegan Paul.

Douglas, M. 1973: *Natural Symbols*. Harmondsworth: Penguin.

Dowler, L. 1998: 'And they think I'm just a nice old lady': women and war in Belfast, Northern Ireland. *Gender, Place and Culture*, 5, 159–76.

Dowling, R. 1993: Femininity, place and commodities: a retail case study. *Antipode*, 25, 295–319.

Driver, F. 1992: Geography's empire: histories of geographical knowledge. *Environment and Planning A: Society and Space*, 10, 23–40.

Duberman, M., Vicinus, M. and Chauncey, G. (eds) 1991: *Hidden from History: Reclaiming the Gay and Lesbian Past*. London: Penguin.

DuCille, A. 1996: *Skin Trade*. London: Harvard University Press.

Duelli-Klein, R. 1983: How to do what we want to do: thoughts on feminist methodology. In D. Bowles and R. Duelli-Klein (eds), *Theories of Women's Studies*. London: Routledge and Kegan Paul.

Du Gay, P. 1996: *Consumption and Identity at Work*. London: Sage.

Duncan, J. 1990: *City as Text*. Cambridge: Cambridge University Press.

Duncan, J. and Duncan, N. 1988: (Re)reading the landscape. *Environment and Planning D: Society and Space*, 6, 117–26.

Duncan, J. and Ley, D. 1994: *Place/Culture/Representation*. London: Routledge.

Duncan, N. 1996a: Renegotiating gender and sexuality in public and private spaces. In N. Duncan (ed.), *BodySpace*. London: Routledge.

Duncan, N. (ed.) 1996b: *BodySpace*. London: Routledge.

Dworkin, A. 1974: *Woman-Hating*. New York: Dutton.

Dyck, I. 1993: Ethnography: a feminist method? *Canadian Geographer*, 37, 50–2.

Dyck, I. 1995: Hidden geographies: the changing life worlds of women with disabilities. *Social Science in Medicine*, 40, 307–20.

Dyck, I. 1996: Women with disabilities and everyday geographies: home space and the contested body. In R. A. Kearns and W. M. Gesler (eds), *Putting Health into Place: Landscape, Identity and Well-being*. Syracuse: Syracuse University Press.

Ehrenreich, B. 1997: *Blood Rites: Origins and the History of War*. New York: Metropolitan Books.

Ehrlich, A. 1987: Israel: conflict, war and social change. In C. Creighton and M. Shaw (eds), *The Sociology of War and Peace*. London: Macmillan.

Eisenstein, Z. 1979: *Capitalist Patriarchy and the Case for Socialist Feminism*. New York: Monthly Review Press.

Eisenstein, Z. 1994: *The Colour of Gender: Reimaging Democracy*. London: University of California Press.

Elshtain, J. 1987: *Women and War*. New York: Basic Books.

Elson, D. and Pearson, R. 1981: 'Nimble fingers make cheap workers': an analysis of women's employment in Third World export manufacturing. *Feminist Review*, 7, 87–107.

Engels, F. 1972: *The Origin of the Family, Private Property and the State* (1884). London: Lawrence and Wishart.

England, K. 1994: Getting personal: reflexivity, positionality and feminist research. *Professional Geographer*, 46, 80–9.

England, K. (ed.) 1997: *Who Will Mind the Baby?* London: Routledge.

England, K. and Stiell, B. 1997: 'They think you're as stupid as your English is': constructing foreign domestic workers in Toronto. *Environment and Planning A*, 29, 195–215.

Enloe, C. 1983: *Does Khaki Become You? The Militarization of Women's Lives*. Boston: South End Press.

Enloe, C. 1989: *Bananas, Beaches and Bases: Making Feminist Sense of International Politics*. London: Pandora.

Enloe, C. 1993: *The Morning After: Sexual Politics and the End of the Cold War*. Berkeley: University of California Press.

Esping-Andersen, G. 1990: *The Three Worlds of Welfare Capitalism*. Cambridge: Polity Press.

Evans, M. 1997: *An Introduction to Contemporary Feminist Thought*. Cambridge: Polity Press.

Evans, M. and Redclift, N. 1987: *Engels Revisited*. London: Tavistock.

Falk, P. 1994: *The Consuming Body*. London: Sage.

Faulkner, A. and Lawson, V. 1991: Employment versus empowerment: a case study of the nature of women's work in Ecuador. *Journal of Development Studies*, 27, 16–47.

Feathersone, M., Hepworth, M. and Turner, B. (eds) 1991: *The Body: Social Process and Cultural Theory*. London: Sage.

Finch, J. 1983: 'It's great to have someone to talk to': ethics and politics of interviewing women. In C. Belland and H. Roberts (eds), *Social Researching: Politics, Problems, Practice*. London: Routledge.

Fincher, R. and Jacobs, J. M. (eds) 1998: *Cities of Difference*. New York: Guildford.

Fine, M., Weis, L., Addleston, J. and Mazuza, J. 1997: (In)secure times: constructing white working class masculinities in the late twentieth century. *Gender and Society*, 11, 52–68.

Fiske, J. 1992: *Reading the Popular* (1989). London: Routledge.

Fiske, J. 1993: *Power Plays, Power Works*. London: Verso.

Fitzgerald, F. 1986: *Cities on the Hill*. New York: Pantheon.

Fitzgerald, S. F. 1971: My lost city. In A. Trachtenberg, P. Neill and P. C. Bunnell (eds), *The City: American Experience*. New York: Oxford University Press.

Flax, J. 1990: *Thinking Fragments: Psychoanalysis, Feminism, and Postmodernism in the Contemporary West*. Berkeley: University of California Press.

Forest, B. 1995: West Hollywood as a symbol: the significance of place in the construction of a gay identity. *Environment and Planning D: Society and Space*, 13, 133–57.

Foucault, M. 1977: *Discipline and Punish*. London: Allen Lane.

Foucault, M. 1979: *The History of Sexuality*, vol. 1: *An Introduction*. London: Allen Lane.

Foucalt, M. 1987: *The History of Sexuality*, vol. 2: *The Use of Pleasure*. London: Penguin.

Foucalt, M. 1988: *The History of Sexuality*, vol. 3: *The Care of the Self*. London: Allen Lane.

Fox-Genovese, E. 1986: The claims of a common culture: gender, race, class and the canon. *Salmagundi*, 72, 119–32.

Frankenberg, R. 1993: *White Women, Race Matters: The Social Construction of Whiteness*. London: Routledge.

Fraser, N. 1990: Rethinking the public sphere: a contribution to the critique of actually existing democracy. *Social Text*, 25–6, 56–80.

Fraser, N. 1991: False antitheses: a response to Seyla Benhabib and Judith Butler. *Praxis International*, 11, 166–77.

Fraser, N. 1994: After the family wage: gender equity and the welfare state. *Political Theory*, 22, 591–618.

Fraser, N. 1995: From redistribution to recognition? Dilemmas of justice in a 'post-socialist' age. *New Left Review*, no. 212, 68–93.

Fraser, N. 1997a: A rejoinder to Iris Young. *New Left Review*, no. 223, 126–9.

Fraser, N. 1997b: *Justice Interruptus: Critical Reflections on the 'Postsocialist' Condition*. New York: Routledge.

Friedman, J. 1997: Simplifying complexity: assimilating the global in a small paradise. In K. F. Olwig and K. Hastrup (eds), *Siting Culture: The Shifting Anthropological Object*. London: Routledge.

Frisby, D. 1985: *Fragments of Modernity*. Cambridge: Polity Press.

Frobel, F., Heinrichs, J. and Kreye, O. 1980: *The New International Division of Labour*. Cambridge: Cambridge University Press.

Fuentes, A. and Ehrenreich, B. 1983: *Women in the Global Factory*. Boston: South End Press.

Fuss, D. 1990: *Essentially Speaking*. London: Routledge.

Game, A. and Pringle, R. 1984: *Gender at Work*. London: Pluto.

Gatens, M. 1991: A critique of the sex/gender distinction. In S. Gunew (ed.), *A Reader in Feminist Knowledge*. London: Routledge.

Gatens, M. 1992: Power, bodies and difference. In M. Barrett and A. Phillips (eds), *Destabilizing Theory: Contemporary Feminist Debates*. Cambridge: Polity Press.

Gavron, H. 1968: *The Captive Wife*. Harmondsworth: Penguin.

Geltmaker, T. 1992: The queer nation acts up: health care, politics and sexual diversity in the County of Angels. *Environment and Planning D: Society and Space*, 10, 609–50.

Gewertz, D. 1984: The Tchambuli view of persons: a critique of individualism in the works of Mead and Chodorow. *American Anthropologist*, 86, 615–29.

Gibson, J. W. 1994: *Warrior Dreams: Paramilitary Culture in Post-Vietnam America*. New York: Hill and Wang.

Gibson, K. 1991: Company towns and class processes. *Environment and Planning D: Society and Space*, 9, 285–308.

Gibson-Graham, J. K. 1994: 'Stuffed if I know!': reflections on postmodern feminist social research. *Gender, Place and Culture*, 1, 205–24.

Gibson-Graham, J. K. 1996: *The End of Capitalism (as we knew it): A Feminist Critique of Political Economy*. Oxford: Blackwell.

Giddens, A. 1991: *Modernity and Self-Identity*. Cambridge: Polity Press.

Giddens, A. 1992: *The Transformation of Intimacy*. Cambridge: Polity Press.

Giddings, P. 1984: *When and Where I Enter . . . : The Impact of Black Women on Race and Sex in America*. New York: William Morrow.

Gilbert, M. 1994: The politics of location: doing feminist research at 'home'. *Professional Geographer*, 46, 90–5.

Gilman, C. Perkins 1966: *Women and Economics* (1898). New York: Pantheon Books.

Gilman, C. Perkins 1979: *Herland* (1915). New York: Pantheon Books.

Gilman, C. Perkins 1981: *The Yellow Wallpaper* (1892). London: Virago.

Gilmore, D. 1990: *Manhood in the Making: Cultural Concepts of Masculinity*. New Haven: Yale University Press.

Gilroy, P. 1987: *There Ain't No Black in the Union Jack*. London: Hutchinson.

Gilroy, P. 1993: *The Black Atlantic: Modernity and Double Consciousness.* London: Verso.

Glenn, E. W. 1992: From servitude to service work: historical continuities in the racial division of paid reproductive labour. *Signs*, 18, 1–43.

Gluck, S. and Patai, D. (eds) 1991: *Women's Words: The Feminist Practice of Oral History.* London: Routledge.

Glucksmann, M. 1995: Why 'work'? Gender and 'the total social organization of labour'. *Gender, Work and Organization*, 2, 275–94.

Gorham, C. 1997: Benign intentions. *The Guardian 2*, 19 Feb., p. 7.

Greed, C. 1991: *Surveying Sisters: Women in a Traditional Male Profession.* London: Routledge.

Greed, C. 1994: *Women and Planning: Creating Gendered Realities.* London: Routledge.

Greer, G. 1970: *The Female Eunuch.* London: MacGibbon and Kee.

Greer, G. 1985: *Sex and Destiny: The Politics of Human Fertility.* London: Picador.

Greer, G. 1997: Do what I say. *Observer Review*, 11 Jan. p. 5.

Gregory, D. 1994: *Geographical Imaginations.* Oxford: Blackwell.

Gregson, N. and Lowe, M. 1994: *Servicing the Middle Classes.* London: Routledge.

Gronow, J. 1997: *The Sociology of Taste.* London: Routledge.

Grossberg, L. 1996: Identity and cultural studies: is that all there is? In S. Hall and P. du Gay (eds), *Questions of Cultural Identity.* London: Sage.

Grosz, E. 1990: Inscriptions and body maps: Representations and the corporeal. In T. Threadgold and A. Cranny-Francis (eds), *Feminine, Masculine and Representation.* Sydney: Allen and Unwin. (There is an edited version of this paper in L. McDowell and J. Sharp (eds), *Space, Gender, Knowledge.* London: Arnold, 1997.)

Grosz, E. 1992: Bodies-Cities. In B. Colomina (ed.), *Sexuality and Space.* New York: Princeton Architectural Press.

Grosz, E. 1994: *Volatile Bodies: Toward a Corporeal Feminism.* Bloomington: Indiana University Press.

Gunew, S. (ed.) 1990: *Feminist Knowledge: Critique and Construct.* London: Routledge.

Gunew, S. (ed.) 1991: *A Reader in Feminist Knowledge.* London: Routledge.

Halford, S. 1989: Spatial divisions and women's initiatives in British local government. *Geoforum*, 20, 161–74.

Halford, S. 1992: Feminist change in a patriarchal institution: the experience of women's initiatives in local government. In M. Savage and A. Witz (eds), *Gender and Bureaucracy.* Oxford: Blackwell.

Halford, S. and Savage, M. 1995: Restructuring organisations, changing people. *Work, Employment and Society*, 9, 97–122.

Halford, S. Savage, M. and Witz, A. 1997: *Gender, Careers and Organisations.* London: Macmillan.

Hall, C. 1982: The butcher, the baker, the candle-stick maker: the shop and the family in the industrial revolution. In E. Whitelegg et al. (eds), *The Changing Experience of Women.* Oxford: Martin Robertson.

Hall, C. 1992: *White, Male and Middle Class: Explorations in Feminism and History.* Cambridge: Polity Press.

258

Hall, S. 1990: Cultural identity and diaspora. In J. Rutherford (ed.), *Identity: Community, Culture, Difference*. London: Lawrence and Wishart. (Reprinted in L. McDowell (ed.), *Undoing Place?* London: Arnold, 1997b.)

Hamnett, C. 1991: The blind man and the elephant: explanations of gentrification. *Transactions of the Institute of British Geographers*, 16, 173–89.

Hannerz, U. 1996: *Transnational Connections: Culture, People, Places*. London: Routledge.

Hanson, S. 1992: Geography and feminism: worlds in collision. *Annals of the Association of American Geographers*, 82, 569–86.

Hanson, S. and Johnston, I. 1985: Gender differences in work-trip length. *Urban Geography*, 6, 193–219.

Hanson S. and Monk, J. 1982: On not excluding half of the human in human geography. *Professional Geographer*, 34, 11–23.

Hanson, S. and Pratt, G. 1995: *Gender, Work and Space*. London: Routledge.

Haraway, D. 1991: *Simians, Cyborgs and Women: The Reinvention of Nature*. London: Free Association Books.

Hareven, T. 1982: *Family Time and Industrial Time*. Cambridge: Cambridge University Press.

Harris, O. 1980: The power of signs: gender, culture and the wild in the Bolivian Andes. In C. MacCormack and M. Strathern (eds), *Nature, Gender and Culture*. Cambridge: Cambridge University Press.

Harrison, C. and Burgess, J. 1994: Social constructions of nature: a case study of the conficts over Rainham Marshes SSSI. *Transactions of the Institute of British Geographers*, 19, 291–310.

Harrison, C., Limb, M. and Burgess, J. 1987: Nature in the city: popular values for a living world. *Journal of Environmental Management*, 25, 347–62.

Harvey, D. 1971: *Social Justice and the City*. London: Edward Arnold.

Harvey, D. 1989: *The Condition of Postmodernity*. Oxford: Blackwell.

Harvey, D. 1992: Social justice, postmodernism and the city. *International Journal of Urban and Regional Research*, 16, 588–601.

Harvey, D. 1996: *Justice, Nature and the Geography of Difference*. Oxford: Blackwell.

Haug, K. 1992: Myth and matriarchy: an analysis of the mammy stereotype. In J. Fuenmayer, K. Haug and F. Ward (eds), *Dirt and Domesticity: Constructions of the Feminine*. New York: Whitney Museum of American Art.

Hayden, D. 1976: *Seven American Utopias: The Architecture of Communitarian Socialism, 1790–1935*. Cambridge Mass.: MIT Press.

Hayden, D. 1981: *The Grand Domestic Revolution*. Cambridge Mass.:MIT Press.

Hayden, D. 1984: *Redesigning the American Dream*. New York: Norton.

Hayden, D. 1995: *The Power of Place*. New Haven: Yale University Press.

Hearn, J. and Parkin, P. 1987: *Sex at Work*. Brighton: Wheatsheaf.

Heilbrun, C. G. 1988: *Writing a Woman's Life*. New York: Ballantine Books.

Herdt, G. 1981: *Guardians of the Flute*. New York: McGraw Hill.

Herdt, G. (ed.) 1992: *Gay Culture in America*. Boston: Beacon Press.

Heron, L. (ed.) 1983: *Streets of Desire: Women's Fiction in the Twentieth Century City*. London: Virago.

Herzfeld, M. 1985: *The Poetics of Manhood*. Princeton: Princeton University Press.

Hewitt, V. 1994: *Beauty and the Banknote: Images of Women on Paper Money*. London: British Museum Press.

Hindle, P. 1994: Gay communities and gay space in the city. In S. Whittle (ed.), *The Margins of the City: Gay Men's Urban Lives*. London: Arena.

Hirst, P. and Thompson, G. 1996: *Globalization in Question*. Cambridge: Polity Press.

Hondagneu-Sotelo, P. and Avila, E. 1997: 'I'm here, but I'm there' the meanings of Latina transnational motherhood. *Gender and Society*, 11, 548–71.

hooks, b. 1982: *Ain't I a Woman: Black Women and Feminism*. London: Pluto Press.

hooks, b. 1991a: Choosing the margin as a space of radical openness. In *Yearning: Race, Gender and Cultural Politics*. London: Turnaround Books.

hooks, b. 1991b: Homeplace: a site of resistance. In *Yearning: Race, Gender and Cultural Politics*. London: Turnaround Books.

hooks, b. 1991c: Representations of whiteness in the black imagination. In *Black Looks: Race and Representation*. Boston: South End Press.

hooks, b. 1994: *Outlaw Culture: Resisting Representations*. London: Routledge.

Humphries, J. 1977: Class struggle and the persistence of the working-class family. *Cambridge Journal of Economics*, 1, 241–58.

Hutton, W. 1995: *The State We're In*. London: Cape.

Ignatieff, M. 1992: Why 'community' is a dishonest word. *Observer*, 3 May.

Irigaray, L. 1987: Sexual difference. In T. Moi (ed.), *French Feminist Thought: A Reader*. Oxford: Blackwell.

Jackson, S. 1993: *Women's Studies: Essential Readings*. New York: New York University Press.

Jacobs, J. 1995: *Edge of Empire*. London: Routledge.

Jacobus, M., Fox Keller, E. and Shuttleworth, S. (eds), 1990: *Body/Politics: Women and the Discourses of Science*. London: Routledge.

Jagger, A. and Bordo, S. (eds) 1989: *Gender/Body/Knowledge: Feminist Reconstructions of Being and Knowing*. New Brunswick: Rutgers University Press.

Jameson, F. 1991: *Postmodernism, or the Cultural Logic of Late Capitalism*. London: Verso.

Jarosz, L. 1992: Constructing the dark continent: metaphors as geographic representation of Africa. *Geografiska Annaler*, 74B, 105–15.

John, A. 1980: *By the Sweat of their Brow: Women Workers at Victorian Coal Mines*. London: Croom Helm.

Johnson, N. 1995: Cast in stone: monuments, geography and nationalism. *Environment and Planning D: Society and Space*, 13, 51–65.

Johnston, L. 1996: Flexing femininity: female body-builders refiguring the body. *Gender, Place and Culture*, 3, 327–40.

Johnston-Anumonwo, I. 1992: The influence of household type on gender differences in work-trip distance. *Professional Geographer*, 44, 161–9.

Jones III, J. P., Nast, H. and Roberts, S. (eds) 1997: *Thresholds in Feminist Geography*. New York and Oxford: Rowman and Littlefield.

Kandiyoti, D. 1988: Bargaining with patriarchy. *Gender and Society*, 2, 274–90.

Kanter, R. 1977: *Men and Women of the Organisation*. New York: Basic Books.

Kanter, R. 1992: *The Challenge of Organisational Change*. New York: Free Press.

Kaplan, C. 1996: *Questions of Travel: Postmodern Discourses of Displacement*. Durham N. C.: Duke University Press.

Katz, C. 1994: Playing the field: questions of fieldwork in geography. *Professional Geographer*, 46, 67–72.

Katz, C. and Smith, N. 1993: Spatializing metaphors: towards a spatialized politics. In M. Keith and S. Pile (eds), *Place and the Politics of Identity*. London: Routledge.

Kaufman, M. 1993: *Cracking the Armour: Power, Pain and the Lives of Men*. Toronto: Viking.

Keith, M. 1992: Angry writing: (re)presenting the unethical world of the ethnographer. *Environment and Planning D: Society and Space*, 10, 551–68.

Kelly, M. P. Fernandez, 1994: Towanda's triumph: social and cultural capital in the transition to adulthood in the urban ghetto. *International Journal of Urban and Regional Research*, 18, 88–111.

Kerfoot, D. and Knights, D. 1994: The gendered terrain of paternalism.In S. Wright (ed.), *Anthropology of Organisations*. London: Routledge.

Kerouac, J. 1992: *On the Road* (1957). London: Penguin.

Kimmel, M. 1988: *Changing Men: New Research on Masculinity*. London: Sage.

Kinsman, P. 1993: Landscapes of national non-identity: the landscape photography of Ingrid Pollard. Working Paper 17, Department of Geography: University of Nottingham.

Kinsman, P. 1995: Landscape, race and national identity: the photography of Ingrid Pollard. *Area*, 27, 300–10.

Kirby, A. 1995: Straight talk on the PomoHomo question. *Gender, Place and Culture*, 2, 89–95.

Kirby, K. 1996: *Indifferent Boundaries: Spatial Concepts of Human Subjectivity*. London: Guilford Press.

Klein, A. M. 1993: *Little Big Men: Body Building, Subculture and Gender Construction*. Albany, N.Y.: SUNY Press.

Knights, D. and Willmott, H. (eds) 1986: *Gender and the Labour Process*. Aldershot: Gower.

Knopp, L. 1987: Social theory, social movements and public policy: recent accomplishments of the gay and lesbian movements in Minneapolis, Minnesota. *International Journal of Urban and Regional Research*, 11, 243–61.

Knopp, L. 1990: Some theoretical implications of gay involvement in an urban land movement. *Political Geography Quarterly*, 9, 337–52.

Knopp, L. 1992: Sexuality and the spatial dynamics of capitalism. *Environment and Planning D: Society and Space*, 10, 651–669.

Knopp, L. 1995: If you are going to get all hyped up you'd better go somewhere! *Gender, Place and Culture*, 2, 85–9.

Kobayashi, A. 1994: Colouring the field: gender, 'race' and the politics of fieldwork. *Professional Geographer*, 46, 73–9.

Kobayashi, A. and Peake, L. 1994: Unnatural discourse: 'race' and gender in geography. *Gender, Place and Culture*, 1, 225–43.

Koolhaas, R. 1978: *Delirious New York: A Retroactive Manifesto for Manhattan*. London: Thames and Hudson.

Koontz, C. 1986: *Mothers in the Fatherland: Women, the Family and Nazi Politics*. London: Cape.

Kristeva, J. 1986: Women's time (1979). In T. Moi (ed.), *Kristeva Reader*. Oxford: Blackwell.

Lacquer, T. 1990: *Making Sex: Body and Gender from the Greeks to Freud*. Cambridge: Harvard University Press.

Lamphere, L., Ragoné, H. and Zavella, P. 1997: *Situated Lives: Gender and Culture in Everyday Life*. London: Routledge.

Laslett, P. (ed.) 1967: *Locke's Two Treatises on Government*. Cambridge: Cambridge University Press.

Lauria, M. and Knopp, L. 1985: Towards an analysis of the role of gay communities in the urban renaissance. *Urban Geography*, 6, 152–69.

Laws, G. 1994: Social justice and urban politics: an introduction. *Urban Geography*, 15, 603–11.

Laws, G. 1997: Women's life course, spatial mobility and state policies. In J. P. Jones III, H. Nast and S. Roberts (eds), *Thresholds in Feminist Geography*. New York: Rowman and Littlefield.

Leavitt, J. and Saegert, S. 1990: *From Abandonment to Hope: Community Households in Harlem*. New York: Columbia University Press.

Lefebvre, H. 1991: *The Production of Space*, trans D. Nicholson-Smith. Oxford: Blackwell.

Leidner, R. 1991: Selling hamburgers and selling insurance. *Gender and Society*, 5, 154–77.

Leidner, R. 1993: *Fast Food, Fast Talk*. Berkeley: University of California Press.

Lévi-Strauss, C. 1983: *The Way of the Masks*, trans. S. Modelski. London: Jonathan Cape.

Lévi-Strauss, C. 1987: *Anthropology and Myth : Lectures 1951–82*. Oxford: Blackwell.

Lewis, C. and Pile, S. 1996: Woman, body, space: Rio Carnival and the politics of performance. *Gender, Place and Culture*, 3, 23–42.

Leyshon, A. and Thrift, N. 1996: *Money/Space: Geographies of Monetary Transformation*. London: Routledge.

Lim, L. 1983: Capitalism, imperialism and patriarchy: the dilemma of third world women workers in multinational factories. In J. Nash and M. P. Fernandez Kelly (eds), *Women, Men and the International Division of Labour*. Albany, N.Y.: SUNY Press.

Little, J. 1994: *Gender, Planning and the Policy Process*. Oxford: Pergamon Press.

Little, J., Peake, L. and Richardson, P. (eds) 1988: *Women in Cities*. London: Macmillan.

Livingstone, D. 1992: *The Geographical Tradition: Episodes in the History of a Contested Enterprise*. Oxford: Blackwell.

Loftus, B. 1990: *Mirrors: William III and Mother Ireland*. Dundrum: Picture Press.

Longhurst, R. 1995: The Body and Geography. *Gender, Place and Culture*, 2, 97–105.

Longhurst, R. 1996: Refocusing groups: pregnant women's geographical experiences of Hamilton, New Zealand/Aotearoa. *Area*, 28, 143–9.

Longhurst, R. 1997: (Dis)embodied geographies. *Progress in Human Geography* 21, 486–501.

Longhurst, R. and Johnston, L. 1998: Embodying places and emplacing bodies: pregnant women and women body builders. In R. DuPleiss and L. Alice (eds), *Feminist Thought in Aotearoa/New Zealand*. Auckland: Oxford University Press.

Lovell, T. (ed.) 1990: *British Feminist Thought: A Reader*. Oxford: Blackwell.

Lowe, M. and Crewe, L. 1996: Shop work: image, customer care and the restructuring of retail employment. In N. Wrigley and M. Lowe (eds), *Retailing, Consumption and Capital: Towards the New Retail Geography*. Harlow: Longman.

Luxton, M. 1980: *More than a Labour of Love*. Toronto: Women's Press.

Lyons, M. 1996: Employment, feminisation and gentrification in London 1981–93. *Environment and Planning A*, 28, 341–56.

Lyotard, J.-F. 1989: *The Lyotard Reader*, ed. A. Benjamin (including passages from *Le Mur du Pacifique*, trans. P. Brochet, N. Royle and K. Woodward), Oxford: Blackwell.

MacCannell, D. 1994: Cannibal tours. In L. Taylor (ed.), *Visualizing Theory*. London: Routledge.

McClintock, A. 1994: *Imperial Leather*. London: Routledge.

MacCormack, C. and Strathern, M. 1980: *Nature, Culture and Gender*. Cambridge: Cambridge University Press.

McDowell, L. 1983: Towards an understanding of the gender division of urban space. *Environment and Planning D: Society and Space*, 1, 15–30.

McDowell, L. 1991a: Life without Father and Ford: the new gender order of post-Fordism. *Transactions of the Institute of British Geographers*, 16, 400–19.

McDowell, L. 1991b: The baby and the bathwater: deconstruction, diversity and feminist theory in geography. *Geoforum*, 22, 123–34.

McDowell, L. 1992a: Space, place and gender relations, part 1: Feminist empiricism and the geography of social relations. *Progress in Human Geography*, 17, 157–79.

McDowell, L. 1992b: Space, place and gender relations, part 2: Identity, difference, feminist geometries and geographies. *Progress in Human Geography*, 17, 305–18.

McDowell, L. 1992c: Doing gender: feminism, feminists and research methods in human geography. *Transactions of the Institute of British Geographers*, 17, 399–416.

McDowell, L. 1994a: Making a difference: geography, feminism and everyday life – an interview with Susan Hanson. *Journal of Geography in Higher Education*, 18, 19–32.

McDowell, L. 1994b: The transformation of cultural geography. In D. Gregory, M. Martin and G. Smith (eds), *Human Geography*. London: Macmillan.

McDowell, L. 1994c: Polyphony or commodified cacophony: making sense of other worlds and pedagogic authority, *Area*, 26, 241–8.

McDowell, L. 1994d: Social justice, organisational culture and workplace democracy. *Urban Geography*, 15, 661–80.

McDowell, L. 1996: Off the road: an alternative view of mobility, resistance and the Beats. *Transactions of the Institute of British Geographers*, 21, 412–19.

McDowell, L. 1997a: *Capital Culture: Gender at Work in the City*. Oxford: Blackwell.

McDowell, L. 1997b: *Undoing Place?* London: Arnold.

McDowell, L. 1997c: The new service class: housing, consumption and life-style among London bankers in the 1990s. *Environment and Planning A*, 29, 2061–78.

McDowell, L. and Massey, D. 1984: A woman's place? In D. Massey and J. Allen (eds), *Geography Matters!* Cambridge: Cambridge University Press.

McDowell, L. and Peake, L. 1990: Women in geography revisited. *Journal of Geography in Higher Education*, 14, 19–30.

McDowell, L. and Sharp, J. (eds) 1997: *Space, Gender, Knowledge: Readings in Feminist Geography*. London: Arnold.

McDowell, L. and Sharp, J. 1999: *A Glossary of Feminist Geography*. London: Arnold.

McKay, G. 1995: *Senseless Acts of Beauty*. London: Verso.

Mackenzie, S. 1989: *Visible Histories: Women and Environments in a Post-war British City*. London: McGill-Queen's University Press.

Mackenzie, S. and Rose, D. 1983: Industrial change, the domestic economy and home life. In J. Anderson, S. Duncan and R. Hudson (eds), *Redundant Spaces and Industrial Decline in Cities and Regions*. London: Academic Press.

McNay, L. 1992: *Foucault and Feminism*. Cambridge: Polity Press.

Madigan, R. and Munro, M. 1991: Gender, house and "home": social meanings and domestic architecture in Britain. *Journal of Architecture and Planning Research*, 8, 116–31.

Maffesoli, M. 1995: *The Time of the Tribes*. London: Sage.

Mairs, N. 1989: *Remembering the Bone House: An Erotics of Place and Space*. New York: Harper and Row.

Malik, S. 1992: Colours of the countryside – a whiter shade of pale. *Ecos*, 13, 33–9.

Malson, M. R., Mudimbe-Boyi, E., O'Barr, J. F. and Wyer, M. (eds) 1990: *Black Women in America: Social Science Perspectives*. Chicago: University of Chicago Press.

Mangan, J. and Walvin, J. 1992: *Manliness and Morality: Middle Class Masculinity in Britain and America 1800 to 1940*. Manchester: Manchester University Press.

Marcus, G. (ed.) 1994: *Perilous States: Conversations on Culture, Politics and Nation*. Chicago: University of Chicago Press.

Martin, E. 1987: *The Women in the Body: A Cultural Analysis of Reproduction*. Boston: Beacon Press.

Marshall, J. 1984: *Women Managers: Travellers in a Male World*. London: John Wiley.

Mascia-Lees, F., Sharp, P. and Cohen C. B. 1989: The postmodern turn in anthropology: cautions from a feminist perspective. *Signs* 15, 7–33.

Massey, D. 1984: *Spatial Divisions of Labour*. London: Macmillan.

Massey, D. 1991: A global sense of place. *Marxism Today*, 24–9 June. (Also reprinted in T. Barnes and D. Gregory (eds), *Reading Human Geography*, London: Arnold, 1996, and in S. Daniels and R. Lee (eds), *Human Geography: A Reader*, London: Arnold, 1996.)

Massey, D. 1992: Politics and space/time. *New Left Review*, no. 196, 65–84.

Massey, D. 1994: *Space, Place and Gender*. Cambridge: Polity Press.

Massey, D. 1995: Masculinity, dualisms and high technology. *Transactions of the Institute of British Geographers*, 20, 487–99.

Massey, D. 1997: Economic/non-economic. In D. Lee and J. Wills (eds). *Geographies of Economies*. London: Arnold.

Massey, D. 1998: Living in Wythenshawe. In I. Borden, J. Kerr, A. Pivaro, and J. Russell (eds), *Unknown City*. Brighton: Wiley.

Massey, D. and Allen, J. (eds) 1984: *Geography Matters!* Cambridge: Cambridge University Press.

Massey, D. and Jess, P. 1995: (eds) *A Place in the World? Places, Culture and Globalisation*. Oxford: Oxford University Press.

Matrix 1984: *Making Space: Women and the Man-Made Environment*. London: Pluto Press.

Mattingly, D. 1996: Domestic service, migration and local labour markets on the US-Mexican border. PhD dissertation, Graduate School of Geography, Clark University, Worcester, Mass.

Maupin, A. 1980: *Tales of the City*. London: Corgi.

Maupin, A. 1984: *More Tales of the City*. London: Corgi.

Maupin, A. 1986: *Babycakes*. London: Corgi.

Mayer, T. (ed.) 1994: *Women and the Israeli Occupation: The Politics of Change*. London: Routledge.

Meigs, A. 1990: Multiple gender ideologies and statuses. In P. R. Danday and R. Goodenough (eds), *Beyond the Second Sex: New Directions in the Anthropology of Gender*. Philadelphia: University of Pennsylvania Press.

Merchant, C. 1980: *The Death of Nature: Women, Ecology and the Scientific Revolution*. San Francisco: HarperCollins.

Mertes, C. 1992: There's no place like home: women and domestic labour. In J. Fuenmayer, K. Haug and F. Ward (eds), *Dirt and Domesticity: Constructions of the Feminine*. New York: Whitney Museum of American Art.

Merves, E. S. 1992: Homeless women: beyond the bag lady myth. In M. J. Robertson, and M. Greenblatt (eds), *Homelessness: A National Perspective*. New York: Plenum.

Messner, M. A. 1992: *Power at Play: Sports and the Problem of Masculinity*. Boston: Beacon Press.

Metcalf, A. and Humphries, M. (eds) 1985: *The Sexuality of Men*. London: Pluto.

Milkman, R. 1987: *Gender at Work: the Dynamics of Job Segregation by Sex During World War II*. Chicago: University of Chicago Press.

Miller, N. 1988: *Subject to Change: Reading Feminist Writing*. New York: Columbia University Press.

Mills, C. 1988: Life on the upslope: the postmodern landscape of gentrification. *Environment and Planning D: Society and Space 6*, 169–89.

Mills, S. 1996: Gender and colonial space. *Gender, Place and Culture*, 3, 125–47.

Mirza, H. S. (ed.) 1997: *Black British Feminism*. London: Routledge.

Mitchell, D. 1995: The end of public space? People's Park, definitions of the public, and democracy. *Annals of the Association of American Geographers*, 85, 109–33.

Mitchell, J. 1974: *Feminism and Psychoanalysis*. Harmondsworth: Penguin.

Moghadam, V. (ed.) 1994: *Identity Politics and Women: Cultural Reassertions and Feminisms in International Perspective*. Boulder Colo.: Westview Press.

Mohanty, C. T. 1991: Cartographies of struggle. In C. T. Mohanty, A. Russo and L. Torres (eds), *Third World Women and the Politics of Feminism*. Bloomington: Indiana University Press.

Momsen, J. 1980: Women in Canadian Geography. *Canadian Geography*, 24, 177–83.

Momsen, J. 1991: *Women and Development in the Third World*. London: Routledge.

Momsen, J. and Kinnaird, V. 1993: *Different Voices, Different Places*. London: Routledge.

Momsen, J. and Townsend, J. (eds) 1987: *Gender and Development in the Third World*. London: Hutchinson.

Monk, J. 1994: Contextualizing feminism: international perspectives. *IGU Working Paper 27*, Commission on Gender and Geography, Washington, DC.

Moore, H. 1986: *Space, Text and Gender*. Cambridge: Cambridge University Press.

Moore, H. 1988: *Feminism and Anthropology*. Cambridge: Polity Press.

Moore, H. 1994: *A Passion for Difference*. Cambridge: Polity Press.

Morgan, G. and Knights, D. 1991: Gendering jobs: corporate strategy, managerial control and the dynamics of job segregation. *Work, Employment and Society*, 5, 181–200.

Morris, L. 1992: *The Workings of the Household*. Cambridge: Polity Press.

Morrison, T. 1992: *Playing in the Dark: Whiteness in the Literary Imagination*. London: Harvard University Press.

Mort, F. 1995: Archaeologies of city life: commercial culture, masculinity, and spatial relations in 1980s London. *Environment and Planning D: Society and Space*, 13, 573–90.

Mort, F. 1996: *Cultures of Consumption: Masculinities and Social Space in Late Twentieth-Century Britain*. London: Routledge.

Morton, M. 1995: *The Tunnel: The Underground Homeless of New York*. New Haven: Yale University Press.

Moss, P. 1995a: Inscribing workplaces: the spatiality of the production process. *Growth and Change*, 26, 23–57.

Moss, P. 1995b: Reflections of the 'gap' as part of the politics of research design. *Antipode*, 27, 82–90.

Moss, P. 1997: Spaces of resistance, spaces of respite: franchise housekeepers keeping house in the workplace and the home. *Gender, Place and Culture*, 4, 179–96.

Moss, P. and Dyck, I. 1996: Inquiry into environment and body: women, work and chronic illness. *Environment and Planning D: Society and Space*, 14, 737–53.

Nash, C. 1993: Remapping and renaming: new cartographies of identity, gender and landscape in Ireland. *Feminist Review*, 44, 39–57.

Nash, C. 1996a: Men again: Irish masculinity, nature and nationhood in the early twentieth century. *Ecumene*, 3, 427–53

Nash, C. 1996b: Reclaiming vision: looking at landscape and the body. *Gender, Place and Culture*, 3, 149–70.

266

Nash, J. and Kelly, M. Fernandez- (eds) 1983: *Women, Men and the International Division of Labour*. Albany New York: SUNY Press.

Nast, H. 1994: Opening remarks on 'women in the field'. *Professional Geographer*, 46, 54–66.

Nast, H. 1998: Unsexy geographies. *Gender, Place and Culture*, 5, 191–206.

Nast, H. and Kobayashi, A. 1996: (Re)corporalizing vision. In N. Duncan (ed.), *BodySpace*. London: Routledge.

Nast, H. and Pile, S. (eds) 1998: *Places through the Body*. London: Routledge.

New, C. 1997: Man bad, woman good? Essentialisms and ecofeminisms. In L. McDowell and J. Sharp (eds), *Space, Gender, Knowledge: Readings in Feminist Geography*. London: Arnold.

Nicholson, L. (ed.) 1990: *Feminism/Postmodernism*. London: Routledge.

Nicholson, L. 1995: Interpreting gender. In L. Nicholson and S. Seidman (eds), *Social Postmodernism: Beyond Identity Politics*. Cambridge: Cambridge University Press.

Nicolson, N. 1973: *Portrait of a Marriage*. London: Weidenfeld and Nicolson.

Nye, R. 1993: *Masculinity and Male Codes of Honour in Modern France*. Oxford: Oxford University Press.

Oakley, A. 1974: *The Sociology of Housework*. London: Martin Robertson.

Oakley, A. 1981: Interviewing women: a contradiction in terms. In H. Roberts (ed.), *Doing Feminist Research*. London: Routledge and Kegan Paul.

Oakley, A. 1985: *Taking It like a Woman*. London: Flamingo.

Oberhauser, A. M. 1995: Gender and household economic strategies in rural Appalachia. *Gender, Place and Culture*, 2, 51–70.

Oberhauser, A. M. 1997: The home as 'field': households and housework in rural Appalachia. In J. P. Jones III, H. Nast and S. Roberts (eds), *Thresholds in Feminist Geography*. New York: Rowman and Littlefield.

O'Hanlon, R. 1996: *Congo Journey*. London: Hamish Hamilton.

Okely, J. 1975a: Gypsy identity. In B. Adams et al., *Gypsies and Government Policy in England*. London: Heinemann.

Okely, J. 1975b: Work and travel. In B. Adams et al., *Gypsies and Government Policy in England*. London: Heinemann.

Okely, J. 1975c: Gypsy women: models in conflict. In S. Ardener (ed.), *Perceiving Women*. London: Malaby Press.

Okely, J. 1996: *Own or Other Culture*. London: Routledge.

Okely, J. and Callaway, H. 1992: *Anthropology and Autobiography*. London: Routledge.

Olwig, K. F. and Hastrup, K. (eds) 1997: *Siting Culture: The Shifting Anthropological Object*. London: Routledge.

Ortner, S. 1974: Is female to male as nature to culture. In M. Rosaldo and L. Lamphere (eds), *Women, Culture and Society*. Stanford: Stanford University Press.

Ortner, S. B. and Whitehead, H. 1981: *Sexual Meanings: The Cultural Construction of Gender and Sexuality*. Cambridge: Cambridge University Press.

Pahl, R. 1984: *Divisions of Labour*. Oxford: Blackwell.

Pain, R. 1991: Space, sexual violence and social control. *Progress in Human Geography*, 15, 415–31.

Park, C., Radford, J. and Vickers, M. 1998: Disability studies in human geography. *Progress in Human Geography*, 22, 208–33.

Parker, A., Russo, M., Sommer, D. and Yaeger, P. (eds) 1992: *Nationalisms and Sexualities*. London: Routledge.

Patai, D. 1991: US academics and Third World women: is ethical research possible? In S. Gluck and D. Patai (eds), *Women's Words: The Feminist Practice of Oral History*. London: Routledge.

Pateman, C. 1987: Feminist Critiques of the Public/Private Dichotomy. In A. Phillips (ed.), *Feminism and Equality*. Oxford: Blackwell.

Pateman, C. 1988: *The Sexual Contract*. Cambridge: Polity Press.

Pateman, C. 1989: *The Disorder of Women*. Cambridge: Polity Press.

Pateman, C. and Grosz, E. (eds) 1987: *Feminist Challenges*. Boston: North Eastern University Press.

Peake, L. 1993: 'Race' and sexuality: challenging the patriarchal structuring of urban social space. *Environment and Planning D: Society and Space*, 11, 415–32.

Pearson, R. 1992: Gender matters in development. In T. Allen and A. Thomas (eds), *Poverty and Development in the 1990s*. Oxford: Oxford University Press.

Phillips, A. (ed.) 1987: *Feminism and Equality*. Oxford: Blackwell.

Philo, C. 1989: 'Enough to drive one mad': the organisation of space in nineteenth century lunatic asylums. In J. Wolch and M. Dear (eds), *The Power of Geography*. London: Macmillan.

Philo, C. and Parr, H. 1995: Mapping 'mad' identities. In S. Pile and N. Thrift (eds), *Mapping the Subject*. London: Routledge.

Phoenix, A. 1988: Narrow definitions of culture: the case of early motherhood. In S. Westwood and P. Bhachu (eds), *Enterprising Women*. London: Routledge.

Phoenix, A. 1991: *Young Mothers?* Cambridge: Polity Press.

Pieterse, J. N. 1995: *White on Black: Images of Africa and Blacks in Western Popular Culture*. New Haven: Yale University Press.

Pile, S. 1991: Practising interpretative geography. *Transactions of the Institute of British Geographers*, 16, 458–69.

Pile, S. 1996: *The Body and the City: Psychoanalysis, Space and Subjectivity*. London: Routledge.

Pile, S. and Thrift, N. (eds) 1995: *Mapping the Subject: Geographies of Cultural Transformation*. London: Routledge.

Pollard, I. 1989: Pastoral interludes. *Third Text: Third World Perspectives on Contemporary Art and Culture*, 7, 41–6.

Pollock, G. (ed.) 1996: *Generations and Geographies in the Visual Arts: Feminist Readings*. London: Routledge.

Porteous, D. 1990: *Landscapes of the Mind*. Toronto: University of Toronto Press.

Power, M. 1983: From home production to wage labour: women as a reserve army of labour. *Review of Radical Political Economics*, 15, 71–91.

Pratt, G. 1993: Reflections on poststructuralism and feminist empirics, theory and practice. *Antipode*, 25, 51–63.

Pratt, G. 1997: Stereotypes and ambivalence: the construction of domestic workers in Vancouver, British Columbia. *Gender, Place and Culture*, 4, 159–78.

Pratt, M. B. 1992: Identity: skin blood heart (1988). In H. Crowley and S.

Himmelweit (eds), *Knowing Women: Feminism and Knowledge*. Cambridge: Polity Press.

Pratt, M. L. 1992: *Imperial Eyes: Travel Writing and Transculturation*. London: Routledge.

Preis, A.-B. S. 1997: Seeking place: capsized identities and contracted belonging among Sri Lankan Tamil refugees. In K. F. Olwig and K. Hastrup (eds), *Siting Culture: The Shifting Anthropological Object*. London: Routledge.

Pringle, R. 1989: *Secretaries Talk*. London: Verso.

Pringle, R. 1998: *Sex and Medicine: Gender, Power and Authority in the Medical Profession*. Cambridge: Cambridge University Press.

Probyn, E. 1990: Travels in the postmodern: making sense of the local. In L. Nicholson (ed.), *Feminism/Postmodernism*. London: Routledge.

Probyn, E. 1995: Lesbians in space: gender, sex and the structure of missing. *Gender, Place and Culture*, 2, 77–84.

Pryke, M. 1991: An international city going 'global': spatial change in the City of London. *Environment and Planning D: Society and Space*, 9, 197–222.

Putnam, T. and Newton, C. (eds) 1992: *Household Choices*. London: Futures.

Raban, J. 1980: *Arabia through the Looking Glass*. London: Fontana.

Raban, J. 1986: *Old Glory*. London: Picador.

Raban, J. 1995: *Coasting*. London: Picador.

Radcliffe, S. 1990: Ethnicity, patriarchy and incorporation in the nation: female migrants as domestic servants in Peru. *Environment and Planning D: Society and Space*, 8, 379–93.

Radcliffe, S. 1996: Gendered nations: nostalgia, development and territory in Ecuador. *Gender, Place and Culture*, 3, 5–21.

Radcliffe, S. and Westwood, S. 1994: *Viva: Women and Popular Protest in Latin America*. London: Routledge.

Radcliffe, S. and Westwood, S. 1996: *Remaking the Nation: Place, Identity and Politics in Latin America*. London: Routledge.

Ramazanoglu, C. 1989: Improving on sociology: the problems of taking a feminist standpoint. *Sociology*, 23, 427–42.

Ramazanoglu, C. (ed.) 1993: *Up against Foucault*. London: Routledge.

Reinharz, S. 1983: Experiential analysis: a contribution to feminist research. In G. Bowles and R. Duelli-Klein (eds), *Theories of Women's Studies*. London: Routledge and Kegan Paul.

Rich, A. 1980: Compulsory heterosexuality and the lesbian existence, *Signs*, 5, 631–60.

Rich, A. 1986: *Blood, Bread and Poetry: Selected Prose 1979–1985*. New York: Norton.

Roberts, E. 1988: *Women's Work 1840–1940*. London: Macmillan.

Roberts, H. (ed.) 1981: *Doing Feminist Research*. London: Routledge and Kegan Paul.

Roberts, M. 1991: *Living in a Man-Made World*. London: Routledge.

Roediger, D. 1991: *The Wages of Whiteness: Race and the Making of the American Working Class*. New York: Verso.

Romero, M. 1992: *Maid in the USA*. London: Routledge.

Roper, M. and Tosh, J. 1991: *Manful Assertions: Masculinities in Britain Since 1800*. London: Routledge.

Rose, D. 1989: A feminist perspective of employment restructuring and gentrification: the case of Montreal. In J. Wolch and M. Dear (eds), *The Power of Geography*. London: Macmillan.

Rose, D. 1993: On feminism, method and methods in human geography: an idiosyncratic overview. *Canadian Geographer*, 37, 57–60.

Rose, D. and Villeneuve, P. 1988: Women workers and the inner city: some implications of labor market restructuring in Montreal, 1971–1981. In B. Andrew and B. M. Milroy (eds), *Life Spaces: Gender, Household and Employment*. Vancouver: University of British Columbia Press.

Rose, G. 1993: *Feminism and Geography: The Limits of Geographical Knowledge*. Cambridge: Polity Press.

Rose, G. 1995a: Making space for the female subject of feminism. In S. Pile and N. Thrift (eds), *Mapping the Subject: Geographies of Cultural Transformation*. London: Routledge.

Rose, G. 1995b: The interstitial perspective: a review essay on Homi Bhabha's *The Location of Culture*. *Environment and Planning D: Society and Space*, 13, 365–73.

Rose, G. 1997: Engendering the slum: photography in East London in the 1930s. *Gender, Place and Culture*, 4, 277–300.

Rowbotham, S. 1973: *Woman's Consciousness, Man's World*. Harmondsworth: Penguin.

Rowbotham, S. 1989: *The Past is before Us: Feminism in Action since the 1960s*. London: Pandora.

Rowe, S. and Wolch, J. 1990: Social networks in time and space: homeless women in Skid Row. *Annals of the Association of American Geographers*, 80, 184–204.

Rubery, J. (ed.) 1988: *Women and Recession*. London: Routledge.

Rubin, G. 1975: The traffic in women: notes on the political economy of sex. In R. Reitner (ed.), *Toward an Anthropology of Women*. New York: Monthly Review Press.

Ruddick, S. 1995: *Young and Homeless in Hollywood*. London: Routledge.

Ruddick, S. 1996: Constructing difference in public space: race, class and gender as interlocking systems. *Urban Geography*, 17, 132–51.

Said, E. 1978: *Orientalism*. London: Routledge and Kegan Paul.

Said, E. 1983: Traveling theory. In *The World, the Text and the Critic*. Cambridge: Harvard University Press.

Said, E. 1994: *Culture and Imperialism*. London: Vintage.

Sandel, M. 1996: *Democracy's Discontent: America in Search of a Public Philosophy*. Cambridge Mass.: Belknap Press.

Sarre, P., Philips, D. and Skellington, D. 1988: *Ethnic Minority, Housing*. London: Avebury Press.

Sassen, S. 1990: *Global City*. Princeton: Princeton University Press.

Sayer, A. and Morgan, K. 1985: A modern industry in a declining region: links between, theory, method and policy. In D. Massey and R. Meegan (eds), *Politics and Methods*. London: Methuen.

270

Scheper-Hughes, N. 1992: *Death without Weeping*. Berkeley: University of California Press.

Scott, A. (ed.) 1994: *Gender Segregation and Social Change*. Oxford: Oxford University Press.

Scott, J. 1988: *Gender and the Politics of History*. New York: Columbia University Press.

Seager, J. 1997: *The State of Women in the World Atlas* (3rd edn). New York: Penguin.

Seager, J. and Olson, A. 1986: *Women in the World Atlas*. London: Pluto Press.

Sedgwick, E. K. 1990: *Epistemology of the Closet*. Berkeley: University of California Press.

Segal, L. 1990: *Slow Motion: Changing Men, Changing Masculinities*. London: Virago.

Sennett, R. 1994: *Flesh and Stone: The Body and the City in Western Civilization*. London: Faber.

Sharp, J. 1996: Gendering nationhood: a feminist engagement with national identity. In N. Duncan (ed.), *Body Space*. London: Routledge.

Shields, R. 1992: *Lifestyle Shopping*. London: Routledge.

Sibley, D. 1981: *Outsiders in Urban Societies*. Oxford: Blackwell.

Sibley, D. 1995: *Geographies of Exclusion*. London: Routledge.

Silverstone, R. (ed.) 1992: *Consuming Technologies*. London: Routledge.

Silverstone, R. (ed.) 1997: *Visions of Suburbia*. London: Routledge.

Simpson, M. 1994: *Male Impersonators*. London: Cassell.

Sinclair, U. 1982: *The Jungle* (1936). Harmondsworth: Penguin.

Skelton, T. and Valentine, G. (eds) 1997: *Cool Geographies*. London: Routledge.

Sklar, J. 1991: *American Citizenship: The Quest for Inclusion*. Cambridge: Harvard University Press.

Smart, C. 1984: *The Ties that Bind: Law, Marriage and the Reproduction of Patriarchal Relations*. London: Routledge and Kegan Paul.

Smith, A. D. 1991: *National Identity*. Harmondsworth: Penguin.

Smith, J. 1989: *Misogynies*. London: Faber.

Smith, N. 1993: Homeless/global: scaling places. In J. Bird, B. Curtis, T. Putnam, G. Robertson and L. Tickner (eds), *Mapping the Futures: Local Cultures, Global Change*. London: Routledge.

Smith, N. 1996: *The New Urban Frontier: Gentrification and the Revanchist City*. London: Routledge.

Smith, N. and Katz, C. 1993: Grounding metaphor: towards a spatialised politics. In M. Keith and S. Pile (eds), *Place and the Politics of Identity*. London: Routledge.

Smith, N. and Williams, P. (eds) 1986: *Gentrification of the City*. London: Allen and Unwin.

Soper, K. 1990: *Troubled Pleasures: Writings on Gender, Politics and Hedonism*. London: Verso.

Spain, D. 1993: *Gendered Spaces*. Chapel Hill: University of North Carolina Press.

Spivak, G. C. 1987: *In Other Worlds: Essays in Cultural Politics*. London: Methuen.

Spivak, G. C. 1988: Can the subaltern speak? Speculations on widow sacrifice. In C. Nelson and L. Grossberg (eds), *Marxism and the Interpretation of Culture*. London: Macmillan.

271

Spring, M. 1995: *Running for Shelter*. London: Orion.

Spring Rice, M. 1981: *Working Class Wives* (1939). London: Virago.

Squires, J. (ed.) 1992: *Principled Positions*. London: Verso.

Stacey, J. 1988: Can there be a feminist ethnography? *Women's Studies International Forum*, 11, 21–7.

Stacey, J. 1990: *Brave New Families*. New York: Basic Books.

Staeheli, L. A. and Lawson, V. A. 1994: A discussion of 'women in the field': the politics of feminist fieldwork. *Professional Geographer*, 46, 96–101.

Staeheli, L. A. and Thompson, A. 1997: Citizenship, community and struggles for public space. *Professional Geographer*, 49, 28–38.

Stasiulis, D. and Yuval-Davis, N. (eds) 1995: *Unsettling Settler Societies*. London: Sage.

Stichter, S. and Parpart, J. 1988: *Women, Employment and the Family in the International Division of Labour*. London: Macmillan.

Stiell, B. and England, K. 1997: Domestic distinctions: constructing difference among paid domestic workers in Toronto. *Gender, Place and Culture*, 4, 339–60.

Stoddart, D. 1986: *On Geography and its History*. Oxford: Blackwell.

Stoddart, D. 1991: Do we need a feminist historiography of geography – and if we do, what should it be? *Transactions of the Institute of British Geographers*, 16, 484–7.

Strathern, M. 1992: *After Nature: English Kinship in the Late Twentieth Century*. Cambridge: Cambridge University Press.

Synnott, A. 1993: *The Body Social: Symbolism, Self and Society*. London: Routledge.

Tannen, D. 1994: *Talking 9 to 5: How Women's and Men's Conversational Styles Affect Who Gets Heard, Who Gets Credit and What Gets Done at Work*. London: Virago.

Taylor, B. 1983: *Eve and the New Jerusalem: Feminism and Socialism in the Nineteenth Century*. London: Virago.

Theroux, P. 1979: *The Great Railway Bazaar*. London: Penguin.

Theroux, P. 1990: *Travelling the World*. London: Sinclair-Stevenson.

Theroux, P. 1992: *Oceania*. London: Penguin.

Thompson, W. 1825: *Appeal on behalf of one half of the human race, women, against the pretensions of the other half, men, to retain them in civil and domestic slavery*. London.

Thrift, N. 1997: The still point: resistance, expressive embodiment and dance. In S. Pile and M. Keith (eds), *Geographies of Resistance*. London: Routledge.

Titmuss, R. 1987: *The Philosophy of Welfare: Selected Writings of Richard Titmuss*. London: Allen and Unwin.

Tönnies, F. 1967: *Community and Society* (1887). New York: Harper and Row.

Townsend, J. G. 1991: Towards a regional geography of gender. *Geographical Journal*, 157, 25–35.

Tringham, R. 1994: Engendered places in prehistory. *Gender, Place and Culture*, 1, 169–203.

Tseelon, E. 1995: *The Masque of Femininity*. London: Sage.

Turner, B. 1996: *The Body and Society: Explorations in Social Theory*, 2nd edn. London: Sage.

Twine, F. W. 1996: Brown-skinned white girls: class, culture and the construction of whiteness. *Gender, Place and Culture*, 3, 205–24.

Valentine, G. 1990: Women's fear and the design of public space. *Built Environment*, 16, 288–303.

Valentine, G. 1993a: Desperately seeking Susan: a geography of lesbian friendships. *Area*, 25, 109–16.

Valentine, G. 1993b: Negotiating and managing multiple sexual identities: lesbian space-time strategies. *Transactions of the Institute of British Geographers*, 18, 237–48.

Valentine, G. 1996: Children should be seen and not heard: the production and transgression of adults' public space. *Urban Geography*, 17, 205–20.

Venness, A. 1992: Home and homeless in the United States: changing ideals and realities. *Environment and Planning D: Society and Space*, 10, 445–68.

Villeneuve, P. and Rose, D. 1988: Gender and the separation of employment from home in metropolitan Montreal, 1971–81. *Urban Geography*, 9, 155–79.

Walby, S. 1986: *Patriarchy at Work*. Cambridge: Polity Press.

Walby, S. 1989: Theorizing patriarchy. *Sociology*, 23, 213–34.

Walby, S. 1990: *Theorizing Patriarchy*. Oxford: Blackwell.

Walby, S. 1997: *Gender Transformations*. London: Routledge.

Walker, L. 1995: More than just skin-deep: fem(me)ininity and the subversion of identity. *Gender, Place and Culture*, 2, 71–6.

Walkowitz, J. 1992: *City of Dreadful Delight*. London: Virago.

Walter, B. 1995: Irishness, gender and place. *Environment and Planning D: Society and Space*, 13, 35–50.

Ward, K. (ed.) 1990: *Women Workers and Global Restructuring*. Ithaca, N.Y.: ILR Press, Cornell University.

Warde, A. 1991: Gentrification as consumption: issues of class and gender. *Environment and Planning D: Society and Space*, 9, 223–32.

Ware, V. 1992: *Beyond the Pale: White Women, Racism and History*. London: Verso.

Waring, M. 1989: *If Women Counted*. London: Macmillan.

Warner, M. 1985: *Monuments and Maidens: The Allegory of the Female Form*. London: Picador.

Watson, S. 1992: Femocratic feminisms. In M. Savage and A. Witz (eds), *Gender and Bureaucracy*. Oxford: Blackwell.

Watson, S. with Austerberry, H. 1986: *Housing and Homelessness: A Feminist Perspective*. London: Routledge and Kegan Paul.

Webster, J. 1986: Word processing and the secretarial labour process. In K. Purcell (ed.), *The Changing Experience of Employment*. London: Macmillan.

Weekes, D. 1997: Shades of Blackness: young Black female constructions of beauty. In H. S. Mirza (ed.), *Black British Feminism*. Routledge: London.

Weeks, J. 1986: *Sexuality*. London: Horwood and Tavistock.

Wekerle, G. and Whitzman, C. 1995: *Safe Cities: Guidelines for Planning, Design and Management*. London: Van Nostrand Reinhold.

Wekerle, G., Peterson, R. and Morley, D. (eds) 1980: *New Space for Women*. Boulder: Westview Press.

273

West, C. and Zimmerman, D. H. 1987: Doing gender. *Gender and Society*, 1, 125–51.

West, J. 1982: *Women, Work and the Labour Market*. London: Routledge and Kegan Paul.

Westwood, S. 1984: *All Day, Every Day*. London: Pluto Press.

Williams, P. 1976: The role of institutions in the inner London housing market: the case of Islington. *Transactions of the Institute of British Geographers*, 3, 23–34.

Williams, P. J. 1991: *The Alchemy of Race and Rights*. London: Harvard University Press.

Williams, R. 1989: *The Politics of Modernism*. London: Verso.

Williams, W. 1986: *The Spirit and the Flesh: Sexual Diversity in American Indian Culture*. Boston: Beacon Press.

Williamson, J. 1985: *Consuming Passions: The Dynamic of Popular Culture*. London: Boyars.

Willmott, P. and Young, M. 1960: *Family and Class in a London Suburb*. London: Routledge and Kegan Paul.

Wilson, E. 1977: *Women and the Welfare State*. London: Tavistock.

Wilson, E. 1991: *The Sphinx in the City*. London: Virago.

Wilson, E. 1992: The invisible flâneuse. *New Left Review*, no. 191, 90–110.

Winchester, H. and Costello, L. 1995: Living on the street: social organisation and gender relations of Australian street kids. *Environment and Planning D: Society and Space*, 13, 329–48.

WING (Women, Immigration and Nationality Group) 1985: *Worlds Apart: Women under Immigration and Nationality Laws*. London: Pluto Press.

Wittig, M. 1992: *The Straight Mind and Other Essays*. London: Harvester Wheatsheaf.

Wolf, N. 1991: *The Beauty Myth: How Images of Beauty are used Against Women*. New York: Anchor Books.

Wolff, J. 1985: The invisible flaneuse: women and the literature of modernity. *Theory, Culture and Society*, 2, 37–46.

Wolff, J. 1992: On the road again: metaphors of travel in cultural criticism. *Cultural Studies*, 7, 224–39.

Women and Geography Study Group 1984: *Geography and Gender*. London: Heinemann.

Women and Geography Study Group 1997: *Feminist Geographies: Explorations in Diversity and Difference*. London: Longman.

Women Working Worldwide (ed.) 1991: *Common Interests: Women Organizing in Global Electronics*. London: Women Working Worldwide.

Woolf, V. 1977: *Three Guineas* (1938). Harmondsworth: Penguin.

Wright, S. 1995: *The Anthropology of Organisations*. London: Routledge.

Wrigley, N. and Lowe, M. (eds) 1996: *Retailing, Consumption and Capital: Towards the New Retail Geography*. Harlow: Longman.

Young, I. M. 1990a: *Throwing like a Girl and Other Essays in Feminist Philosophy and Social Theory*. Bloomington: Indiana University Press.

Young, I. M. 1990b: *Justice and the Politics of Difference*. Princeton: Princeton University Press.

Young, I. M. 1990c: The ideal of community and the politics of difference. In L. Nicholson (ed.), *Feminism/Postmodernism*. London: Routledge.

Young, I. M. 1997: Unruly categories; a critique of Nancy Fraser's dual systems theory. *New Left Review*, 222, 174–60.

Young, I. M. 1998: Race and gender struggles. *Antipode*, 30.

Young, M. and Willmott, P. 1957: *Family and Kinship in East London*. London: Routledge and Kegan Paul.

Young, R. 1995: *Colonial Desire: Hybridity in Theory, Culture and Race*. London: Routledge.

Yuval-Davis, N. 1997: *Gender and Nation*. London: Sage.

Yuval-Davis, N. and Anthias, F. (eds) 1989: *Women–Nation–State*. London: Macmillan.

Zola, Émile 1982: *The Ladies Paradise*, trans. from *Au bonheur des dames* (1882), introd. Kristin Ross. Berkeley: University of California Press.

Zukin, S. 1988: *Loft Living: Culture and Capital in Urban Change*. London: Radius.

Zukin, S. 1995: *The Cultures of the City*. London: Blackwell.

Index

277